CATALOGING CORRECTLY
for Kids

AN INTRODUCTION TO THE TOOLS
FIFTH EDITION

ALA Editions purchases fund advocacy,
awareness, and accreditation programs for
library professionals worldwide.

CATALOGING CORRECTLY
for Kids

AN INTRODUCTION TO THE TOOLS
FIFTH EDITION

Edited by **SHEILA S. INTNER,
JOANNA F. FOUNTAIN, & JEAN WEIHS**

Association for Library Collections
& Technical Services

Matteson Public Library

American Library Association
Chicago   2011

ISBN: 978-0-8389-3589-7

Printed in the United States of America
15 14 13 12 11   5 4 3 2 1

While extensive effort has gone into ensuring the reliability of the information in this book, the publisher makes no warranty, express or implied, with respect to the material contained herein.

Library of Congress Cataloging-in-Publication Data
Cataloging correctly for kids : an introduction to the tools. — 5th ed. / edited by Sheila S. Intner, Joanna F. Fountain, and Jean Weihs.
    p.   cm.
  Includes bibliographical references and index.
  ISBN 978-0-8389-3589-7 (alk. paper)
  1. Cataloging of children's literature. 2. Cataloging of children's literature—United States. I. Intner, Sheila S. II. Fountain, Joanna F. III. Weihs, Jean Riddle.
  Z695.1.C6C37 2011
  025.3'2—dc22

                                                            2010012945

Cover design by Casey Bayer
Text design in Adobe Caslon Pro and Quicksand by Kirstin Krutsch

♾ This paper meets the requirements of ANSI/NISO Z39.48-1992 (Permanence of Paper).

ALA Editions also publishes its books in a variety of electronic formats.
For more information, visit the ALA Store at www.alastore.ala.org and select eEditions.

Sheila S. Intner is professor emerita of the Simmons College Graduate School of Library and Information Science and was the founding director of its MLIS program at Mount Holyoke College. She teaches cataloging at Rutgers University's School of Communication and Information and the University of Maryland's College of Library and Information Science. In 1989, she was elected an ALA councilor-at-large and president of ALCTS. She has also served as chair of the Cataloging and Classification Section of ALCTS. She has received the Margaret Mann Citation Award, the OLAC Annual Award, the NETSL Annual Award, and the Queens College Distinguished Alumna Award. She has written or edited numerous books, including *Cataloging Correctly for Kids, Electronic Cataloging* (2003), *Metadata and Its Impact on Libraries* (2006), and *Standard Cataloging for School and Public Libraries* (1994, 1998, 2001, and 2007). She joined G. Edward Evans and Jean Weihs in preparing the seventh edition of *Introduction to Technical Services* (2002) and, with Peggy Johnson, wrote *Fundamentals of Technical Services Management* (2008).

Joanna F. Fountain is assistant professor of library science at Sam Houston State University. During her career, which began as a library page at Syracuse University, she has worked in children's services and as a bookmobile librarian. She has completed a variety of cataloging projects and served Texas schools as liaison for the K–12 union catalog. Throughout her career, she has sought to combine her dual interests in Spanish and library science. Since she began full-time teaching, she has continued to conduct workshops and has been working on a bilingual subject heading list designed to increase access to library collections for Spanish speakers. Joanna is the author or editor of *Subject Headings for School and Public Libraries* (2001) and, with Elizabeth Haynes, *Unlocking the Mysteries of Cataloging: A Workbook of Examples* (2005). Joanna hopes that this edition of *Cataloging Correctly for Kids* will provide guidance for new librarians and updated information for those who catalog for young readers and researchers.

Jean Weihs has worked as a school librarian and in university, public, and special libraries as a reference librarian and bibliographer. Most of her career, however, has involved cataloging. She served as director of the Library Techniques Program at Seneca College of Applied Arts and Technology and has taught at UCLA and Simmons College. She was a member of the Joint Steering Committee for Revision of AACR for nine years, serving five years as chair. She has written or edited numerous publications, including *Nonbook Materials: The Organization of Integrated Collections* (1970, 1973, 1979, and 1989), *Accessible Storage of Nonbook Materials* (1984), *The Integrated Library* (1991), *The Principles and Future of AACR: Proceedings of the International Conference on the Principles and Future Development of AACR* (1998), and *Standard Cataloging for School and Public Libraries*. She has received the Margaret Mann Citation Award, the 60th Anniversary Award of the University of Toronto Faculty of Library and Information Science, the Queen's Jubilee Medal, OLAC's Nancy B. Olson Lifetime Achievement Award, and the Canadian Association of College and University Libraries' Blackwell's Award for Distinguished Academic Librarian.

CONTENTS

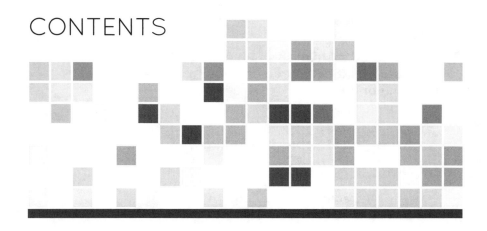

INTRODUCTION

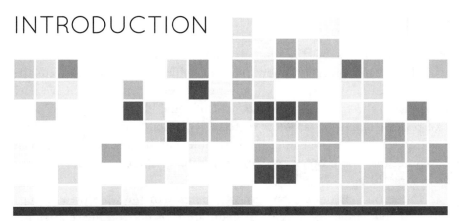

Sheila S. Intner

At this writing, the first decade of the twenty-first century is drawing to a close. It has been a time of productive ferment for the world of cataloging, and cataloging for kids has been no exception. Three developments with roots in the last century have achieved new levels of maturity and converged, affecting the way all library and information services—including cataloging and classification—are performed and delivered to those who use them. The first of these developments was networking.

One might think that bibliographic networks, which have been around since the end of the 1960s, did all the developing they were going to do a long time ago, once the Internet began. It's true that the Internet, which goes back more than twenty years, gave new dimensions to our ideas about sharing bibliographic data. In the past few years, however, the definition of what constitutes bibliographic data has become more complex and sophisticated as well as broader and more flexible. New kinds of materials required new kinds of cataloging. New issues had to be resolved, such as dealing with crossover media and remotely accessed materials (more about them in a moment). The value of subject headings came into question because of the availability of keyword searching. Studies of the materials retrieved using subject headings or keywords, but not both, seemed to show that although either type of subject searching was productive, keyword retrievals gathered numerous off-topic hits and failed to include all the relevant materials available, whereas subject heading retrievals honed in on relevant materials with far greater precision. New types of subject access, such as collaborative folksonomies, sprang up, and reader-generated reviews gave new meaning to the traditional requirement of some libraries to obtain positive reviews before buying new materials. Without a doubt, the Internet has expanded the exchange of bibliographic data hugely, globalizing it in a manner that the prophets of Universal Bibliographic Control could not have foretold.

The second major development was the growth and widespread acceptance of standards. The successful maturation of networking is attributable in part to the large number of libraries that chose to adopt standard cataloging and classification practices. The trend that began at the turn of the twentieth century, sparked by the Library of Congress's sale of its inexpensive printed cards, reached entirely new levels with the distribution of MARC records in the twenty-first century. Exchange of computerized bibliographic information and exploitation of its benefits demanded adherence to cataloging rules and adoption of uniform tools and methods. The MARC format prevailed. Avatars of USMARC (CANMARC, AUSMARC, UNIMARC) merged into one set of markup protocols—MARC 21—so that all users everywhere could plumb the enormous database built by OCLC and its global cohort. Best practices grew more uniform as the advantages of accessing more than 150 million catalog records and one billion holdings became crystal clear. A dramatic example of the development was the British Library's abandonment of PRECIS as its subject authority and adoption of *Library of Congress Subject Headings* in its place. (Today's readers may not be aware how recently this occurred.)

The third development was the rapid change in the materials collected by information agencies—libraries, school library media centers, learning centers, and so forth—that serve kids' needs for learning-related resources, entertainment-related resources, and curiosity-satisfying resources. Not only do libraries now "collect" both local and remote electronic resources of all kinds—e-books, websites, databases, online music and videos, interactive maps, art, and games, to mention a few—but they are still buying (and kids are using) the old faithfuls: books, "hard copy" recordings, print-on-paper journals, and more. Materials in crossover media, such as music videos, video art, digitized maps, and the like, are routinely included in all kinds of library collections, and they must be cataloged and classified just like all the single medium materials.

Kids are, perhaps, the most likely to accept and prefer cutting-edge materials. Today's tweens and teens think e-mail is old-fashioned. Do you want to reach them? Try IMing instead. Notice how quiet and absorbed in thought they appear sitting in the backseat of the family car on a long trip or attending a lengthy school program? If they keep glancing toward their laps, chances are they are texting a friend or two. These days, kids expect to get their information through something they wear in an ear or carry around in a hand. And libraries have responded. In a short time, reference collections have gone from excitedly showing off a few new online resources (frequently duplicated on library shelves by print-on-paper versions) to consisting in large part of online data in multiple formats. After all, not only are kids interested in using the computer-based technologies familiar to them, but librarians and media specialists now know that online resources are more efficient in serving constituents located beyond their traditional borders, and serving them 24/7. Libraries have remote patrons as well as remote resources.

This fifth edition of *Cataloging Correctly for Kids* points the way for librarians working with kids to provide effective cataloging for materials intended for children and young adults. The book begins with the official guidelines for this endeavor, sponsored by the Association for Library Collections & Technical Services (ALCTS), reproduced in chapter 1. Three committees of the ALCTS Cataloging and Classification Section— the Cataloging of Children's Materials Committee, the Committee on Cataloging: Description and Access, and the Subject Analysis Committee (SAC)—as well as their subcommittees and task forces contributed to the guidelines, prepared for this book by Joanna F. Fountain. The guidelines provide the foundation on which the rest of this book's contributors have built. In chapter 2, Lynne A. Jacobsen explores the special ways that children's searching differs from adult searching. These differences must be identified and understood before they can be addressed. Together, these two chapters set the stage for the rest of the book.

In chapter 3, Deborah A. Fritz takes readers beyond generalities, important though they are, to the first specific steps in creating bibliographic data appropriate for kids' materials: describing materials according to current standards in AACR2-2005 and encoding the data using MARC 21. Explanations in the chapter are thorough and well illustrated. In chapter 4, Ms. Fritz describes the process of copy cataloging—finding cataloging records in one of several possible sources and transforming them appropriately for use in local catalogs. Chapter 5 explores the background, structure, and potential uses of *Resource Description and Access* (RDA), the next iteration of cataloging rules still being tested and finalized. Lynnette Fields joined Ms. Fritz in preparing this chapter, which, like chapter 3, is filled with helpful illustrations.

In the next chapter, Kay E. Lowell covers authority control, the process whereby access points used in catalogs (that is, searchable headings) are established in proper form. Chapter 6 forms a bridge between bibliographic description—the focus of chapters 3, 4, and 5—and subject access—the focus of chapters 7, 8, and 9—because authorities include both descriptive and subject-oriented access points.

Chapter 7, by Joanna Fountain, and chapter 8, by Joseph Miller, describe and explain the application of the two most popular subject authorities for kids' materials: the Library of Congress's *Children's Subject Headings* and *Sears List of Subject Headings*, respectively. Both lists of authorized subject headings and cross-references are designed around a core set of subject principles. Both offer alternatives to the more complex *Library of Congress Subject Headings* intended primarily for adult materials, although both can be used with it, as needed.

The Dewey Decimal Classification (DDC) is the focus of chapter 9, by Julianne Beall, one of DDC's assistant editors. Dewey is the familiar choice for classifying collections of numerous school library media centers, learning centers, and public libraries and for arranging the materials on their shelves. Ms. Beall explains the principles and best practices followed at the Library of Congress for assigning DDC numbers to all materials—kids' materials included.

Chapter 10, by Sheila S. Intner and Jean Weihs, describes best practices in the cataloging of nonbook materials. It is the first of six chapters dealing with topics of special interest and importance to librarians who work with kids. The other five chapters cover how the Cataloging-in-Publication (CIP) program helps kids (chapter 11 by Joanna Fountain and Michele Zwierski), cataloging for kids in academic libraries (chapter 12 by Gabriele I. Kupitz), cataloging for kids for whom English is not their first language and preliterate kids (chapter 13 by Pamela J. Newberg), automating the kids' catalog (chapter 14 by Judith Yurczyk), and outsourcing kids' cataloging (chapter 15 by Ms. Newberg and Jennifer Allen).

This fifth edition of *Cataloging Correctly for Kids* closes with a glossary of abbreviations, compiled by editors Intner and Fountain, and an updated bibliography of resources for further study compiled by Virginia M. Overberg and Brigid Burke. The index to the text was prepared by Jean Weihs to aid readers in navigating the subjects they seek throughout the chapters of the book.

A book like this, which, in its preparation, has been read and re-read by many colleagues and friends as well as by the American Library Association's professional editorial staff, should be error-free. Still, to para-phrase Joan Collins, "Show me people who have never made a mistake and I'll show you people who have never achieved much."[1] As the book's princi-pal editor, I beg forgiveness should you come across errors of any kind in its pages. The responsibility is entirely mine, and I offer sincere apologies for them. I also ask humbly to be told about the errors so they can be addressed in the future. (Contact me at shemat@aol.com.)

"CCfK," as we nicknamed it, is the product of the hard work and dedi-cation of many individuals—authors, editors, committee members, sec-tion leaders, and association leaders—all of whom worked hard to bring it into being. Although there are too many people to mention individually on these pages, two stand out and deserve special thanks: Chris Rhodes, our principal editor at ALA Editions, and Charles Wilt, executive director of ALCTS, who guided our work every step of the way.

We dedicate CCfK to you, its readers, and hope it helps kids get the best possible service.

NOTE

1. *21st Century Dictionary of Quotations*, edited by the Princeton Language Institute (New York: Laurel, 1993), p. 292.

CHAPTER 1

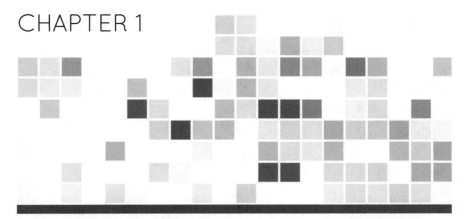

Guidelines for Standardized Cataloging for Children

Joanna F. Fountain for the Association for Library Collections
& Technical Services, Cataloging and Classification Section,
Cataloging of Children's Materials Committee

The library community has long recognized that children have their own unique characteristics and requirements as library users. They are considered a different enough audience, as users of both print and nonprint materials, that special bibliographic treatment of library materials is warranted to meet their developmental needs. Many adult users of libraries—especially parents, teachers, and other caregivers—will also benefit from this treatment when they are using catalogs created to provide simple and full information about the content of library materials for younger and less sophisticated readers.

Adults using catalogs created for adult or general use will already have discovered that such catalogs distinguish children's materials in a library by such mechanisms as subject heading subdivisions indicating that a given work is "juvenile fiction" or "juvenile literature" (nonfiction) as well as through differences in location.

BACKGROUND

In recognition of the unique nature of juvenile library users and in response to their needs, the Library of Congress (LC) established the Annotated Card (AC) program in 1966. Currently administered by the Children's Literature Section, U.S. and Publisher Liaison Division, the program

1

has adapted the Library's cataloging policies and practices to include annotations, modified subject heading use, and some special classification options. The headings LC developed for use with children's materials are now known as Children's Subject Headings (CSH). The AC program was originally accessed through catalog cards that included annotations from the Library of Congress; it is now available through MARC (Machine-Readable Cataloging) records and LC's Cataloging-in-Publication (CIP) program.

During the 1960s, as libraries found it cheaper or more convenient to rely on commercial or centralized processing services, it became apparent that standardization of cataloging practices was necessary. More recently, many libraries began contributing records to shared databases, lending further weight to the need for standardization. A study by the Cataloging of Children's Materials Committee of the Resources and Technical Services Division (RTSD) of the American Library Association (ALA) found that the lack of a uniform standard meant that many libraries developed customized cataloging according to their own perceived needs or that they accepted nonstandard cataloging from other sources.

The cost of customized cataloging, however, cuts into other services, and if the source of cataloging changes, so do the style and standard of cataloging. The Cataloging of Children's Materials Committee also foresaw that the development of MARC standards and widely used bibliographic utilities offered potential for the wider dissemination of standardized cataloging if guidelines for standardization could be developed and followed. In response, the committee recommended in 1969 that LC's practices for cataloging children's materials be adopted as a national standard. This recommendation was subsequently adopted by the Cataloging and Classification Section of the Resources and Technical Services Division (RTSD; in 1989 renamed Association for Library Collections & Technical Services [ALCTS]).

Since the original guidelines were developed, many more libraries have benefited from shared cataloging efforts, either through bibliographic utilities or commercial processors using MARC records, so that it is now even more advantageous in terms of cost and data compatibility to accept this standardization. The creation and exchange of bibliographic data at an international level, and access to these data by commercial processors as well as by libraries, have led the ALA to accept LC's cataloging for children's materials as a standard. In 1982, the Cataloging of Children's Materials

Committee, with the cooperation of the Children's Literature Section (recently renamed the Children's Literature Team, History and Literature Cataloging Division) at LC, developed the "Guidelines for Standardized Cataloging of Children's Materials," which were accepted by the RTSD board of directors on July 14, 1982.

Widespread use of MARC records has made it possible for many smaller libraries to automate their catalogs, converting retrospectively from card catalogs to online and World Wide Web (Web) catalogs and acquiring current machine-readable records from LC, materials vendors, and specialized vendors of cataloging data for use in online computer systems. International developments in content and MARC standards in turn suggest the need for again updating the guidelines for policies and practices for cataloging library materials for children, which were last revised in 2005.

SCOPE

The guidelines are intended for use in cataloging all materials deemed intellectually suitable for children and young people. Although the matter of deciding what materials are suitable for inclusion in a given juvenile collection may be difficult and subjective, these guidelines address the needs of catalog users through ninth grade, or approximately age 15; however, although application of these guidelines to materials for grades ten through twelve is optional, that choice may be convenient in high school libraries to provide uniformity. LC considers materials to be "juvenile" works when they are intended by the author or publisher, or deemed suitable by the cataloger, for use by children and young people in these age and grade ranges. Catalogers in libraries with juvenile collections are encouraged to consider implementing the LC standard for all grade levels and ages newborn through 18, if their collections include materials for teens at all levels.

Agencies that contribute cataloging to a shared database using the MARC format place an appropriate code in the fixed-field character position for target audience (Books field 008 position 22), indicating the intended level of the material. Code j indicates the item is intended for general use by children and young people through the age of 15 or the ninth grade. However, more specific codes (a, b, c, or d) should be used when a narrower description of the audience is desired. If an item is appropriate for more than one audience, the code for the principal target audience is assigned. The audience codes are defined as follows:

a   Preschool (up to, but not including, kindergarten)
b   Primary (kindergarten through grade 3)
c   Preadolescent (grades 4 through 8)
d   Adolescent (grades 9 through 12)
g   General (any audience level, including the general adult population)
j   Juvenile (all through age 15 or grade 9)

These guidelines are compatible with national cataloging tools and should be used in conjunction with them. Currently these tools include the following:

> *Anglo-American Cataloguing Rules,* current edition (AACR2) with its latest revision and amendments, or finalized rules of Resource Description and Access (RDA) when that becomes available to the individual library
>
> *Library of Congress Rule Interpretations* (LCRI)—LC policies and interpretations of AACR2 if they are applied by the individual library
>
> *Cataloger's Desktop*—a web subscription product that includes the most-used cataloging documentation resources in electronic form, if that product is used by the individual library in lieu of printed documentation
>
> *Library of Congress Subject Headings* (LCSH), including AC/CSH modifications and principles for applying them, as issued annually and published daily on the Web at http://authorities .loc.gov when AC/CSH modifications and principles differ from instructions published in *Subject Headings Manual* (intended for application of subject headings in non-juvenile catalogs)
>
> *Abridged Dewey Decimal Classification and Relative Index* (current edition), or *Library of Congress Classification* schedules, if those are applied at the individual library

These guidelines are based on the practices of the Library of Congress for cataloging children's material, and they note or expand on certain rules and options in AACR2 or RDA. Rules, options, and practices that are not touched on are not meant to be excluded. References within this text to individual rules are to rules in the current (second) edition of AACR2. Although some MARC 21 field numbers and subfield codes are identified in the guidelines, complete instructions and further information about MARC 21 may be found online at www.loc.gov/marc/bibliographic/ and in the printed documentation for *MARC 21 Format for Bibliographic Data* and some local system manuals. Some commonly used MARC 21 fields are listed in figure 1.1.

GUIDELINES FOR DESCRIPTION AND ACCESS

These guidelines address the following:

- Description of print and nonprint—including electronic—materials and resources
- Name, title, and series access points for various types of materials

FIGURE 1.1 **MARC 21 BIBLIOGRAPHIC FIELDS COMMONLY USED IN JUVENILE RECORDS**

010	Library of Congress Control Number (LCCN)	521	Target audience note
		526	Study program information note
020	International Standard Book Number (ISBN)	538	System details note
		546	Language note
050	Library of Congress Call Number	586	Awards note
082	Dewey Decimal Classification	600	Subject added entry—Personal name
100	Main entry—Personal name		
110	Main entry—Corporate name	650	Subject added entry—Topical term
130	Main entry—Uniform title		
245	Title statement	651	Subject added entry—Geographic name
246	Varying form of title		
250	Edition statement	655	Index term—Genre/Form term
260	Publication, distribution, etc. (Imprint)	658	Index term—Curriculum objective
		700	Added entry—Personal name
300	Physical description	710	Added entry—Corporate name
490	Series statement	730	Added entry—Uniform title
500	General note	800	Series added entry—Personal name
505	Formatted contents note		
508	Creation/Production credits note	830	Series added entry—Uniform title
511	Participant or performer note		
520	Summary note	856	Electronic location and access

- Subject heading use for juvenile catalogs
- Classification of juvenile collections

Examples show MARC records following AACR2 content (figures 1.2 through 1.5).

FIGURE 1.2 **EXAMPLE OF AN ANNOTATED CATALOG CARD FOR A BOOK**

Fic   Kerby, Mona.
Owney, the mail-pouch pooch / Mona Kerby ; pictures by Lynne Barasch. —
1st ed. — New York : Farrar, Straus and Giroux, 2008.
[42] p. : col. ill., map ; 21 cm.
Summary: In 1888, Owney, a stray terrier puppy, finds a home in the Albany,
New York post office and becomes its official mascot as he rides the mail train
through the Adirondacks and beyond, criss-crossing the United States, into
Canada and Mexico, and eventually traveling around the world by mail boat in
132 days.
ISBN-13: 978-0-374-35685-9
ISBN-10: 0-374-35685-8
1. Owney (Dog)—Juvenile fiction. [Owney (Dog)—Fiction. 2. Terriers —
Fiction. 3. Dogs—Fiction. 4. Mascots—Fiction. 5. Postal service—Fiction.
6. Voyages and Travels—Fiction.] I. Barasch, Lynne, ill. II. Title.
PZ10.3.K4845 Own 2008   [Fic]—dc22   2006047605

DESCRIPTION

Level of Description

The description of the material to be cataloged must follow the second level of description as found in rule 1.0D2 in AACR2 unless there is a special need for third-level (very detailed) description. Although many libraries have previously used abbreviated cataloging similar to the first level of description, the first level of description does not provide for elements that are considered important by many libraries and, therefore, are required by the guidelines. These elements include statements of responsibility (including subsequent statements of responsibility such as "illustrated by …"), dimensions, and series information. Elements that require clarification, or for which specific treatment is suggested, are discussed more fully in the following sections.

FIGURE 1.3 **EXAMPLE OF A MARC 21 RECORD FOR A BOOK**

Leader 01776cam a2200385 a 450	
001	14374812
005	20081124130439.0
008	060512s2008 nyuab j b 000 1 eng
010 __	|a 2006047605
020 __	|a 0374357858
020 __	|a 9780374356859
040 __	|a DLC |c DLC |d DLC |d TxGeoBT
042 __	|a lcac
050 00	|a PZ10.3.K4845 |b Own 2008
082 00	|a [Fic] |2 22
100 1_	|a Kerby, Mona.
245 10	|a Owney, the mail-pouch pooch / |c Mona Kerby ; pictures by Lynne Barasch.
250 __	|a 1st ed.
260 __	|a New York : |b Farrar, Straus and Giroux, |c 2008.
300 __	|a [42] p. : col. ill., map ; |c 21 cm.
520 __	|a In 1888, Owney, a stray terrier puppy, finds a home in the Albany, New York post office and becomes its official mascot as he rides the mail train through the Adirondacks and beyond, criss-crossing the United States, into Canada and Mexico, and eventually traveling around the world by mail boat in 132 days.
650 0_	|a Owney (Dog) |v Juvenile fiction.
650 1_	|a Owney (Dog) |v Fiction.
650 1_	|a Terriers |v Fiction.
650 1_	|a Dogs |v Fiction.
650 1_	|a Mascots |v Fiction.
650 1_	|a Postal service |v Fiction.
651 1_	|a Voyages and travels |v Fiction.
856 42	|3 Contributor biographical information: |u http://www .loc.gov/catdir/ enhancements/ fy0804/2006047605-b.html
856 42	|3 Publisher description: |u http://www.loc.gov/catdir/ enhancements/fy0804/ 2006047605-d.html

GMD

The GMD, or general material designation (rule 1.1C; subfield h of MARC field 245), though optional in AACR2 and selectively applied in LCRI, is strongly recommended in these guidelines for *all* nonbook formats of materials in List 2. The GMD should appear in square brackets immediately following the title proper, because its purposes are to identify the broad class of material to which an item belongs and to distinguish between different forms of the same work early in the description. It precedes any other title information, such as a subtitle. Use of the GMD "text" is optional; however, most agencies do not use it for books.

Notes

AACR2 provides for many optional elements. The note area of the catalog

FIGURE 1.4 **EXAMPLE OF AN ANNOTATED CATALOG CARD FOR A NONBOOK ITEM**

636.752　Grogan, John, 1957-
Marley & me [sound recording] / written and read by John Grogan. —
[New York] : HarperAudio, p2005. —
5 sound discs : digital ; 4 3/4 in. —
Compact discs.
Subtitle on container: Life and love with the world's worst dog.
Abridged reading of the book, published New York: Morrow, 2005.
Summary: Author John Grogan's vivid description of how Marley, a wriggly yellow furball, grew into a large Labrador retriever and changed his family's life.
ISBN-13: 978-0-06-167132-6
1. Grogan, John, 1957- . 2. Labrador retriever—Florida—Biography. [1. Grogan, John, 1957- . 2. Labrador retriever.] I. Title. II. Title: Marley and me
SF429.L3G76 2005x　　　636.752'7'092—dc22

record has the widest range of options. Notes may be provided if the cataloger or cataloging agency deems them necessary; they may be accepted or revised as part of a record from a vendor, with special attention to appropriate language for the potential user of the material.

These guidelines strongly encourage use of the summary or annotation note (MARC field 520), which is part of most Annotated Card program records. It consists of an objective statement of the most important elements of the plot, theme, or topic of the work. A summary, or annotation, should describe the unique aspects of the work and generally justify, whenever possible, the assigned subject headings, but it should not praise or criticize the item's content nor be so vague as to be useless in making a selection. Words in the summary should be chosen to facilitate keyword searching in online catalogs, using synonyms for words found in the title and subject headings, for example. Users of nonbook items are especially dependent on summary notes because of the greater difficulty of browsing such materials. However, a summary note is not required if a contents note (MARC field 505) that describes the nature and the scope of the work is used. A contents note is used to record the titles of individual selections contained in an item such as a book, sound recording, or videorecording.

AACR2 specifies the order in which notes are to be given. If both the summary note (MARC 520) and the contents note (MARC 505) are present, the contents note will often be the last note in the record.

Information about system requirements (MARC field 538, System details note) should be provided for videorecordings, electronic resources, and some sound recordings. One may use or include such common terms as *CD* or *DVD* in notes.

The participant or performer note (MARC field 511) is used to list names of performers or cast members on sound recordings and videorecordings. The cataloger may optionally provide name added entries for any or all names in 511 notes.

Two other notes are especially applicable to juvenile materials. Target audience notes (MARC field 521) contain information about reading grade level, interest age level, or interest grade level of the intended audience of an item. Because more than one may be provided, and measures and

FIGURE 1.5 **EXAMPLE OF A MARC 21 RECORD FOR A NONBOOK ITEM**

Leader	01162nim 2200277a 4500
005	20091026215454.5
007	sd fzngnnmmned
008	091026s2005 nyunnn g a eng d
020 __	|a 9780061571326
028 33	|a CD 4469(5) |b HarperAudio
040 __	|a TxGeoBT |c TxGeoBT
050 04	|a SF429.L3 |b G76 2005x
082 04	|a 636.752'7'092 |a B |2 22
100 1_	|a Grogan, John, |d 1957-
245 10	|a Marley & me |h [sound recording] / |c written and read by John Grogan.
246 3_	|a Marley and me |h [sound recording\
260 __	|a [New York] : |b HarperAudio, |c 2005.
300 __	|a 5 sound discs (6 hrs.) |b digital ; |c 4 3/4 in.
500 __	|a Compact discs

500 __	|a Subtitle on container: Life and love with the world's worst dog.
500 __	|a Abridged reading of the book, published New York : Morrow, 2005.
520 __	|a Author John Grogan's vivid description of Marley, the wriggly yellow furball that grew into a large Labrador retriever that changed his family's life.
600 10	|a Grogan, John, |d 1957-
650 _0	|a Labrador retriever |z Florida |v Biography
600 11	|a Grogan, John, |d 1957-
650 _1	|a Labrador retriever
852 42	|3 Contributor biographical information |u http://www.loc.gov/catdir/enhancements/fy0911/2005040010-b.html

opinions often do not agree, the source of the statement of level must be included. The awards note (MARC field 586) contains information about awards associated with an item, such as the Newbery Medal and Academy Awards, along with the date (year) of the award.

ISBN

The International Standard Book Number (ISBN; MARC field 020) is required when available. If there are two or more ISBNs, they should all be included in separate 020 fields. In a MARC record, the ISBN is given near the beginning of the record, before the rest of the description. On cards, the area for standard number and terms of availability (price) follows the area for notes.

NAME, TITLE, AND SERIES ACCESS POINTS

There is no variation from AACR2 in either choice or form of main entry for children's materials. The form of added entries for names and titles also remains the same. However, for names used as subject access points, follow the guidelines in the section "Subject Headings." The choice of added entries for names and titles and the choice and form of series added entries are discussed here.

Name Access Points

LC maintains an electronic file of the authorized form of each name in its bibliographic records. The authorized form is established according to the rules in AACR2 Part 2, along with various rule interpretations (LCRIs) and options that appear there. As part of the name authority component (NACO) of the Program for Cooperative Cataloging (PCC), many non-LC participants contribute records to the Name Authority File (NAF). The file is more broadly known as the LC/NACO Authority File, found at http://authorities.loc.gov.

Currently, the file contains over six million authority records. Of this total, names, series titles, uniform titles, and name/title combinations are found in the LC/NACO file. These include topical subjects as well as the names of fictitious characters. These authority records are freely available for consultation, copying and pasting, and downloading. Librarians developing catalogs for young and other readers should always verify and use the form of names and titles in the LC/NACO file so that searchers are not confused by multiple forms representing the same person or body.

In bibliographic records, added entries for individuals (MARC field 700) and groups (corporate bodies, MARC field 710) are provided to improve access to names other than those used as main entries, which are authorized forms of entry for the individual or first-named author of a work.

1. Added name entries should be made for all authors if two or three individuals or bodies collaborated on the work. If four or more collaborated, an added entry (called a "tracing" in card catalogs) is made only for the first author named.

2. Added entries for illustrators are required, as their contribution to a work may equal or overshadow that of a writer. Access to the record by illustrators' names is important not only for the artistic content but also for collocating works of artists. If the illustrator is also the author of the work, a separate added entry is not made. For illustrators whose contribution consists only of the cover, frontispiece, or incidental or repeating chapter-head decorations, or for designers who are not also the illustrators, added entries are optional.

3. Added entries should be made for principal performers on sound recordings and for producers, directors, and writers of videorecordings unless there are more than three of each. If there are four or more, make an added entry only under the one named first in each category. However, the cataloger may exercise judgment in the number of added entries, limiting these to those deemed useful for a young audience.

4. Although AACR2 allows the optional use of function designations for editors, compilers, and the like (subfield e of MARC field 700), only the designation ill. (for illustrator) is required by these guidelines.

Title Access Points

Generally, make a title entry for all items in the library. Specifically:

1. Make an added entry for the title even if the title proper (MARC field 245, subfield a) is the same as an assigned subject heading. Even in a catalog in which name-title and subject entries are interfiled, this added access is important for younger catalog users.

It is also essential for divided card catalogs and online catalogs, as the title must appear as an entry in the title index itself, thus allowing for retrieval by title alone.

2. Make an added entry for the title even if the title proper is the same as the main entry heading for a personal or corporate name.

In MARC records, the first indicator setting will be 1 in field 245; this indicates that title entry is made for the title proper. Added title entries (MARC field 246) should be made for other versions of a title under which users are likely to search, whether these actually appear on the item or not. Varying forms of titles are recorded in MARC field 246 with the first indicator set to 3 so that these titles will be indexed and retrievable in a title search. The authorized forms of many names (personal, corporate, etc.) as well as series and uniform titles may be easily verified in the LC/NACO file.

Series Access Points

Series access is particularly important for children's materials because the series title is a source of information about the content and approach of a work.

Make a series added entry for each work in the series that is cataloged if it provides a useful access point. Add the number of the individual work within the series if there is a number. The series added entry (MARC field 490) should use the title as it appears on the item. If the series title is deemed unimportant for searching purposes, as in the case of an imprint name used as a series title, the title is given in MARC field 490. The first indicator in the 490 field specifies whether there will be an added series entry and whether it will be indexed. A first indicator of 0 specifies that the series title will not be indexed. For example,

490 0_ ‡a Pelican books

If, as is most often the case, that title is useful in searching, it is then searched in the LC/NACO authority file; the authorized form of the series is then recorded in field 8XX of the MARC record, whether it is the same as or different from the title that appears on the item. The first indicator setting of 1 in field 490 specifies that the series will be indexed; the second indicator of 0 in field 830 specifies that the authorized form of the title has no nonfiling characters (initial articles or marks of punctuation). For example,

> 490 1_ ‡a Sports stars
> 830 _0 ‡a Sports stars

> 490 1_ ‡a A series of unfortunate events ; ‡v bk. 1
> 830 _0 ‡a Lemony Snicket's A series of unfortunate events

> 490 1 ‡a Kids make a difference
> 830 _0 ‡a Reading expeditions series. ‡p Kids make a difference

When the authorized form of the series has a personal name as the first element, it is entered in an 800 field. The name in subfield a is used as in the LC/NACO authority file followed by a t subfield containing the series title. The entire name-title entry must be used. The first indicator is set to 1 when the first element of the author's name is a surname. For example,

> 490 1 ‡a Alphabet books
> 800 1 ‡a Moncure, Jane Belk. ‡t Alphabet books

Series added entries can be uniform titles, including collective uniform titles, although few of this type are encountered in juvenile collections. For example,

> 800 1_ ‡a Shakespeare, William, ‡d 1564-1616. ‡t Works. ‡f 2008

Authorized forms of many series titles are freely available on LC's website at http://authorities.loc.gov. Each title should be checked against that file to ensure accuracy and to prevent confusion in the catalog.

SUBJECT HEADINGS

Until the Library of Congress's Subject Authority File was made available on the Web, the best print source for subject headings was the most recent edition of *Library of Congress Subject Headings* (LCSH) with its list of Children's Subject Headings (CSH). The online version, which contains records contributed by participants in the Subject Authority Cooperative program (SACO), is now part of the LC/NACO authority file. Although the online version is more current, CSH terms are rarely changed, and the printed version is usually entirely satisfactory. The printed version includes the usage guidelines—including subdivision practice—in addition to the list, so this version is still invaluable. The list is also available on Classification Web, a subscription product.

The CSH list contains terms created as alternatives to terms in the main list; these replacement terms are designed to offer more appropriate subject headings for juvenile catalog users and to afford them easier subject access to materials. Each term includes references to the unused term(s)—that is, those found in the main list and which have been replaced by the bold-font terms.

Any heading chosen from a printed copy of the multivolume LCSH ("big red") books should be checked against the exception list of CSH (in the front of the first volume or in the supplementary volume) or online to see if there is a replacement term.

Records created under the CSH program are updated online daily and are distributed weekly and daily via subscription on the MARC Distribution Service. Although record and card printing programs may be coded to delete or keep the bracketed information, CSH records may be identified easily by the presence of a subject heading with a second-indicator value of 1. For example,

> 600 11 ‡a Lincoln, Abraham, ‡d 1809-1865 ‡x Childhood and youth
> 650 _1 ‡a Holiday cooking
> 651 _1 ‡a Virginia ‡x History

CSH headings are identified in Cataloging-in-Publication (CIP) data and on catalog cards by brackets. For example,

> [1. Family life—Fiction. 2. Christmas—Fiction.]

Subject headings may also be added from the *Sears List of Subject Headings,* either by a vendor or local cataloging agency, with the second indicator set to 7 and the code "sears" provided in subfield 2 to identify the source of the term. For example,

> 650 _7 ‡a Glass manufacture. ‡2 sears

If the cataloger is using OCLC's standards, the second indicator in the 6XX field should be set to 8 for Sears subject headings.

650 _8 ‡a Glass manufacture

APPLICATION OF CHILDREN'S SUBJECT HEADINGS AND SUBDIVISIONS

Some CSH headings are simplified forms of standard LC headings, but the chief difference between CSH and LC heading use is in the rules for application of subject headings. Review the full details, found in the front matter in LCSH volume 1; only a brief summary is provided here.

1. Omit the subdivision **—Juvenile literature,** and related subdivisions such as **—Juvenile films** and **—Juvenile fiction.**
2. Avoid special juvenile form headings, such as **Children's poetry** and **Children's plays.**
3. Avoid the term *American* and the subdivision **—United States** when the subject is universal in nature. Use other geographic terms normally, such as the names of states or provinces and other nations.
4. Delete words in topical headings that would be superfluous in a juvenile catalog. For example, use **Parties** instead of **Children's parties.**
5. Assign subject headings to fiction as well as nonfiction to bring out the most important subject-oriented aspects of the work. For example, use the subdivision **—Fiction** for all fictional material.
6. Assign both specific and broader, general headings (e.g., **Turtles** and **Sea turtles**) to a work if both provide useful subject access.
7. Assign headings designating the literary form (e.g., **Jokes; Stories in rhyme**) whenever access by form of material appears helpful.
8. Assign both popular and scientific terms (e.g., **Cats** and **Felidae**) for the same work if that appears helpful, especially for older children. Note, however, that the CSH list customarily substitutes common names of animals and plants for scientific ones in the LC standard list.
9. Assign CSH replacement subdivisions, such as **—Cartoons and comics,** in juvenile catalogs.

CREATION OF NEW SUBJECT HEADINGS

If the CSH list and LCSH do not provide suitable terminology for the children's materials at hand, the following steps may be taken:

1. Contact LC to suggest new subject headings for the CSH list or LCSH at www.loc.gov/catdir/pcc/prop/proposal.html.
2. Create a term to be used locally, and give it in MARC fields 690 or 653 if your automated system allows searches on these fields.
3. If using the Sears list, create a term to be used locally, and write the term at its alphabetical place in the book.

USE OF MARC FIELD 658 FOR CURRICULAR OBJECTIVES

If it is the policy of the local library or is deemed important to list index terms denoting curriculum or course-study objectives applicable to the materials being described, use terms found in published local or state sources in subfield a and identify the source in subfield 2 of the MARC 658 field. Other subfields in this field, such as subfield c (Curriculum code), are optional. For example,

> 658 _ _ ‡a Earth and space ‡c 1211(b)(7-8) ‡2 txac
> 658 _ _ ‡a Community history ‡2 local

CLASSIFICATION

The following guidelines require the choice of either the Dewey Decimal Classification (MARC field 082) or the Library of Congress Classification (MARC field 050).

Dewey Decimal Classification

1. For fiction for preschool through second grade (K–2) or through age 8, assign the letter E.
2. For fiction for third grade (age 9) and up, assign the classification Fic or F.
3. For nonfiction materials, assign a number from the current abridged edition of the Dewey Decimal Classification (DDC). Treatment of biography is described in item 4 of this list.

4. For biography, assign the class number representing the subject of the person's most noted contribution, as instructed in the current abridged edition of the Dewey Decimal Classification. The Cutter should be based on the subject entry for the individual. For collective biography, assign 920; the Cutter is based on the main entry. Other options included in the Abridged DDC are also appropriate, such as B for individual biographies. LC provides full and abridged DDC numbers for both individual and collective biographies, as well as the B option, in its MARC records.

Library of Congress Classification

1. For fiction, assign numbers from the PZ schedule.
2. For nonfiction materials, assign numbers from the appropriate nonfiction schedule.

Classification of Folklore

Under either Dewey or Library of Congress classification, use the following guidelines to determine whether an item is folklore:

1. Folklore is defined as those items of culture that are learned orally, by imitation or by observation, including narratives (tales, legends, proverbs, etc.). A story about fairies is not folklore unless it meets the criterion of having been handed down orally from generation to generation. It might be a modern piece of fantasy instead.
2. Regard relatively faithful retellings and adaptations of folk material as folklore.
3. Do not consider religious mythology, stories from the Bible or other religious scriptures, modern fantasies, or drastic alterations of folk material as folklore, but class them elsewhere.

LOCAL IMPLEMENTATION

Adopting this standard does not require libraries or catalogers to use records created by LC or to accept all elements of records available online or through commercial vendors. Data manipulation and design of local cataloging profiles are provided by most commercial vendors and utilities and are accommodated by most machine-readable formats. However, libraries that contribute to shared databases and vendors that supply MARC records are expected to conform to those database or union catalog standards. Libraries that do not use computer services now, or that are not currently involved in shared catalogs, may well do so in the future. It is thus to the advantage of all libraries to have and follow a recommended standard for cataloging juvenile materials. As a further benefit, by making children's cataloging compatible with that for adult materials—without sacrificing its unique characteristics—this standard enables the young user to understand the adult catalog, whether it is in a public or academic setting.

These guidelines give sufficient latitude for the individual cataloger or library to meet local needs while remaining within the standard. The recommendations in these guidelines are intended to meet the requirements of young library users, in accordance with the purpose of the catalog record.

RESOURCES

Abridged Dewey Decimal Classification and Relative Index. 14th (or more current) ed. Dublin, OH: OCLC. Summaries are available online at www.oclc.org/dewey/resources/summaries/deweysummaries.pdf.

Anglo-American Cataloguing Rules. 2nd ed. rev. and updates. Chicago: American Library Association, 2002.

Fountain, Joanna F. *Subject Headings for School and Public Libraries: An LCSH/Sears Companion.* 3rd (or more current) ed. Westport, CT: Libraries Unlimited.

Furrie, Betty. *Understanding MARC Bibliographic: Machine-Readable Cataloging.* 7th (or more current) ed. Washington, DC: Library of Congress Cataloging Distribution Service. Also available online at www.loc.gov/marc/umb/.

Gorman, Michael. *The Concise AACR2.* 4th (or more current) ed. Chicago: American Library Association.

Library of Congress. Cataloging Policy and Support Office. *Library of Congress Classification Schedules.* Washington, DC: Library of Congress. Outline available online at www.loc.gov/catdir/cpso/lcco/. Note that the Cataloging Policy and Support Office is now the Policy and Standards Division.

————. Cataloging Policy and Support Office. *Library of Congress Subject Headings.* Washington, DC: Library of Congress. Authority file available online at http://authorities.loc.gov. Updated daily online and annually in print.

————. Cataloging Policy and Support Office. *Subject Headings Manual.* Washington, DC: Library of Congress. Updated online and in print as needed.

————. Network Development and MARC Standards Office. *MARC 21 Format for Bibliographic Data.* Washington, DC: Library of Congress. Also available online at www.loc.gov/marc/bibliographic/ecbdhome.html. Updated online and in print as needed.

CHAPTER 2

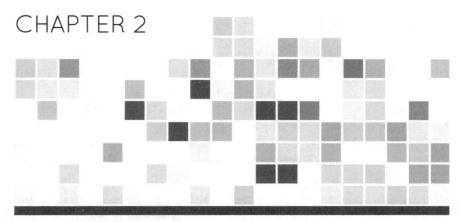

How Children Search

Lynne A. Jacobsen

Understanding how children search and retrieve information is critical to providing quality cataloging and metadata that will enable children to succeed in finding information. Understanding how children search also impacts the design of information retrieval systems, including web search engines, databases, and catalog interfaces. In addition, such understanding provides important insight into how to best teach information literacy to ensure that children become effective researchers.

Children are accessing electronic information now more than ever. "Nearly 75% of all U.S. households reported they had Internet access in 2004 . . . 93% of K–12 classrooms in the United States now have at least one computer connected to the Internet."[1] Children are using the Internet not only to complete homework assignments but also to engage in leisure activities such as playing games, pursuing interests, and communicating with one another. These activities require information literacy skills such as constructing searches, using keywords, selecting synonyms, narrowing topics, navigating web pages, and determining which pages are relevant and authoritative.

IDENTIFYING THE PROBLEMS

Children experience difficulty when searching for information for a variety of reasons. First, young children do not have the cognitive and mechanical skills necessary to search effectively. In addition, most user interfaces are created for adults, not children. Finally, cutting-edge technologies continue to change how we read, write, and communicate.

Though elementary school students are expected to use Google for searches and Microsoft PowerPoint for presentations, children are just beginning to learn to read. They have difficulty reading through extensive amounts of text. They do not have the knowledge base or the vocabulary to construct effective searches. Because children have not yet developed recall memory, they have trouble modifying a search. Although Boolean searching and search limiters will improve the precision of keyword searching, these concepts are too complicated for children age 10 and under. Children are just beginning to enter the developmental stage in which they can classify objects and understand hierarchical structure, so they have trouble determining broader and narrower terms as well as related terms. Children use natural language and thus have problems retrieving information from systems that use controlled vocabularies. LCSH subject headings, for example, require knowledge of words above a sixth-grade reading level.

Reading online text requires different cognitive processes than does reading text in print. Reading online often requires children to click on hyperlinked text, which takes more effort to navigate, read, and fully understand than text presented in a more linear fashion. Catalogs, databases, and web pages that contain hyperlinked information compound the problems children experience when doing research.

In addition to these cognitive skills, children are weak in the mechanical skills needed to access information. They have difficulty typing, spelling, alphabetizing, and even holding down a mouse button for extended periods. They also have trouble determining the form of a word to use, such as *dog* or *dogs*.

Even teenagers experience difficulty when performing online searches. Though they are skilled in using computers, teens don't always have the knowledge to understand more complex information. They haven't yet fully developed their reading skills, and so they have trouble reading extensive amounts of text.

PROVIDING SOLUTIONS

Solutions to the difficulties children experience in searching include enhanced cataloging practices, improved interface design, and focused information literacy instructional programs.

ENHANCED CATALOGING PRACTICES

Enhanced cataloging practices can improve children's access to materials. Catalogers must be cognizant of using language that children can read and understand when assigning subject headings, writing summaries, and establishing headings. Subject headings such as the Library of Congress's Children's Subject Headings assigned using the Annotated Card program are appropriate for children. The "Guidelines for Standardized Cataloging for Children" (see chapter 1) suggest assigning both broad and specific headings and assigning both popular and scientific terms.

A cataloger must be attentive to a book's "aboutness." Applying headings consistently enhances retrieval as does providing topics for fiction as well as nonfiction materials. Sometimes more abstract headings, such as **Fear of the dark—Fiction,** are warranted. Including natural language terms in summary notes and keyword fields will enrich keyword access.

Children's library materials come in a variety of formats. A juvenile collection can contain the same title in the form of a book, a sound recording, a videorecording, a large-print book, a board book, a book/compact disc set, and an electronic book, to name a few. It's essential to apply the same subject headings, summaries, and audience level to the same work in different formats to increase the consistency of retrieval of these items. Other valuable access points are uniform titles and series statements. Uniform titles should be used for stories with many editions and versions (AACR2 25.12B). Also, uniform titles provide important links to motion pictures and television programs. Many items published for children are part of a series. Children often ask for these items by series name, so providing access to series titles is helpful.

Catalogers should consider assigning foreign-language subject headings, at least to foreign-language materials. New subject heading thesauri are being developed, such as the *Sears List of Subject Headings, Spanish Edition; Subject Headings for School and Public Libraries, Spanish-English Bilingual Edition;* and *Bilindex* for subject headings in Spanish. Assigning subject headings from more than one thesaurus has become a common practice.

When cataloging items with collective titles, it is necessary to provide access to the individual titles included in the item. Titles listed in contents notes should be indexed—that is, made searchable for title keyword access. To improve access, make added entries for variant forms of titles, such as cover titles. Titles that include acronyms, numbers, and abbreviations should be spelled out in added-title entries to help children find them.

Catalogers should always ask, "How might children search for this item?" and then provide the necessary access points. Catalogers need to be aware of how fields are indexed in their systems to make sure certain access points are necessary.

IMPROVED INTERFACE DESIGN

Improved interface design will also help children successfully retrieve information. For example, spell-checkers can help children who have spelling difficulties. The "Did you mean . . . ?" and similar software enhancements are found on many catalogs and websites such as WorldCat Local and Amazon.com. A natural language processor can help children overcome the constraints of controlled vocabulary. Ask Kids at www.askkids.com is an example of a children's search engine that uses natural language queries.

Although hierarchical directory structures address the problems children have with spelling and knowledge of subject terms, they often provide limited search results. Subject directories can even frustrate children because the structure doesn't match their own categorizations. The International Children's Digital Library (ICDL) opted to flatten the depth of facet hierarchies because children have trouble navigating top-level, more abstract categories. As a result, ICDL presents simultaneous categories to help children create Boolean searches.

Children can also experience difficulty in determining formats retrieved from federated searches. The use of faceted browsing shows promise in helping guide children as they do research. Facets that collocate format type, author, title, publication year, and subtopic will help children narrow their searches without the need to type or use Boolean operators.

Large and Beheshti discuss many interface design features that appeal to children.[2] For example, metaphors are only useful when children readily understand them. Also important is a clear layout, with bright colors and not too much empty white space. Children like graphics but consider cartoon-like figures "childish." Font size should be easy to read. In addition, search terms should be highlighted in the hit list, and output ranking will help eliminate the need for children to scroll through many pages of results. Alphabetical searching (clicking on a letter) is popular with children as are context-sensitive help and searchable online documentation. However, general help screens are not considered helpful. Finally, children prefer personalization, interactivity, and multilingualism built into the design. Computer game–like interfaces utilizing 3-D may soon be possible, and adapting interfaces for the smaller screens of handheld devices is a current challenge. Young people should always be consulted when designing search interfaces.

FOCUSED INFORMATION LITERACY INSTRUCTION

In addition to improving cataloging practices and interface design, teaching information literacy will help children successfully retrieve information. Teaching information literacy is the responsibility of parents, teachers, and librarians. These skills are complex, and repetition at home, in school, and at the library will produce the best results. Children need to understand the entire search process beginning with having sufficient background knowledge of a subject. Next, they need to understand how a search site works, whether it is a catalog, a database, or a web search engine. They need to learn how to select search words and to try other keywords, such as more specific terms, synonyms, or combinations of terms. Children need to learn how to determine whether a site is authoritative and the information presented is relevant. Practicing reading in an online environment and following links should also be included in an information literacy program. Finally, children need to learn how to synthesize the information they find and cite sources.

CONCLUSION

It is beyond the scope of this chapter to cover specific teaching techniques and strategies, but it is hoped that the suggestions presented here will help you understand how children search and how the combined roles of enhanced cataloging practices, improved interface design, and focused information literacy instruction contribute to successful searching by children.

NOTES

1. Julie Coiro and Elizabeth Dobler, "Exploring Online Reading Comprehension Strategies Used by Sixth-Grade Skilled Readers to Search for and Locate Information on the Internet," *Reading Research Quarterly* 42, no. 2 (April–June 2007): 2.
2. A. Large and J. Beheshti, "Interface Design, Web Portals and Children," *Library Trends* 54, no. 2 (2005): 318–42.

CHAPTER 3

Cataloging Correctly Using AACR2 and MARC 21

Deborah A. Fritz

Imagine this scenario: A cart sits in front of me, piled high with children's books, videos, and sound recordings, along with some educational puzzles, games, and toys, a globe, and ten "Read" posters. All this stuff on the cart (the proper term for which is *resources* rather than *stuff*, of course) cries out to be cataloged, immediately, so it can be put to work. "We should be out there satisfying the informational, educational, and/or recreational needs of our pint-sized library patrons. Please get us cataloged and out on those library shelves!"

But I'm a children's librarian, not a cataloger. I used to make up brief records for the stuff I collected for my kids. I'd file them in my little-used card catalog and get those resources out on the shelves quick-time. Then I'd get on with my real job—don't even begin to ask about all the different things I do in my workday.

Now, however, those days are gone. Although my collection is small, it has become way too big for my kids to browse the shelves to find what they want, even with my help. And I find my magic doesn't work so well anymore—staring at the ceiling and recalling, "Oh yes, we received a video you might like just the other day. . . . It was in a bright blue box and I put it over . . . there."

These days I have to use my catalog to figure out what's in my collection and where I put it. It's looking more and more like past shortcuts and quickie cataloging weren't such good ideas. An author and title, a call number, and a few kid-friendly subject headings aren't proving at all useful these days. My kids want summaries. More contents notes would really help with their keyword searching. They want to find all our videos in Spanish, or books with illustrations of lions. They want to find individual songs on the CDs, for crying out loud! Where do they learn about all of this? They must be going to the library down the road or to other catalogs on the Web, and now they want my catalog to work the same way.

As if that weren't enough, I just found out I'm going to be putting my catalog in with the catalogs of some other libraries in something called a union catalog. It seems that making up brief entries for my records isn't going to work in this union catalog—apparently my records do not "play well" with those from other libraries. If I don't get my information into a form that will fit in the union catalog, I can't add my records. I'll still be able to borrow from other libraries, because that's the library ethos—sharing—but I won't be able to share in return. That wouldn't be right.

I have to start following rules for cataloging my resources—something called AACR. Not only that, but I must also learn how to put the information into computer-friendly form using a standard called MARC. I became a children's librarian to work with children—I'm not a cataloger and I don't want to be one. I don't remember taking a course about cataloging at library school. What am I going to do?

Does this sound familiar? If so, you are not alone. Anyone faced with doing or overseeing the cataloging of children's materials is in the same boat with you. The good news is that help is out there.

CATALOGING STRATEGIES

Copying someone else's cataloging is one source of help. Outsourcing your cataloging to someone else (a book jobber, publisher, cataloging service, anyone but you!) is another. More details about these kinds of assistance are in other chapters of this book. However, no one is perfect, not even the highly trained catalogers at the Library of Congress. So, whether you copy or buy records from elsewhere, you still have to know enough about AACR2 and MARC 21 to recognize problems when they occur.

With all this in mind, this chapter will introduce you to AACR2 and MARC 21, as gently as possible, and show you how important it is to find out how to use them both. Then you, too, can provide your kids (and maybe that union catalog) with the cataloging data they need these days. First, here's a bit of a history lesson. I'll keep it short.

CATALOGING RULES

The cataloging community has been developing and refining rules for a long time to standardize the way bibliographic information is provided. For now, just wrap your brain around the fact that for copy cataloging, outsourcing, and all those other methods of making cataloging faster, easier, cheaper, and better, all catalogers must (as far as humanly possible) provide *the same bibliographic information whenever they describe the same resources*. Try doing that without written rules! The current internationally accepted cataloging rules developed by representatives from the United States, Great Britain, Canada, and Australia, and used by most libraries in those and, increasingly, many other countries, are called the *Anglo-American Cataloguing Rules*, or AACR.[1]

The first edition of AACR, called AACR1, was published in 1967. A new edition, called AACR2, came out in 1978. Since then, there have been no new editions, only revisions—in 1988, 1998, and 2002. In 2002, AACR changed to a loose-leaf format to be updated by replacement pages; updates to the 2002 text were published in 2003, 2004, and 2005. An online version is available as part of *Cataloger's Desktop*,[2] updated through 2005.

A new, third edition of AACR (AACR3) was proposed in 1997, and work was begun to make some fairly radical revisions to the rules. However, by the time that the first draft of AACR3 was finally made public, in 2004, it was immediately clear to the cataloging experts that the library community was (in general) ready for and demanding even more changes than they, the experts, were proposing. A change in direction for the rules was signaled by the choice of a new name: *Resource Description and Access* (RDA), published in 2010.

For more complete historical details, see "A Brief History of AACR," an online document produced by the Joint Steering Committee for Revision of Anglo-American Cataloguing Rules, the international committee responsible for AACR.[3] We will discuss the possible future of cataloging in a new chapter (5) on RDA, but for now, let's concentrate on the rules we *have* and must follow until told otherwise.

The current version of AACR has two parts. Part 1 explains how to describe the materials (aka the resources) collected by our libraries. It is closely based on, but not exactly the same as, another set of cataloging rules called the International Standard Bibliographic Description (ISBD).

Part 2 of AACR2 explains how to add searchable terms to the descriptions of the resources. These terms should be the ones a patron might use in an attempt to find the resources. We call these searchable terms *access points*, *headings*, *tracings*, and other names you may encounter as you read various manuals. (We seem to like having at least two or three names for everything we talk about in cataloging.) AACR2 does not say how to assign subject headings or call numbers. For those instructions we must turn to controlled vocabularies and classification schemes, respectively, described elsewhere in this book.[4]

For a long time, student catalogers were taught how to use the current versions of cataloging rules to provide bibliographic information on three-by-five-inch catalog cards. The cards were then meticulously filed in long, narrow catalog drawers according to yet another set of instructions (the *ALA Filing Rules*). Assuming the cards were correctly filed, patrons could search the card catalog to find the bibliographic information. Using that information, they could decide whether they wanted to take the next step of finding the materials. Lots of steps were involved, but the system worked—as long as scrupulous care was taken with every step along the way. (This scrupulous care gave catalogers a bad reputation as being persnickety and far too attached to their silly cataloging rules. But, read on—vindication is coming.)

Remember, if everyone follows the same rules to provide the same bibliographic information when describing the same resources, then, when one cataloger provides the bibliographic information, other catalogers can copy the information instead of having to create it all from scratch. I ask you, where would we be these days without copy cataloging?

SHARED CATALOGING AND THE RISE OF MARC

Over the years, the cataloging community tried many methods of sharing cataloging information. Some were more successful than others, but all were expensive and by no means simple. Then the Library of Congress (LC) got involved. The clever catalogers at LC began producing card sets for the materials they cataloged and selling the sets at modest cost to other libraries. Any library that could afford these card sets jumped at the chance to speed up its cataloging process, and LC was soon inundated with requests for its printed cards.

More time passed, and computers came along. We progressed from writing cards by hand to using manual typewriters and, eventually, electric typewriters, but in the late 1960s, a group of cutting-edge library and computer people from LC and sixteen other libraries devised a way to use the new computer technology (it was barely out of infancy) to cut down on the drudgery of producing catalog cards. They took the cataloging rules, designed a set of computer codes around them, and called the codes MARC (MAchine-Readable Cataloging). Catalogers could use these codes to enter bibliographic information into computers instead of onto cards. Computers could then print catalog cards or produce book or microform catalogs (fiche or film), along with spine labels, book cards, and other useful by-products. Better yet, once the standards caught on, library vendors began to design circulation systems and computer catalogs (sometimes called OPACs, meaning Online Public Access Catalogs) around the coding standards, forever eliminating the need to file catalog cards.

Before long, catalogers discovered they could share computer records far more easily than they had been able to share cards. To facilitate this record-sharing process, groups of libraries began putting records from LC with the records they made themselves into union catalogs, such as OCLC, RLIN (Research Libraries Information Network), and Utlas (University of Toronto Libraries Automated System). Libraries could then copy the records as long as they allowed everyone else to copy their records in return.

Along the way, someone thought it would be a good idea to add an identifying code to any records we made or copied. This was done, and, suddenly, it became easy to tell what libraries had which records (and therefore the materials those records represented) in their collections. Once we could tell who had which resources, it became a snap to share those resources via interlibrary loan (ILL).

It took a while for this new way of entering cataloging information into computer records to catch on, but gradually more MARC records were made and more computer programs were designed around them. Nowadays, most libraries, no matter how small, already have or are in the process of getting integrated library systems with modules for acquisitions, serials tracking, cataloging, an online catalog, and circulation—and all these modules share the same MARC records for their different functions.

Let us consider the wonder of MARC for a (not so) brief moment.

The MARC standards that were developed in the United States (first called LCMARC, then USMARC) morphed into slightly different standards when they were implemented in other countries, becoming AUSMARC, CANMARC, UKMARC, and so on. Over time, however, most of these variations were either dropped or harmonized with the original format to produce what is now called MARC 21. MARC 21 is currently maintained by the Library of Congress, Library and Archives Canada (LAC), the British Library, and committees of the library associations of the United States, Canada, and Britain: MARBI, CCM, and BIC, respectively.

Because libraries collected more than just books, as time went on, different groups of specialist catalogers developed special MARC formats for different types of materials. For a number of years, this meant that we dealt with slightly different MARC codes for books, visual materials (e.g., videos, graphics), maps, sound recordings, music, serials, and so on. In a massive undertaking called *format integration*, which was almost as difficult as coming up with the standards in the first place, all the discrepancies among the formats for different materials were eliminated, resulting in a unified set of standards for coding the bibliographic information for anything being cataloged.

The most current version of the MARC standards can be purchased from LC in print form or viewed online, free of charge (MARC 21 Format for Bibliographic Data). The print and online versions of the MARC manual are kept in sync and updated annually. In addition, OCLC offers free access to its own online version of the standards, with many good examples and explanations (OCLC Bibliographic Formats and Standards). This is very helpful to OCLC users and non-OCLC users alike.

No sooner were the standards for coding bibliographic information nicely set up to make MARC bibliographic records than we discovered we needed to code more than just bibliographic information for library automation systems. As mentioned earlier, Part 2 of AACR2 tells about providing access points or headings to allow patrons to search the catalogs and find descriptions of resources. These headings must be entered consistently if patrons are to find everything in one place. To make headings consistent, we apply something we call authority control to provide a different type of information (called *authority information*) for headings. One very important type of authority information is a cross-reference that takes patrons from headings we don't use (such as Dr. Seuss) to headings we do use (such as Seuss, Dr.). For example:

Dr. Seuss. Author
See Seuss, Dr. Matches 66 Items

In the computerized MARC environment, it is not efficient to enter authority information into every bibliographic record to which it applies (e.g., entering the Dr. Seuss *See* reference into sixty-six bibliographic records would be quite a task). Instead, the authority information is entered into a different type of record, a MARC *authority* record, and then linked to each applicable bibliographic record (see chapter 6 for more details on authority control).

There are also MARC holdings records for holdings information (barcode numbers, collection symbols, shelf locations, and notes about specific books, videos, or other cataloged items), MARC community records for community information (such as the location and dates of the local chamber of commerce or Kiwanis Club meetings), and MARC classification records for classification information (used by the publishers of the classification schemes). In this introductory chapter we will stick to discussing only bibliographic records and will not go into more detail about the other types of MARC records, but some of the readings at the end of this chapter explain them further.

As you can tell by now, a lot is going on in this process we call cataloging. In the remainder of this chapter, our task is to concentrate on the specific area of providing bibliographic information (description and access points) for resources. It sounds simple, but it relies on strict adherence to two complicated and ever-changing standards—AACR and MARC—as well as more detailed explanations that help catalogers apply the standards uniformly.[5]

That's enough of the history and reasons why cataloging is how it is, so let us boldly dive into the deep end and get down to details. The bottom line is that AACR tells us what bibliographic information to provide, and then MARC tells us how to code it for the computer. You could, if you wished, use MARC and not follow AACR2, or follow AACR2 and not use MARC, but neither of these options is a good idea for any library, large or small, in today's world of shared cataloging. If you want to copy cataloging from others, have others do your cataloging, or both, your records must follow both AACR2 and MARC.

THE CATALOGING PROCESS

Here's how it works: Picture me with a book or video, or some other fascinating library resource in one hand. See me start flipping through AACR2 with the other hand. I begin at part 1, chapter 1 (begin at the beginning, we always say).

Chapter 1 tells me how to describe any type of material or resource I might encounter in the library. That sounds like a pretty useful set of rules, so why look any farther? It's all in the history. Chapter 1 was written way back when we only cataloged books. The chapters on videos, sound recordings, serials, and so forth, were added to cover special features of materials that chapter 1 does not cover. I have to turn to chapters 2–12 for instructions that describe different types of materials (e.g., chapter 2 for books, chapter 7 for videos). So, the first thing to remember about AACR2 is that we must always begin with the general descriptive rules and then turn to the appropriate special rules chapter to see if there are other important details we need to know.

Whatever I am describing, chapter 1 tells me to break my description down into eight broad areas. Instructions for providing the information for these eight areas are given in numbered subrules in chapter 1; the same subrule numbering is used in all twelve descriptive chapters. Now it's time to pull out the MARC manual. There, I see each of the descriptive areas is a field in MARC records.

Figure 3.1 illustrates how it all fits together. Instructions for entering information for the "Title and statement of responsibility" area can be found in AACR2 rule 1.1 (for all materials), 2.1 (for books), 6.1 (for sound recordings), 7.1 (for videos), or 12.1 (for serials). Then MARC says to put the title and statement of responsibility information in a 245 field.

AACR2 rule 1.2 tells us what edition information to provide, and how (for all materials), while more specific details can be found in 2.2 (for books), 6.2 (for sound recordings), 7.2 (for videos), or 12.2 (for serials). Then MARC says to put the edition information in a 250 field. Look closely at figure 3.1 and see where MARC says to put each of the eight areas of information.

No doubt about it, these cataloging rules are detailed! The next thing you need to know about them is that they even tell you exactly where to look on the resource for the information that you are to use to describe the resource. If I am describing a book, for example, chapter 2 tells me where to look on the book for the information for each of the areas shown in figure 3.1. Note that you look in the specific chapters (2–12) rather than the general chapter (1) for instructions on these "sources of information." Figure 3.2 shows examples of these instructions.

FIGURE 3.1
RELATIONSHIP OF AACR2 RULES AND MARC 21 FIELDS

AACR2 Areas of Information	All	Books	Sound Recordings	Videos	Serials	MARC Fields
	Ch 1	*Ch 2*	*Ch 6*	*Ch 7*	*Ch 12*	
Title and statement of responsibility area	1.1	2.1	6.1	7.1	12.1	245
Edition area	1.2	2.2	6.2	7.2	12.2	250
Material/Type of publication specific details area	1.3				12.3	various
Publication, distribution, etc. area	1.4	2.4	6.4	7.4	12.4	260
Physical description area	1.5	2.5	6.5	7.5	12.5	300
Series area	1.6	2.6	6.6	7.6	12.6	490
Note area	1.7	2.7	6.7	7.7	12.7	5XX[a]
Standard number and terms of availability area	1.8	2.8	6.8	7.8	12.8	02X[b]

[a]5XX means any field beginning with 5 (e.g., 502, 504, 505).
[b]02X means any field beginning with 02 (e.g., 020, 022, 024, 028).

Okay, you've got it that you have to divide the bibliographic description of a resource into areas of information, and the information for those areas must come from specific places on the resource. That's the first step. Once that idea is firmly fixed in your mind, the rules take you one step deeper, because each area of information is further subdivided into *elements*. These elements become *subfields* in MARC records.

Figure 3.3 illustrates how the "Title and statement of responsibility" area is divided into elements. It shows that the instructions for entering the information for the "Title proper" element are found in rule AACR2 1.1B (for all materials), 2.1B (for books), 6.1B (for sound recordings), 7.1B (for videos), 12.1B (for serials), and so on. Then MARC says to put that

FIGURE 3.2
AACR2 PRESCRIBED SOURCES FOR DIFFERENT FORMATS

AACR2	Book	Sound
	Ch 2	*Ch 6*
Title and statement of responsibility area	Title page	Physical carrier and labels
Edition area	Title page, other preliminaries, colophon	Physical carrier and labels, accompanying textual material, container (box)
Publication, distribution, etc. area	Title page, other preliminaries, colophon	Physical carrier and labels, accompanying textual material, container (box)
Physical description area	The whole publication	Any source
Series area	Series title page, monograph title page, cover, rest of publication	Physical carrier and labels, accompanying textual material, container (box)
Note area	Any source	Any source
Standard number and terms of availability area	Any source	Any source

information in subfield a ($a) in the 245 field. The figure goes on to reveal that the instructions for entering the information for the *general material designation* (GMD) element are found in rule 1.1C (for all materials), 2.1C (for books), 6.1C (for sound recordings), 7.1C (for videos), 12.1C (for serials), and so on. Then MARC says to put that information in subfield h in the 245 field. I could continue, but I'm sure you get the picture.

Remember I said that the rules tell you where to look on the resource for the descriptions to put in each area of information? There's more: down at the element level, the rules also tell you *how* to enter each piece of information. Once you go to the right place on a resource to find a particular piece of information, the rules then tell you whether to give that information:

FIGURE 3.3
AACR2 RULES AND MARC 21 FORMAT SUBFIELDS

AACR2	All	Book	Sound Recordings	Video	Serial	MARC 21 Subfield
	Ch 1	Ch 2	Ch 6	Ch 7	Ch 12	
Title and statement of responsibility area	1.1	2.1	6.1	7.1	12.1	245
Preliminary rule	1.1A	2.1A	6.1A	7.1A	12.1A	
Title proper	1.1B	2.1B	6.1B	7.1B	12.1B	$a
General material designation	1.1C	2.1C	6.1C	7.1C	12.1C	$h
Parallel titles	1.1D	2.1D	6.1D	7.1D	12.1D	$b
Other title information	1.1E	2.1E	6.1E	7.1E	12.1E	$b
Statements of responsibility	1.1F	2.1F	6.1F	7.1F	12.1F	$c
Items without a collective title	1.G	2.G	6.G	7.G	12.G	$b or $c

- exactly as it is given on the resource (e.g., titles, parallel titles, and subtitles) in the form in which it appears (e.g., statements of responsibility) or
- as found, but using abbreviations from appendix B and numerals from appendix C (edition statements and publication details) or
- as free text (notes)

The makers of the rules aren't intentionally trying to drive you crazy, no matter how it seems. Keep this in mind as we go to the next level of detail, because the rules proceed to tell us exactly what punctuation to put in front of or around each element and subfield in each area (field).

The punctuation is called *ISBD punctuation* and can be very useful for patrons, even kids. If you are looking at a record in your catalog and trying to help someone figure out the title of a resource when that title is in a language you cannot read, just look for one of the ISBD punctuation marks that signal where the title ends and another sort of information begins. For example, suppose the catalog record says, "Rawls : een inleiding in zijn werk / Ronald Tinnevelt & Gert Verschraegen." Using the ISBD punctuation, you can break this title and statement of responsibility area/field into its elements/subfields, as follows:

- **"Rawls"** is the main title, because it is at the beginning of the field.
- **"een inleiding in zijn werk"** is the subtitle (preceded by space-colon-space).
- **"Ronald Tinnevelt & Gert Verschraegen"** is the statement of responsibility (preceded by space-slash-space).

Granted, younger patrons might find punctuation rules hard to remember, but you should not find it too difficult to grasp them, especially if you consider the alternative, without the funny punctuation: "Rawls een inleiding in zijn werk Ronald Tinnevelt & Gert Verschraegen." As you can see, without the ISBD punctuation, we really have no idea where one piece of information (title) ends and another (subtitle, responsibility statement) begins.

Many patterns are found in AACR. These patterns help reveal the big picture, but there's no escaping the need to get down to nitty-gritty details and learn the actual rules. It might be helpful to start with Michael Gorman's *Concise AACR2* or *Maxwell's Handbook for AACR2* or both, and then move up to Deborah A. Fritz's *Cataloging with AACR2 and MARC21*.[6] Eventually, though, you still have to face the full versions of rules and standards. Let's see more examples of how they work together.

MORE ABOUT MARC

We have touched on MARC, showing how areas of information are entered into MARC fields and how elements of these areas are entered into MARC subfields. The same information once entered on cards is now entered in MARC records. Figures 3.4A and 3.4B illustrate how areas and elements from a card display become fields and subfields in a MARC display.

If you try to match each phrase from the card to the MARC record, you'll notice the Title Added Entry on the card seems to be missing in the

FIGURE 3.4A **AREAS AND ELEMENTS IN A CARD DISPLAY**

Main entry for author.
Title [GMD] : subtitle / statement of responsibility for author; another statement of responsibility for illustrator. – Edition statement.
-- Place of publication : Publisher name, date.

Extent of item : other physical details ; dimensions + accompanying material. -- (Series statement)

Notes.
ISBN

1. LC subject heading. 2. Juvenile subject heading. I. Added entry for illustrator. II. Title added entry. III. Series added entry.

                             LCCN

FIGURE 3.4B **FIELDS AND SUBFIELDS IN MARC DISPLAY**

010 ‡a LCCN	300 ‡a Extent of item : ‡b other physical details ; ‡c dimensions + ‡e accompanying material.
020 ‡a ISBN	
1XX 1 ‡a Main entry for author.	490 1 ‡a Series statement
245 10 ‡a Title |h [GMD] : ‡b subtitle / ‡c statement of responsibility for author ; additional statement of responsibility for illustrator.	5XX ‡a Notes.
	6XX 0 ‡a LC subject heading.
	6XX 1 ‡a Juvenile subject heading.
	7XX 1 ‡a Added entry for illustrator.
250 ‡a Edition statement.	8XX __ ‡a Series added entry.
260 ‡a Place of publication : ‡b Publisher name, ‡c date.	

MARC record. Actually, it is present in the coding. The first indicator in the 245 field (the 1 after the 245 tag) tells the OPAC software to make a Title Added Entry. I'll explain indicators, fields, tags, and other MARC coding terms shortly.

Take a deep breath and grit your teeth; this stuff may not be fun, but trust me, you need to know it.

A MARC record begins with a *leader*, which tells a computer program what kind of data the record that follows contains, and a *directory*, which tells the program where to find everything in the record. The leader and directory are followed by the cataloging data, and all of this is stored as one long string of characters. If you save a record in MARC format from the LC OPAC, you see the leader, directory, and long string of data in its raw "communications" format. Figure 3.5 is an example of a record saved in MARC format from the LC OPAC. Fortunately, when catalogers look at MARC, it is displayed in a more readable manner, as shown in figure 3.6.

Even more fortunately, when library users look at MARC records, they see none of this confusing coding, but it is this coding that allows us to specify exactly what information is displayed in the different types of records users see. Figures 3.7 and 3.8 show two very different displays of the same MARC information, depending on the display options a library chooses in the LC OPAC.

FIGURE 3.5 **MARC RECORD FROM THE LC OPAC DISPLAYED IN RAW COMMUNICATIONS FORMAT**

FIGURE 3.6 **MARC RECORD FROM THE LC OPAC DISPLAYED IN MARC FORMAT**

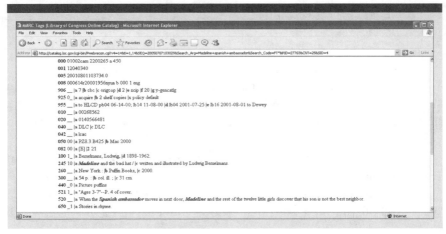

Compare figure 3.8 with figure 3.6 and notice that some of the fields listed in the MARC record do not appear in the LC OPAC's Full Record Display. This occurs because certain MARC fields are included for the use of the computer and are not meant to be seen by library users (e.g., fields 000, 001, 005, 008, 906, 915, 955, 040, 042, and others not shown in this example). The information in these fields is not added because AACR2 tells us to do so; it is added because MARC tells us to do so, illustrating again that we follow two sets of instructions.

As you struggle with understanding all this, please try to remember that MARC coding is vitally important for allowing us to dictate which information is displayed and when, and, equally important, what information is indexed (made searchable) and in which indexes. With these two essential points in mind, let us continue to look at some of the most important things you need to know about MARC coding.

TAGS, SUBFIELDS, AND DELIMITERS

We need fields for entering the different areas of information required by the cataloging rules. In MARC, each field is labeled with a *tag*. Tags are three-digit numbers used to tell programs (and catalogers) what kind of information the field contains. For example, the 245 tag indicates the field

FIGURE 3.7 **A BRIEF RECORD DISPLAY IN THE LC OPAC**

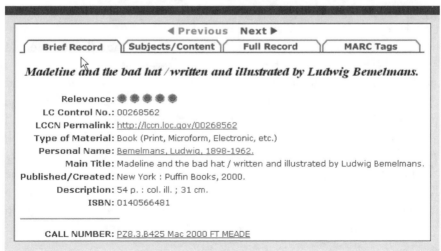

◄ Previous   Next ►

Brief Record   Subjects/Content   Full Record   MARC Tags

Madeline and the bad hat / written and illustrated by Ludwig Bemelmans.

Relevance: ● ● ● ● ●
LC Control No.: 00268562
LCCN Permalink: http://lccn.loc.gov/00268562
Type of Material: Book (Print, Microform, Electronic, etc.)
Personal Name: Bemelmans, Ludwig, 1898-1962.
Main Title: Madeline and the bad hat / written and illustrated by Ludwig Bemelmans.
Published/Created: New York : Puffin Books, 2000.
Description: 54 p. : col. ill. ; 31 cm.
ISBN: 0140566481

CALL NUMBER: PZ8.3.B425 Mac 2000 FT MEADE

FIGURE 3.8 **A FULL RECORD DISPLAY IN THE LC OPAC**

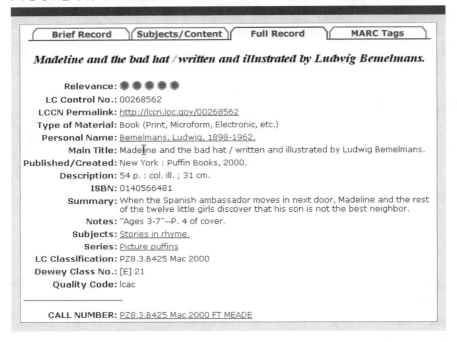

| Brief Record | Subjects/Content | Full Record | MARC Tags |

Madeline and the bad hat / written and illustrated by Ludwig Bemelmans.

Relevance: ● ● ● ● ●
LC Control No.: 00268562
LCCN Permalink: http://lccn.loc.gov/00268562
Type of Material: Book (Print, Microform, Electronic, etc.)
Personal Name: Bemelmans, Ludwig, 1898-1962.
Main Title: Madeline and the bad hat / written and illustrated by Ludwig Bemelmans.
Published/Created: New York : Puffin Books, 2000.
Description: 54 p. : col. ill. ; 31 cm.
ISBN: 0140566481
Summary: When the Spanish ambassador moves in next door, Madeline and the rest of the twelve little girls discover that his son is not the best neighbor.
Notes: "Ages 3-7"--P. 4 of cover.
Subjects: Stories in rhyme.
Series: Picture puffins
LC Classification: PZ8.3.B425 Mac 2000
Dewey Class No.: [E] 21
Quality Code: lcac

CALL NUMBER: PZ8.3.B425 Mac 2000 FT MEADE

that contains title and statement of responsibility information; the 260 tag indicates the field that contains publishing information.

These fields are further divided into *subfields* for entering the specific elements of each area of information. In MARC, each subfield uses a code to tell programs (and catalogers) what kind of information the subfield contains. For example, subfield a in the 245 field contains the title, and subfield c in the 245 field contains the statement of responsibility.

Because subfield codes use letters of the alphabet (in lowercase) and numerals 1 through 9, MARC needs a way to differentiate a subfield code from the actual data in a field. This is done using a symbol called a subfield *delimiter*. The delimiter is a special code that tells the program (and the cataloger) that the character that follows it is a subfield code. A delimiter can look different depending on the cataloging software being used: in the LC example in figure 3.6, it is a pipe sign "|"; in OCLC, it looks like a double dagger "‡"; in BiblioFile, it looks like an upside-down highlighted triangle "▼"; in many other displays, it looks like a dollar sign "$." However it might look, it is the same special character in all cases (ASCII 1F in hex or ASCII 31 in decimal). Be sure to follow your software's instructions for entering this character rather than trying to enter any of the preceding symbols—never enter a dollar sign ($) as a subfield delimiter.

In addition to the tag and the subfield codes, each variable data field has two important codes called *indicators*. The meaning of each indicator depends on the field to which it is attached. Indicators can tell us

- whether a field should be indexed (traced/searchable)
- whether a field should be displayed (printed)
- whether any characters at the beginning of the field should be skipped in indexing (nonfiling characters)
- whether a special label should be displayed (printed) for the field (display constants)
- other equally important things

It is very important that indicator positions are coded correctly. If they are wrong, kids might not be able to find books by their titles (because an indicator told the system to start indexing the title with the word *The* instead of the word that followed), or they might not be able to understand why a particular record is not displayed from their search (because an indicator told the software to index a field, making it searchable, but not to display it, making it invisible).

Figure 3.9 illustrates the main sections of variable data fields (010–9XX).

Control fields (001–009) are an exception to this pattern. They do not have indicators or subfields. Control fields may contain only a single data element, such as a control number (001), a control number identifier (003), or a timestamp (005), or they may contain a series of alphanumeric codes (000, 006, 007, and 008).

FIGURE 3.9
MAIN SECTIONS OF A VARIABLE DATA FIELD (010–9XX)

Tag	1st Indicator	2nd Indicator	Subfield a	Subfield b	Subfield c
245	1	0	$a Title	$b subtitle	$c responsibility

Although difficult for beginners to remember, these coded fields (000, 006, 007, and 008) are very important. For example, a combination of codes in a combination of coded fields (000 and 007) tells OPAC software to show a little CD icon in the catalog for records describing sound recordings. If the coded data that do this are not entered correctly (as is too often the case), the displayed icon is for a book (the default), or, if someone is looking for all the books in Spanish but the language code for Spanish was not entered, the software cannot identify them.

PATTERNS

There are patterns in MARC coding. For example, fields are grouped into blocks of tags, as shown in figure 3.10. Patterns also occur across groupings. For example, all personal name headings are entered in tags that end in 00; all corporate name headings are entered in tags that end in 10; and so on, as shown in figure 3.11.

Combining figures 3.10 and 3.11, you can see the following:

- personal name heading that is a main entry is entered in a 100 field (1XX = main entry; X00 = personal name)
- corporate name heading that is a subject is entered in a 610 field (6XX = subject heading; X10 = corporate name)
- conference that is an added entry is entered in a 711 field (7XX = added entry; X11 = conference name)
- uniform title that is a series added entry is entered in an 830 field (8XX = series added entry; X30 = uniform title), or a 440 (now obsolete)—but that's another story

FIGURE 3.10 MARC FORMAT FIELD TAG GROUPS

001–009	Control fields	4XX	Series statement fields
01X–04X	Number and code fields	5XX	Note fields
05X–08X	Classification and call number fields	6XX	Subject access fields
		70X–75X	Added entry fields
1XX	Main entry fields	76X–78X	Linking entry fields
20X–24X	Title and title-related fields	80X–83X	Series added entry fields
250–270	Edition, imprint, etc. fields	841–88X	Holdings, location, alternate graphs, etc. fields
3XX	Physical description, etc. fields	9XX	Local fields

FIGURE 3.11 **GROUPINGS ACROSS MARC FIELD TAGS**

X00	Personal name headings	**X11**	Conference name headings
X10	Corporate name headings	**X30**	Uniform title headings

FIGURE 3.12 **PATTERNS WITHIN GROUPINGS**

$v	Form subdivision	**$y**	Chronological subdivision
$x	General subdivision	**$z**	Geographic subdivision

Patterns also occur within each grouping. For example, the second indicator of all 6XX fields tells us the source of the subject heading entered in that field (e.g., LCSH, LC Children's, Sears). All the fields in the 6XX also share the same subfields, as shown in figure 3.12. Any of the subject subdivision subfields can be added to any subject heading in a 6XX field.

APPLYING AACR2 AND MARC 21—AN EXAMPLE

There is a great deal more to learn about MARC coding. Two very good places to start are the LC tutorial called *Understanding MARC Bibliographic* and Fritz's *MARC 21 for Everyone.* This short chapter cannot begin to teach all you need to know to create a MARC 21 record following AACR2. To illustrate the complexity involved, let's walk through the steps of how a cataloger applies AACR2 and MARC 21 to provide title and statement of responsibility information for a book.

1. Turn to AACR2 to:
   - find out where to look on the book to find the title and statement of responsibility information (the title page—2.0B)
   - check the general rules for titles (1.1B)
   - check the book rules for titles (2.1B)
   - find out what to enter first (the title proper—1.1B1)
   - check whether to transcribe the title exactly as given or with abbreviations, and so on (transcribe exactly—1.1B2)

2. With the title ready for entering, turn to MARC, which tells how to:
   - enter 245 as the field's tag (to tell the program title information is about to be provided)
   - skip the first indicator until it is clear whether to index the title as a main entry or an added entry
   - look at the first word of the title and decide whether to begin indexing at that word or skip it—if the word is an initial article, such as The, An, A, Los, Las, and so on, use the second indicator to enter the number of characters the program should skip (the number of letters in the article plus one for the space that follows it), or, if the word is not an initial article, enter 0
   - enter subfield a (because information in this field always begins with the title proper), not forgetting the special delimiter character before the subfield (which could display as ‡, ▼, $, etc.)
   - enter the title proper, transcribed exactly as it is given on the title page, just as AACR2 said to do

3. Alternate between AACR2 and MARC to complete the title field:
   - Read on through the rules to find the next bit of information that might be needed: a GMD (general material designation), a word or phrase indicating the physical form of the resource—it is a book and not large print; therefore a GMD is not necessary, so skip it.
   - The next rule says to look for a parallel title—the book is not bilingual (for example, with two titles, one in English and one in Spanish), so skip this, too.
   - The next rule says to look for other title information, such as a subtitle—yes, there is one of those; you already know where to look for the subtitle (the same place as the title—the title page, per 2.0B), so read the general rules for other title information (1.1E), check how you are to transcribe it (1.1E2), and check for any special book rules (2.1E). Then enter it—but where?
   - MARC says subtitles go in tag 245 subfield b; but what about the special separating punctuation (the ISBD punctuation)?

- Go back to AACR2, which says a subtitle is preceded by a space-colon-space (1.1A1).
- Add the punctuation at the end of the preceding subfield (in this case subfield a) and enter the subtitle in a subfield b, transcribing it exactly as given on the title page, just as AACR2 said to do.
- The next AACR2 rule says to look for a statement of responsibility. The book has an author and an illustrator, and you already know where to look for this information (the same place as the title—the title page, per 2.0B). Just check how to transcribe it (1.1F2), read the general rules for the statement of responsibility (1.1F), and check for any special book rules (2.1F). Then enter it—where?
- MARC says statements of responsibility go in tag 245 subfield c; but what about the special separating punctuation (the ISBD punctuation)?
- Go back to AACR2, which says that a statement of responsibility is preceded by a space-forward slash-space, and different functions (such as author and illustrator) are separated by space-semicolon-space (1.1A1).
- There are two statements of responsibility (author and illustrator), so you have to check MARC again for whether you need two subfields c—no, subfield c is not repeatable in the 245 field.
- Enter the statement of responsibility in a single subfield c preceded by a space-slash-space, separating the different statements with space-semicolon-space, and transcribing the statements exactly as they are given on the title page, just as AACR2 said to do.
- Finally, add the end-of-field punctuation. A new area of information is going to follow this field, and because AACR2 says all new areas are preceded by period-space-dash-space (1.0C1), this field must end with a period (the computer will provide the space-dash-space if it is needed).

There you have it—how to enter the title and statement of responsibility for a book into a MARC 21 bibliographic record, in a nutshell. Should you wish to know how to enter an edition statement, publication details, the physical description, series statements, notes, and standard numbers—in other words, the rest of the bibliographic description for your book, much less the headings that allow your patrons to find your carefully crafted descriptions—you should sign up as soon as you can for a continuing education workshop on the subject! You probably have already guessed that this isn't something you can learn by reading manuals on your own or by trial and error. There are too many layers to sort through without some sort of guidance.

Ideally, you will be able to get most of the needed MARC records from somewhere else, whether by doing copy cataloging in-house or from a records vendor, but don't think that you can completely escape your fate by farming your cataloging out to someone else. You still have to know something about the cataloging process if you are going to maintain quality control over the records you are sent. And you do need quality control, because not even LC catalogers are perfect.

CONCLUSION

The bottom line is that the way resources are described is the same for records intended for both adults' and kids' use, with special emphasis on *adding* information particularly useful for kids, such as Summary notes, Contents notes, Audience notes, even Awards notes. Access points are also the same for adults' or kids' use, with the addition of the following:

- Always include added entries for illustrators of children's books.
- Continue to add series added entries, even though LC is no longer doing so, because kids love books in series and want to know about them (use field 490, because the 440 field is now obsolete).
- Add LC subject headings or genre headings or both for everything—fiction and nonfiction (65X Ind 2 = 0)—and add LC Children's Subject Headings for everything (650 Ind 2 = 1) to go in your Kids' Subject Index.

All that said, don't despair. It isn't that hard to grasp all this once someone explains it to you and you have a chance to practice doing it (back to the need for training). Once you've got it, you'll be able to provide your kids with an effective catalog that will perform its function of making your library's resources accessible to those kids, their parents, and anyone else who stumbles upon it.

RESOURCES

Fritz, Deborah A. *MARC 21 for Everyone: A Practical Guide*. Chicago: American Library Association, 2003.

MARC 21 Format for Bibliographic Data (MARC). www.loc.gov/marc/bibliographic/ecbdhome.html.

OCLC Bibliographic Formats and Standards. 1993. www.oclc.org/bibformats/en/.

Understanding MARC Bibliographic. 2009. www.loc.gov/marc/umb/.

NOTES

1. *Anglo-American Cataloguing Rules*, 2nd ed., 2002 rev. and updates (Chicago: American Library Association, 2002–).
2. *Cataloger's Desktop*, available by subscription from the Library of Congress, Cataloging Distribution Service, Washington, DC.
3. Joint Steering Committee for Development of RDA, "A Brief History of AACR," www.rda-jsc.org/history.html.
4. See chapters 7, 8, and 9 for explanations of Library of Congress Annotated Card program subject headings for children's materials, *Sears List of Subject Headings*, and Dewey Decimal Classification, respectively.
5. These include *Library of Congress Rule Interpretations* (2002 cumulation, plus updates for 2003, 2004, and 2005), available on Cataloger's Desktop, www.loc.gov/cds/desktop/; the CONSER Cataloging Manual and CONSER Editing Guide, www.loc.gov/cds/catman.html; and other manuals issued by LC.
6. Michael Gorman, *Concise AACR2* (Chicago: American Library Association, 2004); Robert L. Maxwell, *Maxwell's Handbook for AACR2* (Chicago: American Library Association, 2004); and Deborah A. Fritz, *Cataloging with AACR2 and MARC21* (Chicago: American Library Association, 2003).

CHAPTER 4

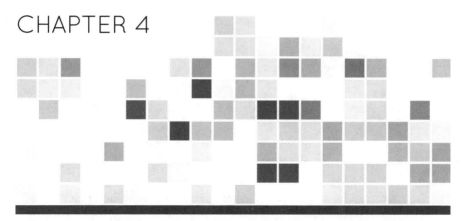

Copy Cataloging Correctly

Deborah A. Fritz

Having read this far, you may now know just enough about AACR2, MARC 21, descriptive cataloging, authority controlled headings, subject headings, call numbers, and the special joys of cataloging nonbook material to realize you'd rather not do it yourself if you don't have to. Outsourcing cataloging is one way of having someone else do it for you. Another way to get the cataloging done is to copy someone else's records. This is perfectly acceptable—even encouraged—behavior in the cataloging world. In fact, library administrators seem to believe the glorious day has already arrived when anyone in the library can catalog, because someone else, somewhere else, has already made a record for every resource in the world. All a cataloger has to do these days is find and copy those records. Would that it were so simple!

WHY COPY CATALOGING?

Let's go back to the beginning (again) to set the stage for how copy cataloging fits into the whole cataloging picture. You have a stack of new items: books, CDs, DVDs, and so on. You need to get those resources out on the shelves. But before you can put them on the shelves, they need to be cataloged. This means you must provide bibliographic information for each resource that accomplishes the following:

- describes it (bibliographic description, such as title, edition, publisher, etc.)
- provides terms by which someone might search for it (access points—for example, names, titles, subjects, etc.)
- provides a call number for it (classification) so that each physical item can be shelved with other materials on similar subjects (e.g., ships) or with other materials of the same physical medium (e.g., large print)
- links the barcode number on the item to the catalog record (holdings information)

This detailed information has to be entered into MARC records so the OPAC can show it to your kids, the circulation system can track loans accurately, and you can share your records and resources with other libraries.

How can it be done? Original cataloging is time consuming and demands a high level of training. Copy cataloging is cost-effective and does not require quite as much training. However, to do a proper job of copy cataloging, at the very least you have to know the following:

- where to find records to copy
- how to search for records to copy
- how to match records with your resources
- how to edit records
- how to add holdings information, such as barcode numbers, locations, and call numbers, to the records
- how to download records from the source site
- how to import records to your library automation system
- how to check that the imported records loaded properly (did not match wrong records already in the database, or, alternatively, loaded as duplicate records)

I can't tell you about the last four steps. How you download from the source for MARC records depends on what the source is. How records are imported to a library automation system is up to that automation system.

How holdings information is added and records are checked to be sure they loaded correctly are also up to local library automation systems. I can and will, however, tell you something about the first four steps.

SOURCES OF MARC RECORDS

There are many records out there that can be copied instead of creating your own—you just have to find them. Here's a list of some sources of MARC records:

> *Shared systems.* If you share a database with other libraries, and another library has already added to the database a MARC record that matches your resource, you simply have to attach your holdings information (barcode, call number, item cost, etc.) to that record; this may be called *add item* or *linking*, but it is still copy cataloging.
>
> *Library of Congress* (LC). The online public access catalog (OPAC) of the Library of Congress (http://catalog.loc.gov) is freely available to any cataloger who has an Internet connection. Records from LC's OPAC can be copied (downloaded) and imported (uploaded) into your local library automation system.
>
> *Bibliographic utilities.* Bibliographic utilities, such as OCLC (www .oclc.org), charge for making their records available for copying but offer many more records than LC. If you are a member of such a utility, you can copy records made by other members (including LC records).
>
> *MARC record vendors.* MARC record vendors offer access to copies of the LC database via CD-ROMs or the Internet or both; MARC records collected from other sources may also be included.
>
> *Z39.50 software.* If the cataloging module of your automation system offers Z39.50 capability, this can be used to search the databases of hundreds of library systems via the Internet and to download MARC records from those databases. If the cataloging module in a local library system does not offer Z39.50, stand-alone software can be purchased to obtain the same capability.
>
> *Outsourcing.* Many libraries contract with book jobbers and publishers to receive a MARC record for every resource that they purchase.

Notice that outsourcing is included in the list of options for copy cataloging. Outsourcing is described in more detail in chapter 15, but be aware it is a type of copy cataloging. When records are received from an outsourcer, they have to be checked just as though they were pulled in from any other source. Outsourcing saves you the step of finding the records, but please don't think that once you get your outsourced records all you have to do is load them. You might *have* to do this and hope for the best if you are doing a retrospective conversion (i.e., converting a card catalog to MARC records) or if you are getting fifty thousand records all at once for an opening day collection. But, if you are receiving small numbers of vendor records on an ongoing basis for the new materials you order, you need to check them to be sure that they truly match your resources and to see if they need editing (for example, are LC's Children's Subject Headings present and properly assigned in every vendor record you receive?).

I'll get to matching and editing shortly, but first let's consider some secrets of searching.

SEARCHING FOR MARC RECORDS

I listed a number of options for sources of MARC records earlier. Unfortunately, each of these sources has its own quirks when it comes to searching. You'll have to read the instructions for each source of records to learn the quirks. Don't be like the cataloger who came to one of my workshops and revealed that for five years she hadn't been able to find any records for ISBNs that ended with an X. The instruction manual for her software had the answer (enter 7 instead of X), but she hadn't read it!

You have to find out what your cataloging interface requires when it comes to searching. Here are a few suggestions about what you might want to research.

- Are hyphens included when searching via an LCCN or ISBN?
- Are there *stopwords* that should not be included in your search?
- Is punctuation, such as apostrophes, commas, and so on, entered or omitted?

Read your software manuals or help screens for the answers to these and similar questions.

Once you know how your search software works, you need to learn the best search terms to use for finding matching MARC records, no matter what the source. Some search terms are great for finding any type of record (for example, ISBNs are good for finding records for books, videos, sound recordings, etc.). Some are extremely useful for certain types of material but not for others (LCCNs are good for books and print serials, but unavailable for videos and sound recordings). On the other hand, publisher's numbers are great for videos and sound recordings, but not helpful for books or serials. Still other search terms can be used for any type of material, but only if previously used terms fail to retrieve the desired records (such as series titles).

To keep things simple and brief, this chapter covers only search terms for finding book records. For more details on search terms for electronic resources, sound recordings, videos, and serials, see the Search Tables in Deborah A. Fritz's *Cataloging with AACR2 and MARC21.*[1]

SEARCHING LIBRARY OF CONGRESS CONTROL NUMBERS

LCCNs are usually found on title page versos if they are present in a book and appear in one of two formats, depending on when the number was assigned:

old format (pre-2001): for example, 96-16774 (two digits representing the year of cataloging + a sequential accession number)
new format (post-2001): for example, 2001-456 (four digits representing the year + a sequential accession number)

An LCCN is a very good choice for searching books published in the United States. If you search the LC database by an LCCN, you should bring up only one record. Usually, this record will match your resource. However, be warned that an LCCN search in any database other than LC's can sometimes bring up more than one record. When an LCCN retrieves multiple records or retrieves a record that does not match your resource, you must flag that LCCN for possible editing later.

SEARCHING ISBNS

An ISBN is usually found on a title page verso or the back cover of a book or both and may take one of two forms, depending on when it was assigned:

old format (pre-2004): ten digits (the last digit can be X, but no other alphabetic characters are valid)

new format (post-2004): thirteen digits (the last digit can be X, but no other alphabetic characters are valid)

ISBNs are very important for searching. If you search by an ISBN, most of the time you will bring up just one record that matches your book. That record may not always match your resource, however. If this is the case, or if the ISBN retrieves multiple records, it must be flagged for possible editing later.

SEARCHING NAMES

Names can be searched, but should only be used if numeric search terms fail, because they are less efficient as search terms. The name you search does not have to be an author. It could be the name of an illustrator, an editor, a translator, and so on. Be careful how you search for compound surnames, because they can be tricky. For example, how would you search for Lynn Reid Banks—as "Banks, Lynn Reid" or as "Reid Banks, Lynn"? Also, watch for authors who have changed their names or have used more than one name (a pseudonym and a real name, or several pseudonyms).

SEARCHING TITLES

If a title is unique, it can be an effective search term, especially when numbers, such as LCCNs or ISBNs, are unavailable. Titles can be much simpler to search than names. However, different authors have been known to use the same title for very different books, so never assume a record found by a title search is sure to match your book.

SEARCHING COMBINED NAMES/TITLES

Combining names and titles (if your search menu permits this) can be much more effective than searching by either names or titles alone. You do not have to use the name of an author for this type of search; you can also use the name of an editor, illustrator, or the like.

SEARCHING SERIES TITLES

Sometimes nothing seems to work, but you know there must be a record somewhere for your resource. If there is a series title on the resource, try searching it. You may get a long list of works in the series, but it still might be better than trying to search by a common name, such as "Smith, John" or "Shakespeare, William," or a common title, such as "The Civil War" (which retrieves 3,300 different records when searched in LC's OPAC).

Figure 4.1 shows what the LC OPAC offers as "Basic Search" options. Note that LCCNs and ISBNs can be searched using the first option "Keyword (match all words)," but be careful, because using a keyword search may bring up multiple hits on a number, whereas choosing "Number Search (LCCN-ISBN-ISSN)" should, usually, bring up only a single hit on a number search. "Browse" searching also provides better results for catalogers than keyword searching when looking for names or titles, or both. Use "Title Begins With" and "Author/Creator Browse" in the LC OPAC search options, as shown in figure 4.1.

FIGURE 4.1
THE "BASIC SEARCH" OPTIONS IN THE LC OPAC

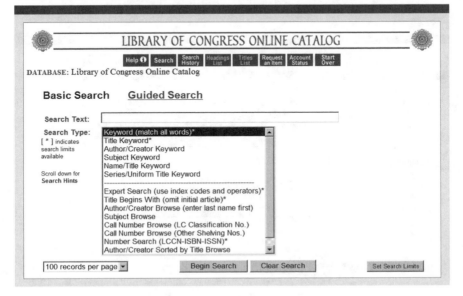

SEARCH QUALIFIERS

DATES

If there is a date on your resource, you can narrow your search by adding the date, if your software will allow you to do so. You may have to go to a more advanced level of searching to do this.

PHYSICAL FORMAT

There is little point in qualifying by "type of material = book" because most records in library catalogs are books. However, if you are looking for the sound recording of *Hamlet* rather than the book, qualifying by the type of material could narrow your results very nicely. Figures 4.2 and 4.3 show how to qualify searches in LC's OPAC and OCLC's Connexion software.

MATCHING MARC RECORDS AGAINST RESOURCES

Once a record is found, you cannot simply say "That looks close enough" and use it, or change a few things to make it match better and then use it. You need to review a list of *match criteria* to be sure that the record truly matches the resource in your hand.

FIGURE 4.2 **SETTING SEARCH LIMITS IN THE LC OPAC**

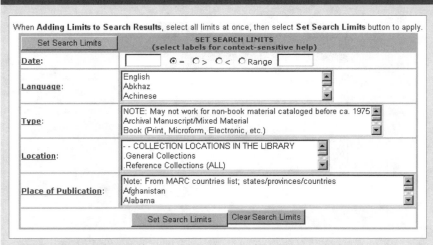

FIGURE 4.3 **SEARCH SCREEN IN OCLC'S CONNEXION**

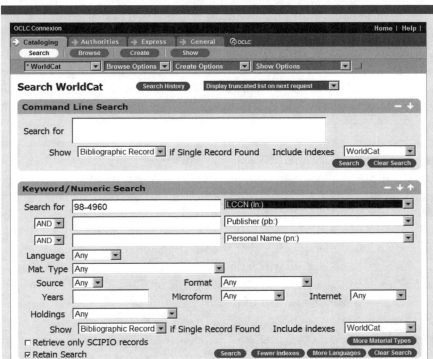

Until the end of 2004, the only official match criteria documenta-tion available was provided by OCLC in its online manual as a chapter titled "When to Input a New Record."[2] The guidelines in this rather long chapter are paraphrased in a series of shorter tables in Fritz's *Cataloging with AACR2 and MARC21*. In late 2004, the Task Force on an Appendix of Major and Minor Changes (part of the Committee on Cataloging: Description and Access of the Cataloging and Classification Section of the Association for Library Collections & Technical Services) produced its own set of guidelines in a document called *Differences Between, Changes Within*.[3]

The guidelines in the three documents just listed are basically the same, just given in different forms. It doesn't really matter which set of guidelines is used, but one of them needs to be followed consistently to be sure you only copy records that really match your resources.

Why? Let's say you understand the general principles of matching records to resources, but instead of following any of the guidelines, you do what seems good sense at the moment. One day you find a record that has the same title as your book, and the same author. The publisher is almost the same but has a slightly different name (because it was recently bought by another publisher and their names are now combined). The pagination is also slightly different, off by six pages. Because the date of publication is the same, however, you decide this record is close enough to be called a match for your resource. The three sets of guidelines listed earlier all agree in saying that this record is not a match and that you need to make a new record because the name of the publisher has changed, the pagination does not match, and, if you look more closely, your book does not have the introduction mentioned in the record. Not knowing about the need for this level of detail in matching, you take the record as is, or you might change the publisher to the name on your book and change the pagination to match yours, and you may or may not get rid of the wording about the introduction.

Either way, the record works fine in your own catalog, because your kids don't care about the picky details just described. But, if you are, or might someday be, a part of any sort of resource sharing arrangement (for example, a union catalog, such as OCLC or SUNLINK, or a virtual union catalog, such as AlleyCat), picture what happens when your record joins other records in the union catalog. Because your record has the same LCCN/ISBN as the record you copied and changed, your record will be linked to that original record.

Let's say that one day John, a student, searches and finds the record to which you are linked, and requests the item from your library to write a paper. John gets your version of the work, finds it lacks the introduction (which is really what he was looking for), and is now up the creek—with no time to go back to the library to get the version he really needs. He loses all faith in the interlibrary loan process, decides to purchase the item, and never darkens the door of a library again, all because you did not follow the guidelines for matching records.

Wouldn't it be better to follow the match criteria guidelines than to lose John as a library patron forever? Even if he is not your patron, we want the interlibrary loan system to work for all libraries, not just our own. So, even if you say you are cataloging for kids and kids don't care about introductions to books, remember the needs of other patrons in other libraries and the implications of your actions on the entire interlibrary loan process.

When matching records, always be sure to look at the MARC record view. No matter what source you copy from, use the MARC view, such as the one shown in figure 4.4, to match records to resources. The fields in bold print are the ones, in this record, that must be carefully checked for matching.

Figure 4.4 gives a brief list of the most important fields that you must check when you are matching any book against a record. Note that, contrary to the expectations of many, neither the LCCN nor the ISBN is listed in figure 4.4 as a field that is to be used for matching. Both are great for searching and machine matching, but they do not matter for human matching.

It would take far more than the limited space allowed by this chapter to explain all the details of how to match records, with examples. To learn more than is given here, turn to one of the previously mentioned guidelines, attend a continuing education workshop, or do both. In particular, two seemingly minor, but very important, steps need your attention: matching to Cataloging-in-Publication (CIP) records and to Encoding Level 3 records.

FIGURE 4.4 **MARC RECORD HIGHLIGHTING FIELDS USED FOR MATCHING**

000 01185cam 2200361 a 4500	**245 10** ‡aHenry the fourth /‡cby Stuart J. Murphy ; illustrated by Scott Nash.	
001 98004960		
003 DLC	**246 3** ‡aHenry the 4th	
008 980109s1999 nyua j 000 0 eng	**250** ‡a1st ed.	

Entrd: 980109	DtSt: s	Dates: 1999,
Ctry: nyu	Ills: a	Audn: j
Form:	Cont:	GPub:
Conf: 0	Fest: 0	Indx: 0
M/E:	LitF: 0	Biog: Lang:
eng	MRec:	Srce:

010 ‡a 98004960	**260** ‡aNew York :‡bHarperCollins Publishers,‡cc1999.
020 ‡a006027610X	**300** ‡a33 p. :‡bcol. ill. ;‡c21 x 26 cm.
020 ‡a0064467198 (pbk.)	**440 0** ‡aMathStart
020 ‡a0060276118 (lib. bdg.)	**521 1** ‡a"Level 1, ages 3 up"—P. [4] of cover.
040 ‡aDLC‡cDLC‡dDLC	**520** ‡aA simple story about four dogs at a dog show introduces the ordinal numbers: first, second, third, and fourth.
042 ‡alcac	
050 00 ‡aQA141.3‡b.M87 1999	
082 00 ‡a513‡221	**650 0** ‡aNumbers, Ordinal‡vJuvenile literature.
100 1 ‡aMurphy, Stuart J.,‡d1942-	**650 1** ‡aNumbers, Ordinal.
	700 1 ‡aNash, Scott,‡d1959-‡eill.

MATCHING TO CIP AND TO ENCODING
LEVEL 3 RECORDS

When looking at a record you think might match your book, the very first
thing to check is the record's Encoding Level, which indicates the degree
of completeness of the MARC record. This is found at position 17 in the
leader of the record. To find position 17, first remember that the leader
is the first tag in a record, usually represented as tag 000. Next, when you
are looking for positions in a leader string, count like a computer and start
at zero (0). In the leader of the record shown in figure 4.4, position 17 is
blank. This means that the record is Full Level according to LC's standards:
"The most complete MARC level created from information derived from
an inspection of the physical item."[4]

In an OCLC MARC record (e.g., figure 4.5), look for leader position
17 in the fixed field area, labeled "ELvl."

In figure 4.5 the ELvl (leader position 17) contains an 8. This means the
record is a CIP record. See figure 4.5 for additional signs that tell you a record
is a CIP record, including the presence of a 263 field (projected date of publication) and the presence of "p. cm." as the only information in the 300 field.
The publication of the book hasn't been completed; therefore, the number of
pages and the height of the spine can't be determined and are left blank.

CIP records are created when a publisher sends LC (or another national
library) a draft of a book that hasn't been published yet, or fills out a form
with information about the book. The cataloging agency makes a CIP cataloging record from that draft or form and sends it to the publisher, which
prints a copy of the CIP record in the book when it is published. This means
that CIP records are created without the finished book in hand. Anything
can change—and often does—between the time the publisher sends the
draft or form to the cataloging agency and the time when the book is actually published. This means you should be more lenient about the match
criteria for such a record. If a record is CIP, you can accept it as a match *as
long as the LCCN (010) or the National Bibliographic Agency Control Number
of another national library (016) matches what you find in the book and the rest
of the record looks as though it could be for your book.*

If leader position 17 contains a 3, as shown in figure 4.6, it means that
the record is abbreviated. Abbreviated records can be created by libraries,
in which case catalogers have to use their best judgment to decide whether
what the record describes matches the resources they have in front of
them. But, publishers have also started to create abbreviated records, intend-

FIGURE 4.5
AN OCLC MARC RECORD VIEWED USING CONNEXION

OCLC 316772138

Books ▼		Rec Stat c	Entered 20090320	Replaced 20090519032220.6		
Type a	**ELvl** 8	**Srce**	**Audn** a	**Ctrl**	**Lang** eng
BLvl m	**Form**	**Conf** 0	**Biog**	**MRec**	**Ctry** nyu
	Cont	**GPub**	**LitF** 1	**Indx** 0	
Desc a	**Ills**	**Fest** 0	**DtSt** s	**Dates** 2009 ,	

```
>010   2009009606
>040   DLC $c DLC $d BTCTA
>020   9780545115100 (alk. paper)
>020   0545115108 (alk. paper)
>042   lcac
>050 00 PZ7.W64816 $b Hug 2009
>082 14 [E] $2 22
>100 1 Wilhelm, Hans, $d 1945-
>245 10 Hugaboo, I love you / $c by Hans Wilhelm.
>260   New York : $b Scholastic, $c 2009.
>263   0912
>300   p. cm.
>520   Lift-up flaps reveal a different kind of hug each baby animal receives from his or her parent.
>650 0 Lift-the-flap books $v Specimens.
>650 1 Hugging $v Fiction.
>650 1 Animals $v Fiction.
>650 1 Lift-the-flap books.
>650 1 Toy and movable books.
```

ing them to be used as pre-order records for resources before they are published. See figure 4.6 for examples of additional signs identifying a record as a pre-order/Level 3 record: the 260 field (publication data) is incomplete, with the place of publication (subfield a) usually missing and the physical description absent or abbreviated.

Like CIP records, pre-order/Level 3 records are created before the resources they describe are published, so anything can change between the time a record is created and the time a resource is published. Once again, be more lenient about the match criteria for these pre-order/Level 3 records. If a record is pre-order/Level 3, it can be accepted as a match *as long as the ISBN (020) matches and the rest of the record looks as though it could be for the book, video, or sound recording being cataloged.*

If none of the CIP or pre-order/Level 3 "signs" is present in a record you have found, you must follow very carefully one of the aforementioned sets of match criteria guidelines for the fields outlined by figure 4.4 to determine whether the record really matches your book.

FIGURE 4.6 **A PRE-ORDER/LEVEL 3 RECORD**

000	00502nam 22002053a 4500	020	|a 0786018720
001	ocn176886230	040	|a BTCTA |c BTCTA |d BAKER
003	OCoLC	100 1	|a Johnstone, William W.
008	070929s2008 xx 000 0	245 10	|a Blood Bond: Texas Gundown.
	eng d	260	|b Pinnacle Books |c 2008.
020	|a 9780786018727	700 1	|a Johnstone, J. A.

To sum up matching, it is *very* important that matching is done properly. Obtain a copy of the match criteria from one of the sources listed earlier. Look carefully at your resource and at any record(s) you find that might match it. Decide whether each field/subfield listed in the match criteria list is okay or not okay. If a field/subfield is okay, move on to the next field/subfield. Continue in this way until you reach the end of the list. If all fields are okay, you have a match. If any are not okay, it is not a match, and you need to find another record or, if no other records are available, enter a new record.

CHOOSING AMONG MARC RECORDS

It used to be, when we first began copy cataloging (many years ago), that we would be grateful to find one record that matched a resource being cataloged. It might seem that finding more than one record that matches a resource would be even better, but this turns out not to be a good thing. Just about everywhere we look (except, perhaps, the LC OPAC), we now find more and more duplicate records from which we have to choose.

Fortunately, subfield a (Original cataloging agency), subfield c (Transcribing agency), and subfield d (Modifying agency) in the 040 field (Cataloging Source) can help us to decide which of two or more matching records to choose. Look for the DLC code in any of these three 040 subfields to indicate that the Library of Congress either created or edited the record. But be careful. We can no longer assume that just because LC has been involved in a record it is perfect. We can only hope it might be better than records made by other libraries. Many libraries make excellent records, however, and if you pay attention to the codes in the 040 subfields, you will start to recognize which they are. Then, you can choose their records over records made by other libraries. See the MARC list of organization sources for the codes in the 040 field that identify the libraries that create or modify records.[5]

Another good place to look for indications that a record should be good is the 042 field (Authentication Code). See figure 4.4 for an example of this field. A list of the meanings of the codes provided in this field is found in the *MARC Field Index to Source Code Usage.*[6] Look for "pcc" (Program for Cooperative Cataloging) and, of course, any code beginning with the letters "lc" (Library of Congress); but, be aware that "lccopycat" indicates that LC copied the record and might have missed important edits needing to be done (yes, even LC catalogers miss things).

These days, you also have to be very careful about using records that have been cataloged in another language. These are not records for the resources written, spoken, or sung in a language that is different from yours, but are records in a language that is different from the language or script used in your catalog. It is easy to pick out records cataloged in a different script, such as Chinese or Japanese, but harder to pick out records cataloged in a different language.

You might not notice the difference until you get to the 300 (Physical description) field or a 5XX (Note) field. With all the records available in many different languages, you need to train yourself to look for the most important clue of all: the 040 subfield b (Language of cataloging). Figure 4.7 shows a record cataloged in French. You might not notice the strange-looking note or the French subject heading, but "fre" in the 040 subfield b tells you that you must not choose this record—look for the English equivalent of the record. If there is no English equivalent (or a record in whatever language your catalog uses), then clone the French record to make a new one in your own language. Do *not* simply copy the French record.

EDITING MARC RECORDS

Many bosses don't want us to edit records we copy. "Don't be so picky, good enough is good enough," they say. "If it's an LC record, it must be okay," they bleat. "You don't have the time to check records," they intone, "so don't let me catch you doing it." My advice: don't let them catch you doing it, but do it, just the same.

Here's another tragic scenario: you work your way quickly and efficiently through an entire book cart in one day, and repeat this achievement day after

FIGURE 4.7
AN OCLC MARC RECORD CATALOGED IN FRENCH

Books	Rec Stat n	Entered 20070420	Replaced 20090710014127.8		
Type a	ELvl M	Srce d	Audn j	Ctrl	Lang eng
BLvl m	Form	Conf 0	Biog	MRec	Ctry bcc
	Cont	GPub	LitF f	Indx 0	
Desc a	Ills	Fest 0	DtSt s	Dates 2007,	

040		U9S ‡b fre ‡c U9S
020		9781551929781 (Cloth)
020		1551929783 (Cloth)
050	_4	PR6068 O85H38 2007
082	04	823/.914 ‡2 22
100	1_	Rowling, J. K.
245	10	Harry Potter and the deathly hallows / ‡c J.K. Rowling.
260		Vancouver : ‡b Raincoast Books, ‡c 2007.
300		607 p. ; ‡c 20 cm.
500		Suite de: Harry Potter and the half-blood prince.
650	_6	Potter, Harry (Personnage fictif)

day after day. Everyone is thrilled, especially your boss, who promotes you to head of cataloging. Then, the complaints start flooding in:

Why can't I find that new best seller by its title? It turns up if I search by author, but half our patrons can't spell that surname—did you forget to check for incorrect indexing or filing indicators in the title field of the record you copied?

Where have all the Spanish books gone? I know we ordered a bunch of bilingual kids' books, but I qualified a search by "language = Spanish," and I can't find the book I distinctly remember seeing on the cart last week—did you forget to check the Language code in the 008 of the record you copied?

A patron checked out and returned a book last month, and now needs to look at it again, but I can't find it anywhere in the catalog no matter what I search. Oh, dear, we must have loaded another record with the same LCCN or ISBN and overlaid that record—did you check that file of outsourced records after you loaded it to be sure that none of the records matched and overlaid incorrectly?

A patron received an overdue notice for a book she would never dream of borrowing. Again, another unchecked record was loaded that caused two different records to match and the barcode for one to be added to the record for the other.

Are you getting the picture that errors in MARC records can have a negative impact on customer satisfaction? In the late 1980s, Arlene Taylor studied accuracy in CIP records and found that "46.2 percent of the sample LC records had at least one error or discrepancy from current practice somewhere in the MARC record. . . . [S]ignificant errors, defined as errors that would affect any kind of access points, were found in 19.6 percent of the records. The difficulty was that there was no way to predict which records would fall into this group without examining every record."[7] It would be nice to think things have gotten better since then, but most catalogers will assure you that does not appear to be the case. So, check the records you copy (or purchase from a vendor) and edit them as needed.

Whatever the source from which records are copied, catalogers must go to a MARC view to do their editing. Figure 4.5 shows in bold print the fields that need to be checked when editing. Notice that nearly every field in the record is in bold type. That's because every one of them needs to be checked!

EDITING MARC RECORDS—SOME EXAMPLES

In the following paragraphs are examples of the most important things to watch for when editing a matching record, but don't think it is a complete list. Such a list doesn't exist, but more detailed instructions on editing can be found in the "editing/cloning/creating records cheat sheets" in Fritz's *Cataloging with AACR2 and MARC21.*

Type of record (000/06). The code in this leader position must match the physical description of the item that the patron sees in the 300 field. If a record you are copying has a Type of Record code and a 300 $a that do not match, the record has to be edited so they match. You'll need to find a MARC manual to find out what codes go in the Type of Record position. This code is very important for showing those cute little icons in the catalog that indicate whether a resource is a book, sound recording, video, and so forth.

Encoding level (000/17). If the code in this leader position is an 8 or a 3, the record is CIP or Abbreviated and, either way, will need to be examined and updated from top to bottom (see the preceding explanation).

Date (008). The first date in the 008 is the one your system uses for qualifying an OPAC search by Date of publication. This date must match the first date in the 260 $c (except for a few situations, such as serials). If, in a matching record you are copying, the first 008 Date does not match the first date in the 260 $c, either the 008 date or the 260 $c date needs to be edited (based on the date on the book, video, etc.).

Country code (008). The Country code in the 008 is what your system uses for qualifying an OPAC search by Place of publication. This code (Ctry in OCLC fixed fields) must match the place of publication that displays to patrons in the 260 $a. If, in a matching record you are copying, the Ctry code does not match the place in the 260 $a, the code must be edited. The complete list of country codes can be found in the *MARC Code List for Countries.*[8] The three-letter code for any state in the United States is easy to formulate: take the postal code (in lowercase) for the state and add the letter u (for United States) to it. For example, the code nyu is for New York State (ny) in the United States (u).

Language code (008). The Language code in the 008 is what your system uses for qualifying an OPAC search by language. This code (Lang in OCLC fixed fields) must match the language of the resource. Catalogers do not determine the Lang code by looking at the language of the title of the work, but by determining the language of the resource itself. If, in a matching record you are copying, the Lang code does not match the language of the resource you have, the code must be edited. The complete list of language codes can be found in the *MARC Code List for Languages.*[9] The language codes for the most common languages are mnemonic: for example, English = eng; Spanish = spa; French = fre; German = ger.

245 indicators. The first indicator of the 245 is very important. It tells the system whether to index the title. If a record has no other main entry in a 1XX field, the title is the main entry. When a title is a main entry, it is automatically indexed, so you do not need a title added entry. Setting the first indicator of the 245 to 0 (245 I1 = 0) tells the system not to make a title added entry, because the title in the record is already indexed. If, in a matching record you are copying, no 1XX is present, but the first indicator of the 245 is 1, this indicator must be edited (changed to 0), or the title may be indexed twice in your OPAC.

If, on the other hand, there is a 1XX in a record, then the title is not the main entry. In this instance, if you want the title to be indexed, you need a "title *added* entry." Setting the first indicator of the 245 to 1 (245 I1 = 1) tells the system to make the title added entry. If, in a matching record you are copying, a 1XX is present, but the first indicator of the 245 is 0, this indicator must be edited (changed to 1) if you want an added entry for the title in your catalog.

The second indicator of the 245 is also *very* important. It tells the system where to begin indexing the title. If a title begins with an article (known as an *initial article*—in English, *A, An,* or *The*) and you don't want the title indexed under that word, you have to tell the system how many characters to skip before beginning indexing.[10]

We skip initial articles in all languages, but there are some exceptions. For example, we don't skip initial articles that begin proper names, such as Los Alamos, Las Animas County, and El Cid. Watch out for words that sometimes function as initial articles and other times have different roles; for example, "Die" is an initial article in German, but not in English. LC provides a list of initial articles online titled *Initial Definite and Indefinite Articles.*[11]

Summary notes (520). Everyone, kids and adults too, loves summary notes (which are supposed to be brief and objective). If a record you are copying does not have such a note, either find another record for a different version of your resource and copy the note from that record, or paraphrase the blurb on the back of the resource, or write a summary yourself. These notes are useful for keyword searching as well as being informative about the contents of the resource.

Intended audience notes (521). The intended (or target) audience (IT) note is another useful note, both for providing information and for facilitating keyword searching. IT is, technically, only supposed to be entered in a record if it is provided on the resource, but it is all right to determine the intended audience of a resource and add the note as long as you take responsibility for the note by adding a subfield b with the "Name or abbreviation of the agency or entity that determined the target audience of the item."

Subject heading fields (6XX). The second indicator of all subject heading fields (6XX) represents the source of the subject heading (e.g., 0 = LCSH; 1 = Children's Subject Headings; 4 = Local Subject Headings). Your system looks at this second indicator to determine whether to index the subject heading. For example, your system might be programmed to index *Library of Congress Subject Headings* (6XX I2 = 0) and *Children's Subject Headings* (6XX I2 = 1) in a separate index, but not *Medical Subject Headings* (6XX I2 = 2). You must train yourself to check the value of this second indicator in each 6XX of a record to make sure the record has subject headings that will be indexed in your system. If, in any matching record you are copying, none of the subject headings present is indexed by your system, you need to add subject headings that will be indexed. Do this by consulting your subject heading authority and adding the headings in new 6XX fields, with the appropriate indicators. (No, you cannot just change the indicator!)

Many records for resources intended for children lack Children's Subject Headings. As chapter 7 of this book explains, these subject headings make it more likely that younger readers will find what they want in terms they use and understand, so such headings should be provided in all records describing resources intended for children. If there are no Children's Subject Headings in a record you are copying, add them.

These examples provide a taste of what you need to know and illustrate why you really do have to edit records, but they are only a taste. Here are a few more hints:

> The indicators for the 246 are equally important (and as problematic in their own way) as the indicators for the 245.
>
> Watch for other useful notes and add them if they are missing, especially those that really help kids, such as 505 Contents notes and 526 Study Program Information notes. This last field, 526, was added to the MARC format to make it possible to identify the curriculum with which a resource is to be used. Teachers will find it helpful, but so will kids and parents trying to find resources related to classroom subjects.
>
> Be careful with editing. If the only record you can find does not completely match the resource that you have, editing it to make it match is the wrong thing to do. If a record you find is a close, but not exact, match to your resource, you may *clone* a "different edition" record. This may seem just like editing, but it isn't,

because cloning a record means that you use the nonmatching record as a foundation to create a *completely new* record. Because you are creating a new record, we are back to chapter 3 and, once again, encouraging you to get proper training to do it right.

Many more instructions and examples are provided in copy cataloging workshops. Try to attend one of these, if you can.

DOWNLOADING AND UPLOADING

Downloading/exporting the records that you copy from an outside source has recently become a little bit trickier with the implementation of Unicode, indicated in MARC by the code value of "a" in position 09 of the leader (Character coding scheme). Position 09 is identified by the following underscore:

000 00876nam_200277 I 4500

The code in the leader position tells your library automation system whether a record represents diacritics using the MARC-8 character encoding or the UTF-8 character encoding. Your system will have been set up to expect either MARC-8 or UTF-8. If it is set up for MARC-8, you must ensure that all records loaded from outside your system have a blank in leader position 09. If it is set up for UTF-8, you must ensure that all records loaded from outside your system have an "a" in leader position 09.

Ask your system administrator or information technology person or system vendor contact what encoding scheme your system uses. The important point is this: you must not ever manually change this code. Always export records that already contain the correct format. When you download records from the LC OPAC, for example, you must choose one of these two character coding schemes when you save a record. Figure 4.8 shows where you enter your choice: either "MARC (non-Unicode/MARC-8)" or "MARC (Unicode/UTF-8)."

If you download records from OCLC WorldCat, this choice is set up in the Connexion options, so it only has to be done once. Just remember, *never* manually change this code in a record you are copying/editing. The code cannot be changed if you are using Connexion—this position does not show up at all. Never change this code locally—if you do so and any diacritics are present in the record, they will not display properly, and the record will cause problems when it is loaded to any other database.

FIGURE 4.8 **SELECTING THE CHARACTER CODING SCHEME DOWNLOAD FORMAT IN THE LC OPAC**

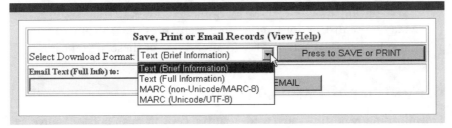

Finally, when it comes to uploading, what I am about to tell you is not new, but it has been sadly neglected by libraries in the past. You truly should make sure the records you load into your system load correctly and do not do any of the following:

- get added as duplicates
- get attached to records that they do not match
- overlay and replace records they do not match

It is true that checking for these problems slows you down, but loading records as duplicates seems to happen with increasing frequency, and duplicate records confuse patrons. Also increasing in frequency is machine-matching incoming records to existing records that are not matches. When this happens, the result is even worse than loading a duplicate record, because either the incoming record is lost when its holdings information gets attached to an existing record, or the existing record is lost when the incoming record replaces it in the database. Either way, you have lost all knowledge of one of the resources you have in your collection. If a patron happens to check out an item that has been wrongly attached in this way, and then receives an overdue notice for it (and the notice refers to something very different from what he or she actually borrowed), the results can be embarrassing for the library.

BACK TO THE BEGINNING

The bottom line for copy cataloging is that you need to know the principles of cataloging to do a decent job of it. If this point differs from what you've been told, then what you've been told is wrong. Familiarize yourself with the cataloging rules, the MARC standards, and the other cataloging resources described elsewhere in this book. Attend some continuing education workshops that teach the practical application of all of them. Join the AUTOCAT discussion list and ask questions, no matter how simple and rudimentary they might seem. (AUTOCAT subscribers love answering all questions posted on the list.) Find out if you have a local or regional cataloging special interest group (CatSIG) in your area and, if so, join it and attend its meetings.

Whatever you do, don't make the mistake of thinking that copy cataloging is something a volunteer, a student assistant, or a typist can do without solid training—no matter how smart or educated the person might be. Outsourcing your copy cataloging helps, but you still must check the records your vendor supplies and make the vendor accountable for the quality of the records, even if you have to pay a little more for it.

Stand up for standards! Defend your database against those who say there's no need to spend time on it because everything is automated now. Proper cataloging isn't a snap, but you can do it—you just have to learn how.

NOTES

1. Deborah A. Fritz, *Cataloging with AACR2 and MARC21* (Chicago: American Library Association, 2003).
2. "When to Input a New Record," in *Bibliographic Formats and Standards,* www.oclc.org/bibformats/en/input/default.shtm.
3. Differences Between, Changes Within: Guidelines on When to Create a New Record, www.ala.org/ala/mgrps/divs/alcts/resources/org/cat/differences07.pdf.
4. MARC 21 Format for Bibliographic Data, www.loc.gov/marc/bibliographic/ecbdhome.html.
5. MARC 21 Format for Bibliographic Data, www.loc.gov/marc/bibliographic/ecbdhome.html.
6. MARC Field Index to Source Code Usage, www.loc.gov/marc/sourcelist/.
7. Arlene G. Taylor, *Cataloging with Copy,* 2nd ed. (Englewood, CO: Libraries Unlimited, 1988), 21.
8. MARC Code List for Countries, www.loc.gov/marc/countries/.
9. MARC Code List for Languages, www.loc.gov/marc/languages/.
10. To determine the number of characters to ignore in filing, count the number of letters in the word and add one character for the space that follows it. If

the initial article is *The*, four characters (3 + 1) should be ignored; if it is *A*, two characters (1 + 1) should be ignored; if it is the Spanish *La*, three characters (2 + 1) should be ignored.

11. Initial Definite and Indefinite Articles, www.loc.gov/marc/bibliographic/bdapp-e.html.

CHAPTER 5

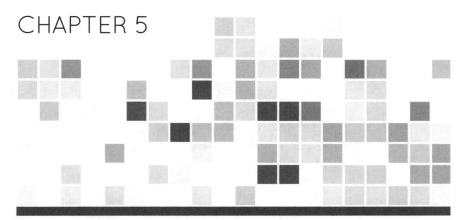

Cataloging Correctly (Someday) Using RDA

Deborah A. Fritz with Lynnette Fields

Disclaimer: Print is such a static medium. By the time this chapter is published, we will know a great deal more about *Resource Description and Access* (RDA): what it is really trying to do, how it will affect us as catalogers, how it will affect our catalog users, how it will affect our current cataloging infrastructure. In the meantime, please realize that what follows is just one attempt to interpret what seems to be an RDA vision of our cataloging future.

WHY RDA?

Perhaps, after reading chapter 3 ("Cataloging Correctly Using AACR2 and MARC 21") you are ready to run screaming for cataloging help. Even chapter 4 ("Copy Cataloging Correctly") might be seeming scary—telling you that you have to learn all sorts of strange and curious things in order to be sure that the bibliographic information in the records that you copy (or get from a record supplier) will function properly in your library catalog.

"Can't you make this any simpler?" you plead.

The cataloging rules people (the Joint Steering Committee, or JSC, mentioned in chapter 3) seem to have heard your pleas, and they are determined to "make it simpler" for us to:

- provide bibliographic information about resources
- enable software designers to develop:
  - cataloging software that will simplify providing bibliographic information
  - catalogs that will use our bibliographic information more effectively
- enable anyone and everyone to use our bibliographic information on the Web, in any creative way they choose

In 1997, the cataloging experts began talking about putting out a new edition of *Anglo-American Cataloguing Rules* (AACR, to be called AACR3). Catalogers were requesting additional instructions that would help us catalog the exciting new resources that modern technology was throwing our way. Back then it was websites, enhanced CDs, and dual discs; as time has gone by, MP3, streaming video, podcasts, and webcasts have come along; any time now, we'll probably be seeing holograms.

In 2004, the JSC made an initial draft of AACR3 available for public review and then sat back and waited for responses. They certainly got responses, surely more than they ever anticipated, ranging from "You are making too many changes" to "You are not making anywhere near enough changes" to "It is too late to make any changes, there is just too much stuff out there, we can't keep up, the whole idea of cataloging is dead."

It certainly is true that there is far too much stuff out there for us to hope to describe it all. It doesn't help that every individual cataloger has to spend so much time and effort providing or checking minute details (like coding and punctuation) in our resource descriptions. We all know that we need the details to make the records display and function properly in our current OPACs. We all (or at least some of us) go to great lengths to make the best MARC records that we possibly can, following the rules and standards to the letter. But the fact is that none of our library automation systems seems to be able to make our bibliographic records work as well as we would like them to.

WHAT SHOULD BIBLIOGRAPHIC RECORDS DO?

The JSC response to the criticism leveled at AACR3 was to shift its focus back to the basics of what it is that we actually want our bibliographic records to *do*.

In 1998, IFLA (the International Federation of Library Associations and Institutions) released a report called *Functional Requirements for Bibliographic*

Records (FRBR).[1] This report identified four very specific tasks that our bibliographic records should help a user to do:

- **F**ind descriptions of things that match a user's search.
- **I**dentify that a description that has been found is for the thing that was sought, or allow the user to pick among multiple similar descriptions.
- **S**elect from multiple possible descriptions the thing that best suits the user's needs (e.g., large print vs. regular print vs. an e-book/digital print).
- **O**btain the actual thing or item (e.g., by using a call number to find the item on a shelf or by clicking on a link to find a virtual item on the Web).[2]

These FISO (Find, Identify, Select, Obtain) user tasks represent an extension of the catalog objectives stated by Charles Cutter way back in 1876, the cataloging principles published in Paris in 1961, and other great ideas put forth by Seymour Lubetzky, Julia Pettee, Anthony Panizzi, S. R. Ranganathan, and many other cataloging luminaries. So, rather than continuing to try to tweak the existing AACR rules to cover new materials, in 2005, the JSC made the radical decision to restructure the new rules to align them with the recommendations set out by the FRBR report.

The FRBR approach to bibliographic information is very different from our current method of cataloging (as we will explain shortly). To highlight the change in direction (and to make the name seem more international in scope), the committee decided to change the name of the new instructions from *Anglo-American Cataloguing Rules* to *Resource Description and Access* (RDA).

IMPROVING THE ORGANIZATION OF BIBLIOGRAPHIC DATA

The way we currently describe resources and provide access to them certainly doesn't seem to meet the FISO objectives as well as it should. In this section, a few of the most irksome problems with the bibliographic information currently being provided are considered.

Multiple versions: Under current cataloging rules, separate records are made for every different version of a work. Unfortunately, this approach makes it difficult for someone to find the work and select *any* available version of it. For example, we have been hearing for years that kids (and adults) are frustrated when they have to say, "I want *Harry Potter and the Sorcerer's Stone*, and I don't care whether it is in large print, regular print, or a paperback. I'll even take an audiobook if that is all you have available, but all your copies are checked out. How do I put a hold on whichever version becomes available first?"

To resolve this difficulty, we hear that some libraries have given up making separate records when they have a work issued in different versions by different publishers. They say it is bad enough to have to make different records for large print and regular print (though they accept that some people care deeply about that particular difference). These libraries have gone to the extreme of adding a note to a single record, such as: "Published by various publishers." This is not a good thing to do! But, they say their OPACs won't let them place holds for all versions any other way. We know we can't let the shortcomings of computer systems drive development of cataloging rules, but how can this situation be improved?

"Based on" relationships: Wouldn't it be nice to be able to tell a kid who loves the movie *Clueless* that it is actually based on Jane Austen's *Emma*? Yes, we know that is done in MARC records now (with a 500 "Based on" note and a 700 Author/Title added entry), but the relationship isn't very clear in the OPAC. Is there a better way of handling this situation?

Adaptations, sequels/prequels, and series relationships: What about all the adaptations (Disney versions of *Winnie-the-Pooh*), sequels and prequels (will *Star Wars* ever end?), and the series that aren't *really* series but everyone thinks they are (e.g., *Jimmy Neutron*)? Can all these relationships be pulled together more effectively?

Obscure technical terms: Why can't we use the terms kids use to describe a DVD or a CD? Can you really imagine any kid texting another kid to ask, "Have you seen the new Spiderman videodisc?" Surely modern technology can allow us to show descriptions that use the terms people in our audience will recognize without worrying about whether the records will match other records that use different terms for the same thing (e.g., sound disc or audio disc).

Updating bibliographic information: Wouldn't it be marvelous if there was a better way of updating and enhancing records so that every cataloger didn't have to add the same missing information to CIP and pre-order records, or death dates to authors' names, or a note about a newly won award? We don't have time to revisit records, and we can't afford to pay for and figure out how to download, upload, and machine match and overlay replacement records. There has to be an easier way.

Simplifying the bibliographic information we need to provide: Wouldn't it be great if we didn't have to remember all that stuff about the order of entering title information and the punctuation separating different bits of information, and those hard-to-remember fixed field codes and indicators?

And, while we are talking about simplifying things, wouldn't it be absolutely fabulous if we didn't have to repeat the same summary notes, contents notes, audience notes, awards notes, and subject headings in every record for every version of the thing being described?

The good news is that RDA has been designed to allow software developers to build:

- OPACs that organize and present bibliographic information more effectively
- cataloging software that helps to simplify how bibliographic information is entered

MORE ABOUT MULTIPLE VERSIONS

Concentrating, for now, on the multiple versions issue, it turns out that with the RDA approach to cataloging, the library catalog might be able to do better in satisfying the needs of someone who doesn't care which version of a work she gets when she simply wants:

- the Work (**W**) (the story, the song, the poem, the essay, the biography, etc.)
- but, she does care which Expression (**E**) she gets, because she probably doesn't want the Spanish translation (or maybe she actually *does* want the Spanish translation)
- and she might even care about a particular Manifestation (**M**), because she might be looking for the illustrations that come with a particular manifestation
- but, at least we know she won't care which Item (**I**) we loan her, unless it is the one with page 36 missing

We'd better explain the FRBR concept of Works, Expressions, Manifestations, and Items (WEMI) before we go any farther.

WORKS, EXPRESSIONS, MANIFESTATIONS, AND ITEMS—WHAT ARE THEY?

A work is, at the most basic level, just a germ of an idea in the mind of a person or group of people. But, for us to know anything about this idea, much less to be able to collect it, the idea has to be expressed in some form. It could be expressed in words or music or pictures or stone or in a combination of ways, but once an idea has been expressed somehow, it can be said that the person or group of people has created a "work."

All expressions of works are not recorded for posterity. For instance, a music jam session may never be recorded, or written down in musical notation; or, a story told around a fire may neither be written down nor captured on audio- or videotape. In either case, we may never know about those works. But, if an expression of a work is recorded in some way (written on a page, typed into a computer document, spoken or sung into a device that can record sound, filmed by a camera, etc.), then that expression is made manifest—that is, made apparent to human senses (there for us to see, hear, or feel)—in a form that allows it to be accessed many times.

A FEW WEMI POSSIBILITIES

Some works are only expressed in one way (e.g., written words), only manifested in one form (e.g., a collection of pages, which we call a volume), and only produced as a single item (e.g., a handwritten manuscript).

Other works are only expressed in one way (e.g., written words) and only manifested in one way (e.g., a collection of pages, which we call a volume), but are produced as multiple items (e.g., many copies of a published book).

Still other works are expressed in many different ways (e.g., as written words and spoken words, or translated into different languages), manifested in different forms (e.g., the written words are in large print and regular print or the text of a digital format or both; the spoken words are released on a CD and on an audiotape), and available as millions of multiple copies or items for each expression and manifestation.

Figure 5.1 shows an example of a classic children's story (or work), expressed, manifested, and itemized in multiple formats and languages. These are the kinds of works that could use a better form of organization than we are able to manage in our catalogs thus far. Notice the large number of formats and languages listed on the left side of the screenshot.

FIGURE 5.1 BEMELMANS' *MADELINE* IN WORLDCAT: A WORK WITH MANY EXPRESSIONS, MANIFESTATIONS, AND ITEMS

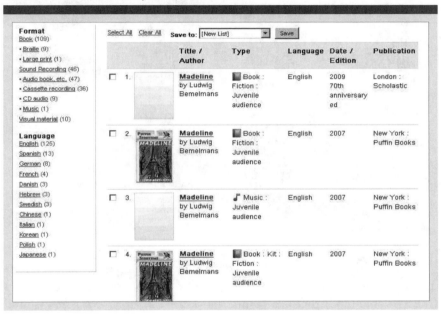

Next, let's try to look at WEMI from the point of view of catalog users. Have a look at figure 5.2 as you read the next section.[3]

Imagine someone comes up with an idea and writes a book. He or she finds a publisher to publish that book, and then the library purchases it. At this point we have a physical *item* in hand (the book: item A in figure 5.2) that is a *manifestation* (something published by a particular publisher that we can see, touch, hear, smell, or taste) of an *expression* (a specific intellectual or artistic form—in this case, text in English-language words) of a *work* (in this case, a story for children, titled *Madeline*).

Then, let's say, a different publisher publishes the same work. Now there is another physical *item* (the book: B) that is a *different manifestation* of the *same expression* of that work.

FIGURE 5.2 **BEMELMANS' *MADELINE* SHOWING WEMI RELATIONSHIPS**

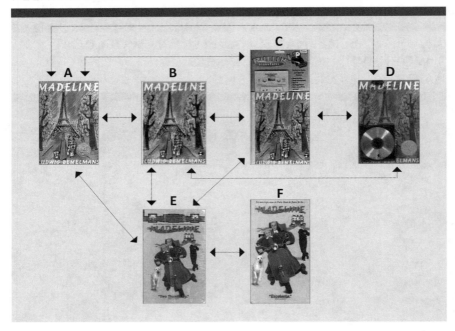

If one of those publishers (or a completely different publisher) then produces a sound recording (a book-on-tape) of this work, we have an item (the audiobook: C) that is a manifestation of a *different expression* (sound in English) of the work.

And if someone produces the book-on-CD, we will have an item (the audiobook: D) that is a *different manifestation* (because of the different carrier—a CD instead of cassettes) of the *same expression* of the work.

But, if someone (e.g., Peter Jackson) were to make a movie of the work—because a movie is never the same as the original book—we would have another item (the video: E) that is a manifestation of an expression of a *different work* that is *related* to the original work.

Finally, the soundtrack to that movie could be issued on a CD, which would also be an item (the sound recording: F) that is a manifestation of an expression of a *different work* that is related to the movie.

The challenge is to take the user who finds his way to *any* of these things also to *all* the other, related things.

The writers of the original FRBR report and the developers of RDA both declined to take the responsibility for dictating exactly how an OPAC should apply the concept of WEMI. But, figures 5.3 to 5.8 display an example of how an OPAC might apply WEMI to make it easier for catalog users to find any of the following:

- a whole work
- specific expressions of a work
- a particular manifestation of an expression of a work
- an exact item

(Keep in mind that this WEMI catalog is theoretical and doesn't exist anywhere . . . yet.)

Figure 5.3 shows all of Ludwig Bemelmans's works listed under his name (we dropped a few of his works in the interest of space). The title of each work has a plus (+) sign, indicating there is more to be seen under the title.

Figure 5.4 shows (after clicking on the plus sign to expand the entry for *Madeline*) that the library has expressions of that work in text and in audio, as well as one or more related works.

FIGURE 5.3 **THEORETICAL FRBR DISPLAY OF LUDWIG BEMELMANS'S WORKS**

Bemelmans, Ludwig, 1898-1962.
+ Blue Danube
+ Father, dear father

+ Madeline
+ Madeline in London
+ Madeline's rescue

FIGURE 5.4 **A THEORETICAL FRBR DISPLAY OF THREE EXPRESSIONS OF LUDWIG BEMELMANS'S WORK *MADELINE***

Bemelmans, Ludwig, 1898-1962.
+ Blue Danube
+ Father, dear father
- Madeline
+ Text, English

+ Text, German
+ Text, Spanish
+ Audio
+ Related works

Figure 5.5 shows (after we expand the expression entries for "Text, English" and "Audio") two different manifestations of the text expression and two different manifestations of the audio, all for Bemelmans's work *Madeline*. (You might notice that different terms are displaying than those you are used to seeing in the description field, but don't worry about them, for now.)

FIGURE 5.5 A THEORETICAL FRBR DISPLAY OF FOUR MANIFESTATIONS OF LUDWIG BEMELMANS'S WORK *MADELINE*

Bemelmans, Ludwig, 1898-1962.

+ Blue Danube

+ Father, dear father

- Madeline

  - Text, English

     Madeline / Ludwig Bemelmans.

       Imprint: New York : Simon and Schuster, 1939.

       Description: [46] p. : colour illustrations ; 31 cm.

     Madeline : story & pictures / Ludwig Bemelmans.

       Imprint: [New York] : Puffin Books, 1993.

       Description: 1 volume (unpaged) : colour illustrations ; 21 cm.

       ISBN: 0140548459

  + Text, German

  + Text, Spanish

  - Audio

     Madeline [sound recording] / Ludwig Bemelmans.

       Imprint: Pine Plains, N.Y. : Live Oak Media, p1998.

       Description: 1 audio disc (16 min.) : digital ; 12 cm.

       ISBN: 1591128056

       Imprint: [New York, N.Y.] : Viking Penguin, [1980-1989?]

       Description: 1 audio cassette : analog ; 10 x 7 cm, 4 mm tape.

       ISBN: 0140950672

+ Related works

FIGURE 5.6 A THEORETICAL FRBR DISPLAY OF TWO WORKS THAT ARE RELATED TO LUDWIG BEMELMANS'S WORK *MADELINE*

Bemelmans, Ludwig, 1898-1962.
+ Blue Danube
+ Father, dear father
- Madeline.
  + Text
  + Audio
  - Related works
    Madeline (Motion picture : 1998)
      Madeline [videorecording] / TriStar Pictures presents a Jaffilms
      production ; story by Malia Scotch Marmo and Mark Levin & Jennifer
      Flackett ; screenplay by Mark Levin & Jennifer Flackett ; produced by
      Saul Cooper, Pancho Kahner and Allyn Stewart ; directed by Daisy von
      Scherler Mayer.
        Imprint: Culver City, CA : Columbia TriStar Home Video, [1998]
        Description: 1 videodisc (89 min.) : sound, colour ; 12 cm.
        ISBN: 0767819659
    Madeline (Television program : 1960)
      Madeline [videorecording] / produced by Legend Films ; an NBC
      Television Production ; executive producer, William H. Brown, Jr.
        Imprint: Del Mar, CA : Genius Entertainment, c2005.
        Description: 1 videodisc (55 min.) : sound, colour ; 12 cm.

Figure 5.6 shows (if we expand the "Related works" heading) two new works that are based on the original work, Bemelmans's *Madeline*: a motion picture and a television program.

If we select the entry for the motion picture (in figure 5.6), we can see the FRBR hierarchical display for that work. Figure 5.7 shows that it also has a Related works heading.

Finally, figure 5.8 shows (if we expand that Related works heading) first, an audio expression of the soundtrack from the motion picture (considered a different work) and second, a link back to the original work (Bemelmans's *Madeline*) that we started with.

FIGURE 5.7 A THEORETICAL FRBR DISPLAY OF THE MOTION PICTURE *MADELINE*, A WORK THAT IS RELATED TO LUDWIG BEMELMANS'S WORK *MADELINE*

Madeline (Motion picture : 1998)
    Madeline [videorecording] / TriStar Pictures presents a Jaffilms production ;
        story by Malia Scotch Marmo and Mark Levin & Jennifer Flackett ;
        screenplay by Mark Levin & Jennifer Flackett ; produced by Saul Cooper,
        Pancho Kahner and Allyn Stewart ; directed by Daisy von Scherler Mayer.
        Imprint: Culver City, CA : Columbia TriStar Home Video, [1998]
        Description: 1 videodisc (89 min.) : sound, colour ; 12 cm.
        ISBN: 0767819659
+ Related works

The WEMI logic behind these displays should make it easier for both adults and kids to accomplish the FISO user task objectives, and perhaps even make it possible, at last, for users to place holds at whatever level they choose. We'll see in a moment how this approach is also good for catalogers, possibly saving both time and effort.

WEMI ENTITIES

Just as you have to learn the meanings of important terms to understand how the AACR cataloging rules and MARC coding standards work together, you now have to grasp some new terms to understand the RDA documentation.

In RDA-speak, each of the different WEMI levels we have mentioned is describing a different *entity* (aka *thing*).

In other words, the Work is one thing (entity) because you can say, "Don't you think *Emma* is Jane Austen's best book?"—and here you would be talking about *Emma*, the work.

But you might also say, "Don't you think *Emma* is Juliet Stevenson's best reading?"—and here you would be talking about a different thing (entity): the specific sound recording expression of Jane Austen's *Emma* that was read by Juliet.

Or you might say, "You need to get the *Emma* with the Richard Church introduction"—and here you would be talking about another thing (entity)

FIGURE 5.8 **A THEORETICAL FRBR DISPLAY OF TWO WORKS THAT ARE RELATED TO THE MOTION PICTURE WORK *MADELINE***

Madeline (Motion picture : 1998)
  Madeline [videorecording] / TriStar Pictures presents a Jaffilms production ;
    story by Malia Scotch Marmo and Mark Levin & Jennifer Flackett ;
    screenplay by Mark Levin & Jennifer Flackett ; produced by Saul Cooper,
    Pancho Kahner and Allyn Stewart ; directed by Daisy von Scherler Mayer.
    Imprint: Culver City, CA : Columbia TriStar Home Video, [1998]
    Description: 1 videodisc (89 min.) : sound, colour ; 12 cm.
    ISBN: 0767819659
 - Related works
  Madeline
      Madeline [sound recording] : music from the motion picture / score
        composed and conducted by Michel Legrand.
          Imprint: New York : Sony Wonder/Sony Music Soundtrax, p1998.
          Description: 1 audio disc : digital ; 12 cm.
          ISBN: 1573305782
  Bemelmans, Ludwig, 1898-1962. Madeline
      + Text, English
      + Text, German
      + Text, Spanish
      + Audio
      + Related works

again: the specific manifestation of *Emma*, published in 1962 by the Folio Society, that contains this introduction.

Each copy (item) of *Emma* is yet another thing (entity)—that concept is easy to grasp, because you can actually hold that thing (the item) in your hand. The other "things" (works, expressions, and manifestations) are more abstract, but because you can refer to them, they are, indeed, entities, or things.

We will come back to entities in just a minute (yes, we know you can't wait!), but first we have to learn another term. Think back to chapter 3, where we explained that AACR talks about descriptive areas and elements of areas and that these terms translate into fields and subfields in a MARC record. In RDA terminology we speak of these areas (AACR) or fields (MARC) as separate *data elements*. So, the title field is a title element, the edition field is an edition element, the publisher field is a publisher element, and so on.

Going one step farther, each of these elements can be subdivided into other elements. For example, a publisher element can be broken down into a place of publication element, a publisher's name element, and a date of publication element.

The RDA data elements are the building blocks of cataloging in the new scheme of things. These elements can be assembled in a field in a MARC record—

    260 ___ $aAuckland : $bFlying Kiwi Press,$c2008.

—but they can just as easily be put together in an XML document:

```
<originInfo>
    <place>Auckland</place>
    <publisher>Flying Kiwi Press</publisher>
    <dateIssued>2008</dateIssued>
</originInfo>⁴
```

Don't let this XML example scare you—you won't have to enter data in something that looks like that. Instead, you'll have a nice form to fill out, which might look like this:

    Place: **Auckland**
    Publisher: **Flying Kiwi press**
    Date issued: **2008**

In computer terms, a set of data elements is called a *record*. But most catalogers are so programmed to think "record = MARC record" that we are going to use the term *entity record* in this chapter to keep the options open for the carrier of the RDA elements (MARC, XML, etc.).

SEPARATE SETS OF RDA ELEMENTS FOR EACH WEMI ENTITY

Now, let's put the RDA elements and WEMI together. In FRBR, the four WEMI levels are called Group 1 Entities, and the idea is that catalogers will describe each of the Group 1/WEMI entities separately.

"Wait a minute!" you squeak. "Do you actually mean that *each* of these things (Work, Expression, Manifestation, Item) will get its own descriptive record (oops, I mean entity record)?"

Well, yes, which is a major change from AACR because instead of making (or finding and copying) a single record for the book in your hand, we will now need four sets of descriptive data elements.

Look at it this way: under AACR2 and MARC 21, we have to describe and provide access to every resource with a full and complete MARC Bibliographic (Bib) record, putting the very same information that applies to each Bib record *in each* Bib record over and over again. Figure 5.9 shows how we currently repeat the same information in three different MARC Bibliographic records for the story *Madeline*.

We show only three Bib records here, but there are Bib records for seven manifestations of just the English text in the LC OPAC and seventy-eight manifestations of the same English text in WorldCat.

Surely, it would be simpler if we could make:

- one set of data elements describing the Madeline story/work itself, with only the information that applies to every version of the Work
- one set of data elements describing each different way that the work is expressed (e.g., regular print text, digital text, large print text, sound, etc.), with only the information that applies to that particular Expression of the work
- one set of data elements describing each different production of each expression (the Puffin publication using regular print, or the Scholastic-TAB publication using large print, or the Seeing Hands publication using braille, etc.), with only the information that applies to that particular Manifestation of the expression of the work
- one set of data elements describing each physical or virtual item, with only the information that applies to that particular Item

Figure 5.10 shows how a cataloger's view of the WEMI data elements for Bemelmans's *Madeline* might look in the future (underscored text in the illustration indicates a link).

FIGURE 5.9 **THREE MANIFESTATIONS OF MARC BIBLIOGRAPHIC RECORDS FOR BEMELMANS'S** *MADELINE*

Type of Material: Book (Print, Microform, Electronic, etc.)
Personal Name: Bemelmans, Ludwig, 1898-1962.
Main Title: Madeline, story & pictures by Ludwig Bemelmans.
Published/Created: New York, Viking Press [1963]
Description: [48] p. col. illus. 32 cm.
Summary: Madeline, smallest and naughtiest of the twelve little charges of Miss Clavel, wakes up one night with an attack of appendicitis.
Notes: Caldecott Honor Book
Subjects: Sick --Fiction.
Stories in rhyme.
France --Fiction.
LC Classification: PZ8.3.B425 Mag3
Dewey Class No.: [E] 19
Geographic Area Code: e-fr---

Type of Material: Book (Print, Microform, Electronic, etc.)
Personal Name: Bemelmans, Ludwig, 1898-1962.
Main Title: Madeline / story & pictures by Ludwig Bemelmans.
Edition Information: Giant ed.
Published/Created: New York, N.Y., U.S.A : Puffin Books, 1993.
Description: 1 v. (unpaged) : col. ill. ; 44 cm.
ISBN: 0140548459
Summary: Madeline, smallest and naughtiest of the twelve little charges of Miss Clavel, wakes up one night with an attack of appendicitis.
Notes: Caldecott Honor Book
Subjects: Sick --Fiction.
Stories in rhyme.
France --Fiction.
LC Classification: PZ8.3.B425 Mag 1993
Dewey Class No.: [E] 20

Type of Material: Book (Print, Microform, Electronic, etc.)
Personal Name: Bemelmans, Ludwig, 1898-1962.
Main Title: Madeline : story & pictures / by Ludwig Bemelmans.
Published/Created: [New York] : Puffin Books, 1977, c1939.
Description: [46] p. : col. (some ill.) ; 21 cm.
ISBN: 0140501983 : $1.75
Summary: Madeline, smallest and naughtiest of the twelve little charges of Miss Clavel, wakes up one night with an attack of appendicitis.
Notes: "Caldecott honor book."
Subjects: Sick --Fiction.
Stories in rhyme.
France --Fiction.
Series: Picture puffin
LC Classification: PZ8.3.B425 Mag 1977
Dewey Class No.: [E]

FIGURE 5.10 **WEMI DATA ELEMENTS FOR BEMELMANS'S** *MADELINE:* WORK, EXPRESSION, AND TWO MANIFESTATIONS

Work ID: W001
Creator: Bemelmans, Ludwig, 1898-1962
Preferred Title: Madeline
Children's subject: Sick—Fiction
Children's subject: France—Fiction
Genre: Stories in rhyme
LC Classification: PZ8.3.B425
Dewey Class No.: [E]

Expression ID: E001
Language of expression: English
Content type: Text
Illustrative content: illustrations
Awards: Caldecott honor book
Summary: Madeline, smallest and naughtiest of the twelve little charges of Miss Clavel, wakes up one night with an attack of appendicitis
Link to Work ID: W001

Manifestation ID: M001
Title proper: Madeline
Responsibility: story & pictures by Ludwig Bemelmans

Place of publication: New York
Publisher: Viking Press
Date of publication: [1963]
Media type: unmediated
Carrier type: volume
Extent: [48] pages
Dimensions: 32 cm
Color content: colour
Link to Expression ID: E001

Manifestation ID: M002
Title proper: Madeline
Responsibility: story & pictures by Ludwig Bemelmans
Edition: Giant edition
Place of publication: New York
Publisher: Puffin Books
Date of publication: 1993
Media type: unmediated
Carrier type: volume
Extent: 1 volume (unpaged)
Dimensions: 44 cm
Color content: colour
ISBN: 0140548459
Link to Expression ID: E001

As figure 5.10 shows, we only have to enter:

- the subject headings and classification numbers once, in the Work entity record
- the summary and the fact that the work is illustrated, along with the award note, once, in the Expression entity record
- the qualities that are specific to a particular manifestation in the Manifestation entity record (e.g., the specific title, edition, and

publication information; the specific physical description; the ISBN, etc.)

If another publisher releases another English-text version of Bemelmans's *Madeline*, then all we will have to do is create another manifestation entity record for it (M003) and link that entity record to the same E001 expression entity record shown in figure 5.10. And if a new expression (e.g., an Estonian audiobook version) is ever released, then we will:

- create a new expression entity record for it (E002) and link that entity record to the W001 work expression record from figure 5.10
- create a new manifestation entity record for it and link that manifestation entity record to E002 (the new expression entity record)

From here, it is up to the OPAC designers to figure out how to link each of those sets of data elements and display them, perhaps, as shown in figures 5.2 to 5.8.

GROUP 1 ENTITIES, GROUP 2 ENTITIES, AND GROUP 3 ENTITIES

We hope you grasp the concept of Works, Expressions, Manifestations, and Items as separate entities because things are about to get a bit more complicated. As was said earlier, FRBR designated the WEMI entities as Group 1 entities to make it easy to refer to them as a group.

Now, consider this question: "Who is responsible, in any way, shape, or form, for each of these Group 1 entities?" The answer could be one of the following:

- one person is responsible for this particular Work (the author)
- another person is responsible for this Expression of the work (a translator)
- a corporate body is responsible for this Manifestation (the publisher)
- a family is responsible for a particular Item (a donor)

These other entities fall nicely into a separate group of their own and so are called *Group 2* entities.

Think of it this way: Group 2 entities (persons, families, corporate bodies) are responsible for creating or producing Group 1 entities (works, expressions, manifestations, items), and, looking at it the other way around, Group 1 entities are created/produced by Group 2 entities.

FIGURE 5.11 **LINKED GROUP 1 AND GROUP 2 ENTITIES FOR BEMELMANS'S *MADELINE* IN SPANISH**

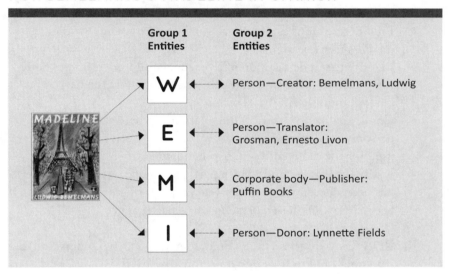

Let's say that we have the Spanish text (the expression) of Bemelmans's *Madeline* (the work), published by Puffin Books (the manifestation), with a copy of this book (the item) having been donated to our library. Figure 5.11 illustrates how we can think of Group 2 entities linked to Group 1 entities.

To express this sort of linking in our current cataloging environment, a main entry or an added entry (as appropriate) is created for each person or corporate body responsible for a resource and added to the MARC Bibliographic record that we make for the resource. Then separate MARC *Authority* records are made for each of these persons or corporate bodies to ensure the headings used for them are consistent.

FRAD AND FRSAD

This process brings up the question of how authority records will fit into the new cataloging picture. Once the FRBR group came up with the functional requirements for *bibliographic* records, it soon became clear that another report was needed, this time on the functional requirements for *authority* records. In the end, because these requirements take us well beyond the information currently provided by MARC Authority records, the name of the report was changed from *Functional Requirements for Authority Records* to *Functional Requirements for Authority Data* (FRAD).

The FRAD report explains the user tasks that Group 2 entities should satisfy:

- Find descriptions of persons, families, and corporate bodies that match a user's search.
- Identify that a description of a person, family, or corporate body that is found is the one that was sought, or allow the user to pick among multiple similar descriptions.
- Contextualize (or Clarify) the relationship between entities (a person who is a member of a family) or between different names used for the same entity (e.g., pseudonyms).
- Justify (or Understand) why a particular name or form of name has been chosen for an entity (e.g., explain that a new name has been chosen because a person's name has changed).

The RDA terms for these tasks (Find, Identify, Clarify, Understand) are easy to remember (and to turn into an acronym—FICU).

Like the FRBR FISO user tasks, the FRAD FICU user tasks provide a philosophical foundation for the different data elements that RDA declares are necessary for each Group 2 entity (**P**erson, **F**amily, or **C**orporate body).

It's obvious we can't stop with just Group 1 and Group 2 entities; at least one more group of entities (Group 3) is needed to answer "what is this thing about?" FRSAD, or the *Functional Requirements for Subject Authority Data*, fulfills this need.

Group 3 entities "represent an additional set of entities that serve as the subjects of works,"[5] including concepts, objects, events, and places:

- **C**oncept—an idea that can be the subject of a work (field of knowledge, discipline, school of thought, theory, process, technique, and practice; e.g., philosophy, biology, kayaking, cooking)

- **O**bject—a material thing that can be the subject of a work (e.g., rock, tree, dog, cat, rowboat)
- **E**vent—a happening, action, or occurrence (e.g., World War II)
- **P**lace—a geographic location (e.g., Jamaica)

A work can be about another work or about a particular expression of a work or about a particular manifestation of a work or even about a particular item, so Group 3 also includes the WEMI entities from Group 1. And, because a work can also be about a person or persons, a family or families, a corporate body or corporate bodies, Group 3 (entities that serve as the subjects of works) also includes those Group 2 entities.

Just as each Group 1 WEMI entity is described by its own set of data elements, each Group 2 and Group 3 entity is also described by its own designated set of data elements. Now, wrap your brain around the idea that any of those sets of data elements for any of those entities can be linked to any other set of data elements for any other entity. This can make your brain hurt, so figure 5.12 is a simplified illustration of the potential relationships.

Picture each of the linked boxes in figure 5.12 as a set of data elements (an entity record) connected to another set of data elements (another entity record), and you begin to grasp how RDA's approach to cataloging differs from that of AACR and other cataloging rules.

The links and connections are very important in FRBR, where they are called *relationships*.[6] They are no less important in RDA, where over half the chapters in the new manual teach catalogers how to record relationships. If this sounds fascinating and a bit like setting off on a web search and following links until you end up in interesting but unexpected places—you are right! All that is needed now to start building this web of bibliographic relationships is widespread implementation of RDA and the software to make it simple (and perhaps fun) to create, find, and link the Group 1, 2, and 3 entity records.

RDA STRUCTURE AND LAYOUT

Let's look briefly at a broad outline of the structure of RDA's instructions.

Introduction
- explains the underlying principles of the instructions (it is very important to understand these)

FIGURE 5.12 **LINKED ENTITIES FROM GROUP 1, GROUP 2, AND GROUP 3**

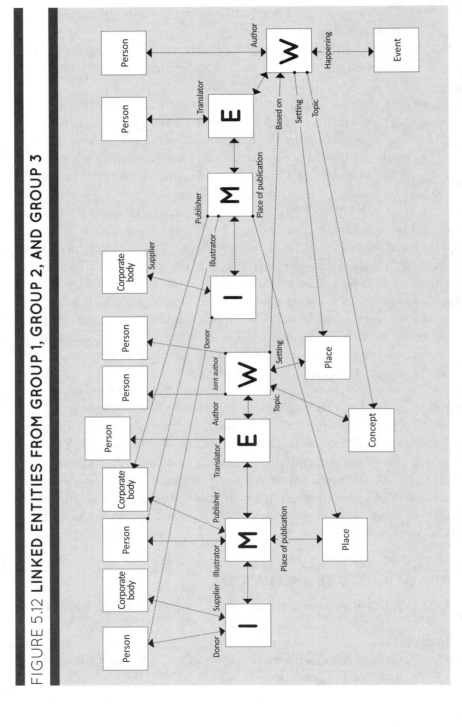

- outlines the core data elements that must be provided in order to describe:
  - the attributes (characteristics) of items, manifestations, expressions, and works (Group 1 entities) and of persons, families, and corporate bodies (Group 2 entities)
  - the relationships between Group 1 entities and Group 2 entities
  - subject relationships
  - relationships between items, manifestations, expressions, and works and other items, manifestations, expressions, and works
  - relationships between persons, families, and corporate bodies and other persons, families, and corporate bodies

Sections 1–4 explain how to describe the following, including how to identify what they are:

Section 1: manifestations and items
Section 2: works and expressions
Section 3: persons, families, and corporate bodies
Section 4: concepts, objects, events, and places

Sections 5–10 explain how to describe relationships:

Section 5: how to connect a work, expression, manifestation, and item
Section 6: how a particular person, family, and/or corporate body might be related to a work, expression, manifestation, or item
Section 7: how a particular subject (concept, object, place, or event) might be related to a work, expression, manifestation, or item
Section 8: how a work, expression, manifestation, or item might be related to another work, expression, manifestation, or item
Section 9: how a person, family, or corporate body might be related to another person, family, or corporate body
Section 10: how a concept, object, event, or place might be related to another concept, object, event, or place

As is apparent from this outline, RDA is structured very differently than AACR2. This is one reason why it is vital that this cataloging tool be provided as an online product. We'll talk more about it later; for now, let's look at a few areas where RDA is similar to AACR2 and where it is quite different.

AACR2 AND RDA: SIMILARITIES AND DIFFERENCES

The good news for experienced catalogers is that most of the actual instructions in AACR2 carry over into RDA unchanged. The RDA website lists the instructions that have changed in a document titled "Changes to AACR2 Instructions."[7]

Like AACR2, RDA tells catalogers where to look on a resource for information to use in entering the data elements for a work, expression, manifestation, and item associated with a resource.

Unlike AACR2, RDA does not want us to think about "areas" of information anymore (e.g., putting title and statement of responsibility information into one area or field). Instead, we are to think *separately* about each piece of information. For example, title proper, other title information, parallel title information, and statement of responsibility are each to be seen as separate data elements.

Like AACR2, RDA directs *how* to enter each data element. Having located the designated place on a resource to find a particular piece of information, RDA offers three choices for recording that information:

- exactly as it is given on the resource in the form in which it appears
- as found on the resource, but using abbreviations
- as free text (notes)

Unlike AACR2, RDA does not go into details about the order in which to enter the data elements nor does it address the issue of providing separating punctuation for the elements (ISBD order and punctuation). RDA recommends that "the *presentation* of data be in accordance with ISBD specifications" and provides guidelines for this presentation in an appendix. The plan is that catalogers will not have to enter the data elements using ISBD order and punctuation; rather, OPAC software developers will study the RDA appendix and present the data using ISBD order and punctuation.

Like AACR2, RDA gives many examples and contains many references to other rules for clarification. But, in the RDA documentation available as an online tool, these examples will be keyword searchable. Every reference to another rule will be a clickable link to that rule. This capability is one of the main reasons that RDA needs to be an online tool rather than a printed text. In addition, with an online tool, cataloging software can be programmed to prompt us with appropriate RDA instructions for each data element as we enter it. Think how this simplifies finding the right rule!

Like AACR2, RDA has appendixes with instructions for capitalization, abbreviations, initial articles, and the like. But, unlike AACR2, RDA eliminates many of the abbreviations used now, requiring the words to be spelled out in full. For example:

The AACR2 abbreviation	Becomes in RDA
ed.	edition
p.	page or pages
v.	volume or volumes
ill.	illustration or illustrations

This means more typing for us (although cataloging software should be able to provide shortcuts to help), but it simplifies things for catalogers, who won't have to remember the abbreviations and the areas where they can and can't be used, and for members of the public, who won't have to guess what the abbreviations mean.

Unlike AACR2, RDA does not separate its instructions for different types of materials into different chapters. This shifts attention from the fact that a work is provided in a particular carrier (book volume, cassette, disc, etc.) to focus instead on recording the important attributes of each of the WEMI entities for the work.

Under AACR2, catalogers think: "This is a sound recording CD; how is a CD cataloged?" Then they follow the special "Sound recording" rules and "General" rules to describe the CD and provide access points for it.

Under RDA, catalogers will think more along these lines: "Here is this work, with this title, created by this person (link to her entity record). This particular expression of the work has Content type: 'sounds,' in Spanish, translated by this person (link to his entity record). This particular manifestation is published on this date by this publisher (link to its entity record), and is read by this person (link to her entity record). It is Media type: 'audio' and Carrier type: 'audio disc,' and these are the additional physical details that need to be added." See figure 5.10 to remember how the data elements are entered for different WEMI entities.

Like AACR2, RDA uses many obscure cataloging terms. But unlike AACR2, RDA tries to define all its terms, explain its concepts, and provide clear instructions about what the data elements being provided are supposed to do in a catalog. For example, RDA is designed to work with online data registries of terms. In these registries, all the common terms used to describe the attributes of an entity—content type (e.g., sounds), media type (e.g., audio), carrier type (e.g., audio disc), dimensions, types of illustrations, and so forth—are defined, and all alternate terms (including the terms in different languages) are provided. In a sense, each common term will have its own authority record. This will allow OPAC software to display whatever term is preferred, in any language, perhaps even to the level of individual options chosen by each user. Some examples are these:

English: CD *or* audiodisc *or* audio disc
French: disque visuel
Spanish: disco audio
German: videodiskette

RDA AND MARC

How will RDA work with MARC? The MARC people insist that MARC can continue to have a place in the brave new RDA world. They say that MARC has proven itself a stable and reliable format for transferring bibliographic data, so whenever records need to be moved from place to place (e.g., between host sites for the linked entity records), using MARC is the best way to pull all the separate entity records into a neat package in order to send that package somewhere. With this in mind, some relatively minor changes have been made to the MARC format to accommodate RDA. A list of these changes is given at the MARC Standards website in a document titled "MARC 21 Format 2009 Changes to Accommodate RDA."[8]

However, one of the main goals of RDA is to make bibliographic data more accessible and understandable to nonlibrary people who might want to use it in interesting ways. An author might like to create a Google Maps mash-up of all the settings used in his works. A fan might like to compile a list of all the movies in which a certain actress appears, sorted by publication place and date. But, one of the complaints about current bibliographic data locked away in MARC records is that those data are not easily understood by humans or software. The MARC manual is freely available online, but its terminology and concepts are so closely tied to AACR2 and other cataloging rules that even ILS (integrated library system) programmers find it difficult to understand. What data are meant to be indexed and where? What data are meant to be displayed or hidden? (This is one reason why so many library automation systems are not designed as well as they should be.)

MARC has been truly invaluable to the library community for the past forty years. Because of MARC we can share cataloging (copy cataloging) and resources (ILL). We can also move MARC data to a new ILS without having to convert them to a different format, and we can send the data from place to place (in the library world) with relative ease.

A complex and vitally important infrastructure is also built around using MARC records:

- They are obtained from publishers, resource suppliers, and record vendors.
- We copy them from one another.
- They are filed in library catalogs and used by every module of the ILS: acquisitions, serials tracking, cataloging, the online catalog, and circulation.
- They appear in OCLC WorldCat and other union catalogs where they are used for resource sharing/ILL.

It is hard to imagine how this infrastructure can be reshaped. But, conceptually, MARC records are "flat," which means all the information about a resource is provided in a single MARC bibliographic record. This means catalogers think about only that one bibliographic record for a resource when it is being cataloged. RDA, however, does not want catalogers to think about data packaged in single, comprehensive records. It wants them to think about how data about one entity relate to data about other entities:

- how a creator entity relates to the work entity he created
- how a translator entity relates to the expression entity for which she did the translation
- how a manifestation entity relates to the illustrator entity who illustrated it

For RDA to work as it is designed, as mentioned, its ultimate goal is to have separate sets of data elements (entity records) for each of the entities associated with a resource (creator, work, translator, expression, illustrator, manifestation, donor, item). Each entity record is linked to any other entity records with which it is associated, and the relationships between the entities are explicitly defined in the data about each linked entity. Isn't it good that you understand the concept of entities? (If not, go back and read the explanations of the term again.) Figure 5.13 illustrates the kinds of

FIGURE 5.13 LINKED AND RELATED GROUP 1 AND GROUP 2 ENTITIES FOR BEMELMANS'S *MADELINE* IN SPANISH

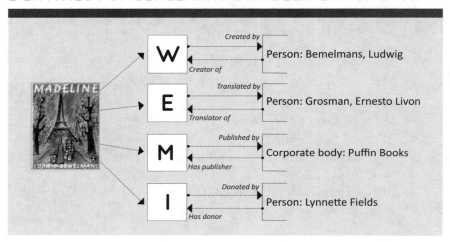

relationship information to be added to entity records to clarify how each entity relates to others.

When the cataloging world switches to RDA, we will, indeed, think differently about the cataloging process. The RDA goal is that, instead of downloading, uploading, and machine matching MARC records, we will eventually switch to sharing cataloging by creating and linking to entity records stored outside local catalogs, out there on the Web.

If all the entity records are stored on the Web, the following will be possible:

- Instead of downloading, uploading, and machine matching MARC records, local libraries can link their holdings to the appropriate manifestation entity record that describes their item, and all the information from the linked Group 1, 2, and 3 entity records will be instantly available in the OPAC.
- Entity records will be updated and enhanced once, for the benefit of everyone, and changes will be immediately available whenever

the data in one of those records are used for a search or displayed in an OPAC record.

But, RDA entails a lot less local control over our data, and it requires a lot more trust that:

- the system (i.e., the Web) will stay up
- Internet access will be fast enough to handle the traffic for all participants
- all the linked data will always be available (can I make a copy?)
- others won't mess up the shared data (the Wikipedia model)

This linked entity record scenario is not yet in place. A new infrastructure must be set up and totally new software designed that will, for example:

- manage (in computer terms) all this linked data
- allow fast, free (?) access to the linked data (not just for libraries but also for anyone who wants to work with the data)
- make it easy to find matching entity records and attach holdings to them
- allow catalogers to create and link new entity records when necessary
- enable OPAC searches that bring up display records that are comprised of data elements from different entity records (stored on sites all over the world?)
- provide ILL capabilities

Once RDA is published and cataloging software is available to make it simple, we can start making linked entity records; and once some linked entity records are available to experiment with, software developers can start designing new ILS modules that use the linked entity records; and once ILS systems that can use linked entity records exist, we can work toward building an infrastructure that is based on these linked entity records.

CAUTIONARY WORDS

It may sound as though we are advocating switching to RDA as soon as there is software help to facilitate making linked entity records, but there are still outstanding questions about this brave new world of RDA:

1. Where can new entity records to link to be found, and what will it cost to use them?
2. How will we search for the new entity records?
3. When will instructions be given on how to match against the bibliographic information in each WEMI entity record (a decision process currently called "when to create a new record")?
4. Will catalogers be able to edit data elements and add local data elements to entity records that are not in their local catalogs?
5. When will local library automation systems be able to use linked entity records instead of MARC records?
6. How will we work with both linked entity records and MARC records until the switch to linked entity records is complete?
7. How will we learn the new RDA instructions and approach?
8. Will catalogers still be able to outsource cataloging to vendors (link local item data to the correct WEMI entity records)?
9. When will all this happen?
10. Do we have to do this?

The first six questions can't be answered yet. Catalogers have to wait and find out as things develop.

A huge amount of information about RDA, FRBR, FRAD, FRSAD, and all those other acronyms is already available online, coming from many different sources—too many to list individually. Have no fear—there will be plenty of training opportunities available, once RDA is released and the time line for implementation is settled. If we can learn the new cataloging approach, so can the vendors on whom we rely.

Although at this writing the RDA online product is soon slated for release, an extended time of training, testing, and evaluation is planned, and widespread implementation of RDA is unlikely before late 2010 or 2011. No one must switch to RDA as soon as it is officially implemented. Probably, only the most sophisticated and ambitious catalogers will do so. Many catalogers will wait until tried and tested software is available for finding, editing, creating, and using data created under the new RDA approach.

Most currently available integrated library systems are designed around MARC records and need MARC records to function. As long as this is the situation, newly created linked entity records will have to be converted into MARC records. For now, catalogers can continue to download, upload, and machine match MARC records. But, as new software becomes available and as libraries gradually generate more linked entity records, a tipping point will be reached, and catalogers, taking a leap of faith, will step out into the new world of linked entity records.

A final question is, unfortunately, unanswerable at this writing: will RDA make it simpler or more difficult for catalogers to provide bibliographic information about resources? Only time will tell. But the future of cataloging certainly looks interesting. Catalogers must be prepared for a certain level of confusion and turmoil over the next few years. It will be up to each cataloger (and library administrator) to decide whether to dive in early or sit back and wait until things settle down. Either way, catalogers must find out as much as they can about RDA and keep in touch with developments, even as they continue following AACR2 and MARC to catalog resources and get them out to users.

NOTES

1. IFLA Study Group on the Functional Requirements for Bibliographic Records, *Functional Requirements for Bibliographic Records, Final Report* (München: K. G. Saur, 1998). Hereinafter cited as FRBR. Also available at www.ifla.org/en/publications/functional-requirements-for-bibliographic-records.
2. The RDA wording (from the 2009 final draft) for these user tasks is:

   - "Find—i.e., to find resources that correspond to the user's stated search criteria
   - Identify—i.e., to confirm that the resource described corresponds to the resource sought, or to distinguish between two or more resources with similar characteristics
   - Select—i.e., to select a resource that is appropriate to the user's needs
   - Obtain—i.e., to acquire or access the resource described."

3. From a workshop designed by Deborah A. Fritz: Book Blitz III.
4. This snippet of XML is based on MODS (Metadata Object Description Schema), developed by the Library of Congress. www.loc.gov/standards/mods/.
5. FRBR, 17.
6. "Relationships serve as the vehicle for depicting the link between one entity and another, and thus as the means of assisting the user to 'navigate' the universe that is represented in a bibliography, catalogue, or bibliographic database." FRBR, 55.

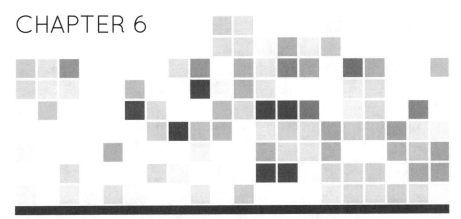

CHAPTER 6

Authority Control and Kids' Cataloging

Kay E. Lowell

WHAT IS AUTHORITY CONTROL?

Authority control often is a difficult term for people to grasp. In this online age, it may be easier to understand authority control by looking at a common experience of what authority control *isn't*. Do a search—any search—on the World Wide Web and you will retrieve hundreds, even thousands of hits. Many of these will leave you scratching your head, because although the term you typed will be in the page somewhere, it may be used in an entirely different sense than you intended. In searching a person's name, for example, you may retrieve a completely different person by the same name or may miss material by or about the person because the form of the name is slightly different. The Internet, in general, has no authority control—that is, no method for assigning terms in a standardized manner or for distinguishing between identical terms with different meanings.

Doris Clack, in her classic work on authority control, defines it as "the process of ensuring that every entry—name, uniform title, series, or subject—that is selected as an access point for the public catalog is unique and does not conflict, by being identical, with any other entry that is already in the catalog or that may be included at a later date."[1] Robert Maxwell describes it thus: "Authority work is so called because it deals with the formulation and recording of *authorized* heading forms in catalog records . . . to ensure consistency in the catalog so that the catalog user has to search under one and only one heading to find records associated with names, subjects, and other access points."[2]

Authority control for names and titles brings together all the works by and about people who have been known by varying forms of their names or by pseudonyms or stage names. It sets the form of name for corporate bodies so that materials issued by that body can be located even when the name of the body changes. It assigns *uniform titles* to works that exist in hundreds of different versions, such as Shakespeare's works, or that are so common that finding the specific one you want could be nearly impossible, such as a symphony.

Subject authority control directs catalogers to choose a term, define its meaning and scope, and apply it consistently whenever they catalog a work. Authority control also provides references for the users of the catalog so that if, for example, they want a book on pigs and enter that search term into a catalog using Library of Congress Subject Headings, the catalog will steer them gently to the word *swine*. The subject authority record often includes references to broader, narrower, and related headings, which can be invaluable to a person just beginning research in a new area of interest. "Authority records also provide cross references to lead users to the headings used in the catalog, e.g., a *search under:* Snodgrass, Quintus Curtius, 1835-1910 will lead users to the authorized form of heading for Mark Twain, i.e., Twain, Mark, 1835-1910."[3]

Catalogers need to understand that "we are dealing here with *access points*, not description."[4] In other words, the form of a name appearing on the title page—which is transcribed into the body of the record—may not be the authorized form of the name that appears in the main or added entries. The rules for constructing name and uniform title access points are in chapters 22 through 25 of AACR2. Guidelines for providing cross-references from one form of a name or title to another are found in chapter 26. Rules governing subject authority work are specific to the thesaurus or subject heading list being used.

WHY IS AUTHORITY CONTROL IMPORTANT?

Consider this: when most libraries used a card-based catalog, it was easy for the human brain to adjust for the occasional slight difference in the form of a heading. If two letters were transposed, the filer could mentally correct that error and file the card in its correct sequence. Computers, however, cannot ignore slight differences. If there is a misspelling in a heading in an online catalog, the item will not be located with the rest of the works that use that access point. The item may as well not be in the collection. Even if a particular catalog includes uncontrolled fields (notes, publisher information, etc.) in its keyword indexing, a misspelled word will result in a hit only if the searcher searches for the misspelling; and the result will not be located in the same set of results as a correctly spelled word. Likewise, if a name is entered in several different ways in an online catalog, the searcher will have to do separate searches or look in separate groups of hits to see everything the library has by or about that person—and this assumes that the searcher even recognizes different entries as potentially referring to the same individual.

Now that most library catalogs can be accessed remotely and that Internet search engines like Google can locate materials in many of them with just a keyword search, authority control is even more important. Why should this be true? Because, in one's home library, if a person doing a search comes across an incorrectly indexed entry or retrieves a record for no obvious reason, he or she can ask a librarian for assistance in interpreting the results. For catalog users outside the library, however, the only assistance available is provided by on-screen help built into the catalog software.

Increasingly, traditional library catalogs are being enhanced by new types of spell-checking, relevance-ranking, sorting and filtering options, and Google-esque help prompts ("Did you mean . . . ?"). Although people who have grown up using Google find such features comfortable to use, the search software still cannot distinguish between Madonna the singer and Madonna the religious icon without *something in the underlying record* upon which to base the distinction. "Implementing a system that performs good relevancy ranking, however, can be incredibly difficult. Especially in response to a broad query, the number of potential results can be very large. Determining the ones most relevant poses a difficult technical problem."[5] Additionally, research has demonstrated that even with the increasing availability of complete keyword indexing of bibliographic records, the exact subject-related concept searched for will not appear in the record in up to one third of instances. "The fact is that the assignment of descriptive language in the subject heading fields frequently attaches important terms and concepts to a bibliographic record that the record will not otherwise contain."[6]

Improving the signal-to-noise ratio of a keyword search still relies in part on the cataloger who has done authority control work, adding records with explanatory notes and cross-references. Authority control, therefore, is still a vital public service.

AUTHORITY CONTROL AND CHILDREN'S CATALOGING

For the children's catalog, the primary issue to consider is children's ability to use language. A growing body of literature reports studies of children's information-seeking behavior and its applicability to library catalogs. Paul Solomon, for example, investigated why so many of children's catalog searches fail. He found that children generally do not have the depth of knowledge needed to navigate subject headings properly or to make effective responses to failed searches.[7] Frances Jacobson pointed out that because the structures of bibliographic records and controlled vocabularies are highly different from and at a much higher reading level than the natural language of catalog users, children require an interpreter, guide, or mental model in order to use them.[8] In one study, researchers "developed categories with age-appropriate science texts for eight- to eleven-year-olds. They found that the children misunderstood the vocabulary even though the science textbooks were supposedly written for their age group. This suggested that adult assumptions about what children will understand do not necessarily hold."[9] The implication is that making library materials truly accessible to children needs special attention and care by those who are cataloging them.

In 1995, Pam Sandlian reported the results of research that prompted the creation of the CARL Corporation's Kid's Catalog product, one of the more successful early graphical interfaces for children's libraries. Seventy-seven percent of children's searches on standard online catalogs failed, primarily because "children often found the language in both bibliographic records and help screens incomprehensible."[10] The Kid's Catalog and similar products from other companies work on the premise that a visual interface to the catalog helps children succeed where a textual interface does not. This premise has been validated and strengthened by further research studies: "children need tools to search digital libraries in multiple ways (e.g., categorical browsing, keyword search), but categories expressed visually through icons are most important to develop; . . . additional search criteria specific to how children see the world need to be considered in the cataloging (metadata), for example, how books make children feel and book color, shape, and length."[11] Early efforts to design software to address these issues often met with limited success, in part because the underlying search categories represented by the icons were created by adults using adult language.

Attempts to accommodate children's thought processes into a truly usable library interface have often involved add-on software that uses a child's own search terms to create new interconnections between bibliographic records—a kind of custom-built authority control (see, e.g., Shuyuan Zhao's dissertation of 2000).[12] One such proposed interface would use advanced semantic relationships recognition software to mine the information already in bibliographic records and display results in a graphically pleasing way that also shows a term's relationship to other terms. This proposed interface would incorporate "helper ontologies" that could deal with the differences between user-supplied terms and other, controlled-vocabulary terms, making results simple for the user to interpret.[13]

With the recent explosion of social networking sites and "tagging" of photos and blog content (even if the taggers "haven't gotten with the program" of using official tags),[14] many more opportunities for expanding access to materials are being explored. This sort of folksonomy tagging is basically what had been envisioned as the perfect enhancement for kids' cataloging: allow a child to add "sad story" to the record for a favorite book. Solomon recommended that catalogs use local authority records or a similar input structure to build a flexible system of references based on children's language or a school's focus.[15] But will it work? Elaine Peterson explored whether folksonomy tagging by the authors of electronic dissertations and theses might suffice to the extent that Montana State University could discontinue adding LCSH controlled headings for these records. The results indicated that little overlap occurred between controlled vocabulary and user-supplied tags and that user-supplied tags tended to be much more specific than LCSH. Of concern, though, were variations in terms, misspellings, and the inconsistency in users' willingness to supply their own subjects. Furthermore, "few databases exist that allow the use of both hierarchical subject headings, such as LCSH, as well as patron-applied folksonomy tags,"[16] a situation that also exists for a catalog that uses multiple controlled-vocabulary thesauri.

It seems that, although technological developments are moving us ever closer to an ideal resource discovery tool, we have not yet reached that goal. For the library without access to the latest technology, add-on programs, or programmers to implement them, one of the best tools for assisting children to use library catalogs is still good, careful authority control that provides excellent cross-referencing and consistency, using whatever vocabulary list is best suited for the audience.

DECISIONS IN AUTHORITY CONTROL

As with all other areas of cataloging, decisions must be made. How will you create your authority file? Will you do your authority work in-house or purchase records from a vendor? Which subject thesaurus will you adopt? What records will you keep in your system and display to the public? How will you keep up with changes in the form of headings?

For many, if not most, libraries, budgetary constraints dictate the answers to their authority control questions. Most libraries do very little of their cataloging from scratch; rather, they purchase preexisting cataloging records through bibliographic utilities or other sources and spend their cataloging dollars on local adjustments to the records. The same can be said for authority control. Clack describes in detail the processes required to create authority records and cross-references from scratch; however, for all but the largest libraries such work is cost-prohibitive. In a school library or other small library, available staff is often hard-pressed just to keep up with public services demands.

CREATING THE AUTHORITY FILE

Fortunately, there is no reason to reinvent the wheel. Thousands of large library catalogs with authority control are available for searching via the Internet. Finding the current correct form of a heading to apply to a bibliographic record is very easy. Even better, the Library of Congress's own authority files—for both adult and juvenile headings—are available, free of charge, at http://authorities.loc.gov. These authority records can be saved in MARC format and loaded into a local system. "The only limitation is that authority records may only be saved, printed or emailed one at a time."[17]

A good choice for creating a library's initial authority file is to find a commercial authority control vendor and pay the vendor to do the work. Vendors can automatically replace incorrect headings with correct ones and supply matching authority records. If the purchaser chooses, the vendor also can apply a number of automatic corrections that reflect changes in cataloging rules, bringing the bibliographic file up to current standards. This option is very worthwhile if many years have passed since the file was originally created or if the library's collection is quite old.

An important consideration in choosing an authority vendor is whether it can supply records for the type of subject headings you use. Most vendors work with some subset of the Library of Congress headings files, supplemented with headings created by libraries or by the vendors themselves. Many also handle LC's Children's Subject Headings. Fewer vendors can provide authority control for Sears subject headings, although the number is increasing. Because Sears uses a vocabulary specifically designed for very small collections and is more accessible to children than some alternatives, this increased availability is welcome.

Another consideration when planning authority control projects is whether your library uses more than one thesaurus—for example, regular LC subject headings for the main collection and Children's Subject Headings (CSH) for children's materials. If so, the local system will have to support two separate authority indexes, each of which will need to be maintained. Because many of the headings in the Sears or CSH lists are in direct conflict with LCSH, loading both types of headings into the same index will create *circular references*: instances in which one heading points to another, which points back to the original heading (CSH's *pigs* versus LCSH's *swine* being the classic example). This is a major disservice to your patrons. If you have no choice other than to load all subject headings into one index, be prepared to do a large amount of manual cleanup to remove the circular references.

Finally, you must decide which authority records to keep in your system. Loading the entire *Library of Congress Subject Headings* file, for example, requires a system able to handle a huge file. For most libraries, a subset of headings will do. Many libraries load only those authority records that include cross-references or scope notes or both that will display and that patrons can use directly.

Do not expect perfection from an authority vendor. No matter how sophisticated the matching algorithms are, there are always names for which no authority record has ever been created, or subject headings that have changed so many times since an item was originally cataloged that no computer in the world can match it to its current authorized form. Your vendor will supply you with lists of no-match headings that need to be manually checked and corrected.

MAINTAINING THE AUTHORITY FILE AND BIBLIOGRAPHIC RECORDS

Work does not stop once the initial authority control project is done. First, each name, series title, uniform title, and subject heading in every new cataloging record must be checked against the catalog and the authority file to provide consistency and accuracy. This process can be handled in the library itself, or batches of records can be sent periodically to the authority control vendor for processing.

If your library uses a card catalog, you need to verify the accuracy of each heading as each item is cataloged. Otherwise, you will be pulling and correcting cards as headings are found to conflict with others already in the catalog. In an online catalog, there are several methods of doing ongoing authority work in-house. Records can be checked during the cataloging process, as is done with a card catalog. Many integrated library systems can provide lists of headings newly added to the catalog, which can then be checked for accuracy on a daily, weekly, or even monthly basis depending on the volume of cataloging being done.

Some systems, because of the way they store bibliographic and authority records, are able to automatically correct headings that exactly match a *see* reference (an unused form of the heading) in an authority record as the records are loaded into the catalog. Many systems, however, have no direct linkage between a bibliographic record and its related authority records. Bibliographic records containing incorrect headings must be manually corrected, either one by one or, in some cases, via a *global update* function. In a card catalog, the equivalent of global updating can be as elaborate as retyping every card or as simple as filing a new reference or guide card explaining the change.

A second consideration for ongoing authority control work is how to handle changed headings. Subject headings change frequently to reflect changes in language, to make subject headings more consistent with one another, to accommodate new areas of knowledge, or to maintain accuracy (a situation that occurs frequently with place names). The library needs a way to be aware of and make these changes. Again, a number of choices are available.

A librarian may ask the authority control vendor to retain a copy of the library's authority and bibliographic records. Then, whenever one of the headings changes, the vendor sends a new copy of the record or any associated authority records or both to the library. A variation on this theme is a *notification service,* in which the vendor sends lists of changes to the library and the library makes the changes in-house. A low-tech but more time-consuming method is for the librarian to use the Library of Congress weekly lists (of subject heading changes), the quarterly *Cataloging Service Bulletin,* or other available sources that list the changes and manually revise authority and associated bibliographic records. "All issues . . . of *Cataloging Service Bulletin* (CSB) are now available at no cost at www.loc.gov/cds/PDFdownloads/csb/."[18] Most libraries rely on some combination of options.

Finally, there is the question of the level of detail in authority maintenance. How exhaustive should your authority control be? In theory, a true authority-controlled catalog has an associated authority record for every single access point it contains. Additionally, every cross-reference in every one of those authority records is checked for accuracy and deleted or enhanced as required. It should be obvious that this level of rigor is next to impossible for all libraries to achieve. In 1995, Jennifer Younger proposed that the concept of *utility* be applied to authority control, focusing authority control efforts on names that are most likely to lead to confusion for the patron if they are not controlled.[19] This advice is even more pertinent for a children's catalog, where confusion should be avoided as much as possible.

CONCLUSION

Remember, no matter what decisions you make for applying authority control to your catalog, you should keep the needs of your users foremost in mind. Particularly for a children's catalog, expend your efforts first in those areas that will help children deal with confusing levels of language used to retrieve information. The work you do in the background may make the difference between a frustrated child and a happy one who will see the library and its catalog as a valuable tool he or she can use successfully.

NOTES

1. Doris Hargrett Clack, *Authority Control: Principles, Applications, and Instructions* (Chicago: American Library Association, 1990), 2.
2. Robert L. Maxwell, *Maxwell's Guide to Authority Work* (Chicago: American Library Association, 2002), 1.
3. Library of Congress, "Library of Congress Authorities, Help Pages, Frequently Asked Questions: What Is an Authority Record?" http://authorities.loc.gov/help/auth-faq.htm#1.

4. Maxwell, *Maxwell's Guide to Authority Work*, 3.

5. "Introduction," *Library Technology Reports* 43, no. 4 (July 1, 2007): 13.

6. Jeffrey Garrett, "Subject Headings in Full-Text Environments: The ECCO Experiment," *College and Research Libraries* 68, no. 1 (January 2007): 74.

7. Paul Solomon, "Information Systems for Children: Explorations in Information Access and Interface Usability for an Online Catalog in an Elementary School Library" (PhD diss., University of Maryland, College Park, 1990), abstract in *Digital Dissertations*: AAT 9133166.

8. Frances F. Jacobson, "From Dewey to Mosaic: Considerations in Interface Design for Children," *Internet Research: Electronic Networking Applications and Policy* 5, no. 2 (1995): 68.

9. Christine L. Borgman, M. Chignell, and F. Valdez, "Designing an Information Retrieval Interface Based on Children's Categorization Knowledge: A Pilot Study," in *Proceedings of the American Society for Information Science* (Medford, NJ: ASIS, 1989), 81–94. Cited in Allison Druin, "What Children Can Teach Us: Developing Digital Libraries for Children with Children," *Library Quarterly* 75, no. 1 (2005): 23.

10. Pam Sandlian, "Rethinking the Rules: The Story behind 'Kid's Catalog,'" *School Library Journal* 41, no. 7 (1995): 24.

11. Allison Druin, "What Children Can Teach Us: Developing Digital Libraries for Children with Children," *Library Quarterly* 75, no. 1 (2005): 36.

12. Shuyuan Zhao, "Use-Based Virtual Reorganization of a Library Collection: An Empirical Study" (PhD diss., Rutgers, The State University of New Jersey, New Brunswick, 2000), abstract in *Digital Dissertations*: AAT 9974003.

13. Ioannis Papadakis, Michalis Stefanidakis, and Aikaterini Tzali, "Visualizing OPAC Subject Headings," *Library Hi Tech* 26, no. 1 (2008): 19–23.

14. Mary Ellen Bates, "Authority Control to the People!" *EContent* 32, no. 3 (April 2009): 43.

15. Solomon, "Information Systems for Children."

16. Elaine Peterson, "Patron Preferences for Folksonomy Tags: Research Findings When Both Hierarchical Subject Headings and Folksonomy Tags Are Used," *Evidence Based Library and Information Practice* 4, no. 1 (2009): 53.

17. Library of Congress, "Library of Congress Authorities, Help Pages, Frequently Asked Questions: Are Authority Records Available Free of Charge?" http://authorities.loc.gov/help/auth-faq.htm#2.

18. Barbara B. Tillett, "Library of Congress Report, ALA ALCTS Committee on Cataloging: Description and Access (CC:DA), Annual Meeting, Chicago, Illinois, July 13, 2009," www.libraries.psu.edu/tas/jca/ccda/docs/lc0907.pdf.

19. Jennifer A. Younger, "After Cutter: Authority Control in the Twenty-first Century," *Library Resources & Technical Services* 39, no. 2 (April 1995): 144–51.

CHAPTER 7

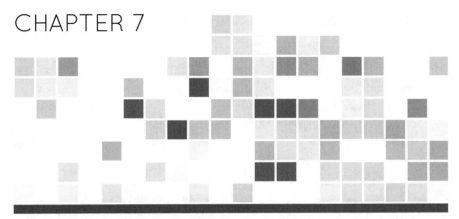

Using LC's Children's Subject Headings in Catalogs for Children and Young Adults: Why and How

Joanna F. Fountain

One of the most challenging and interesting areas of cataloging is the creation and enhancement of machine-readable cataloging records for children's materials. The cataloger must address the needs of multiple audiences while juggling complicated rules, rule interpretations, special guidelines for children's catalogs, classification options, and curriculum-enhancement features. For the school or public librarian who is not a full-time or highly experienced cataloger, this can be a daunting task. Fortunately, many have the opportunity to purchase cataloging records from a variety of sources. Still, the quality of the records available for purchase varies from excellent to seriously erroneous, and children's catalogs—which should be the most helpful—often contain entries that mislead rather than assist younger library users in finding what they seek.

The intent of this chapter is to walk through the guidelines for using the list of subject headings for children's catalogs compiled by the Children's Literature Section (CLS) in the U.S. and Publisher Liaison Division of the Library of Congress (LC).[1] The Cataloging and Classification Section (CCS) of the Association for Library Collections & Technical Services (ALCTS) of the American Library Association (ALA) has recommended similar policies and practices for use in catalogs for children and young adults. These guidelines address the needs of children and youth, librarians, teachers, parents, and others interested in working with young readers and catalog users. Such varied audiences call for several levels and types of information; however, once the principles are understood, catalogers can apply them, knowing they have a sound basis for making the judgments that go into creating useful and usable bibliographic records.

In order to catalog children's materials according to ALA and LC guidelines, one must have access to particular cataloging tools. These include (a) the latest revision of the *Anglo-American Cataloguing Rules* (AACR2) and its amendments, (b) the newer rules when they become generally available for use in small-library settings (RDA—*Resource Description and Access*), (c) ALA's "Guidelines for Standardized Cataloging for Children" (see chapter 1 in this book), (d) a copy of the *Abridged Dewey Decimal Classification and Relative Index,* (e) applicable Library of Congress rule interpretations if the library's policy is to follow these, (f) the *Library of Congress Subject Headings* (LCSH), and (g) if the policy is to provide curricular information, a copy of the curriculum-enhancement guidelines approved by ALA's Machine-Readable Bibliographic Information (MARBI) Committee for use in children's catalogs.[2]

Specific instructions for applying the Children's Subject Headings (CSH) list in children's catalogs are provided in the supplementary volume of the print edition of LCSH. That section describes LC's policies for subject analysis and application of the LCSH list to children's materials in their collection, as well as for the valuable Cataloging-in-Publication (CIP) program. The CSH list itself provides modifications and exceptions to the main list, but does not replace it. Policies applied to children's books and other library materials at the Library of Congress are spelled out in section D500 of the *Subject Cataloging Manual: General Cataloging Procedures,* titled "Juvenile Materials." Selection for CSH program treatment is based on the stated or presumed audience level of the work. The CLS catalogs items within its scope by creating the complete bibliographic citation, including subject headings and brief noncritical summaries. When the need arises, the CLS also develops new children's subject headings and proposes changes to existing headings. In addition, the CLS monitors policies and practices in children's subject cataloging.

Once the "juvenile" determination and citation have been made, the record is processed using current MARC 21 (MAchine-Readable Cataloging) protocols, and the work is classified according to instructions in section F615 of the *Classification and Shelflisting Manual,* selecting the appropriate PZ classification and supplying the E (Easy) and Fic (Fiction) optional classifications from the Dewey Decimal Classification (DDC) schedules. These appear in CIP records and on printed cards in brackets, as do headings from the CSH list. Subject analysis follows instructions in section H1690 of the *Subject Headings Manual.* For example, subdivisions such as **—Juvenile literature,** which would be added to standard subject headings, are not included among the bracketed headings because they are not used in catalogs for children and young adults. Whenever possible, juvenile works—except those receiving a descriptive contents note—receive a brief, noncritical annotation or summary, entered in the Summary note field (MARC field 520).[3] Curriculum enhancements are not provided as part of CSH program cataloging.

The CLS generally has complete responsibility for juvenile literature. However, fictional works are not always assigned subject headings by the CLS when there are budget constraints. When they are omitted, the task of assigning subject headings to fiction is left to local librarians, as it is generally agreed such headings are especially useful in children's catalogs. Works of nonfiction do receive a full array of subject headings and appropriate classification numbers. When the team completes its work on an item, unique book numbers (Cutters) are assigned according to guidelines in LC's *Classification and Shelflisting Manual* (formerly *Subject Cataloging Manual: Shelflisting*), and the item is sent on for shelving.

Although librarians in other settings usually do not work in teams or route materials to other staff members, aspects of LC's procedures may be useful to emulate. Three general procedures are followed: (1) each item is described; (2) subject headings are added to the record; and (3) the work is classified. Beginning with the title page, or the chief source of information for nonbook materials, the cataloger first drafts the bibliographic description, following current rules (AACR2). Codes for level, illustration, and so on are added to the MARC record according to instructions online at www.loc.gov/marc/, or in the printed MARC documentation and manuals that accompany the automated catalog program being used.

Next, subject headings are added. If a local library makes any modifications or additions, these must be noted in the local authority file, and care must be taken to enter these only in "local" fields of the MARC record. Authority files (lists of valid headings and subdivisions) are then checked to ensure consistency in the form of all names and titles used as main and added entries, whether these are used as name, title, or subject entries.

Finally, call numbers are assigned: first the classification is determined, and then the Cutter number (alphabetizing or other sequencing feature) is added. If a shelflist is maintained, that list is checked for appropriate placement within the collection, and any other information, such as an item's copy or volume number, is added.

The remainder of this chapter focuses on processes for the selection and assignment of subject headings for children's catalogs, using LCSH and CSH as the authority. After writing down or mentally noting possible terms to describe what the work is about, the cataloger begins by verifying each term in *both* the main LCSH list (currently five printed volumes) and the CSH list, to prevent conflicts within the catalog. After some practice, the cataloger will frequently guess (or remember) that an alternative term exists in the CSH list and will save time by checking that list first, keeping in mind that headings from both lists are needed. It is important to note and read scope notes in order to be sure that specific instructions for each term are not overlooked. It is wise to review the usage instructions in the "Introduction to Children's Subject Headings," as these vary in significant ways from standard practice. This caution is valid even when the online authority file is used as the source of headings and subdivisions. Standard practice for all categories of headings and free-floating subdivisions is presented in detail in the *Subject Headings Manual,* an essential reference for identifying LC subject cataloging practice.

In many ways LC's instructions are self-explanatory and include representative illustrations. Still, it helps to study them at some length and read portions of the list to gain a working understanding for their application, keeping in mind the varied audiences the children's cataloger must address. These audiences include (1) children and young adults, (2) librarians and cataloging support staff, (3) teachers, (4) college students and faculty members, and (5) the general public, especially parents.

All subject headings in MARC 21 records are entered in fields with three-digit tags beginning with a 6, usually referred to generically as 6XX fields. The tag is followed by two additional numeral positions, known as *indicators*. The first indicator is usually blank.[4] The second identifies the source of the heading. A second indicator set to 1 indicates that the heading is from the CSH list, and the heading and any subdivisions have been entered according to CSH practice. You can usually expect a MARC record for a juvenile work to have at least two sets of subject headings: one with a second indicator 0 (for regular LCSH headings), and one with a second indicator 1. The first set (0) is for entries in standard catalogs; the second set is for entries in catalogs for children and young adults. In addition, it should be noted that CSH procedures have broad appeal and could be considered for use in public catalogs intended for the general adult population. A library serving a broad population might retain both types of entry in its catalog if its automated system can differentiate them and prevent conflicts. School and other children's catalogs should not include subject headings with the second indicator 0, so that subject headings lead directly to CSH entries.

Personal names used as subjects are entered in field 600. Although many Library of Congress records for works of fiction have not been assigned subject headings, librarians are encouraged by ALA guidelines to do so. This may be done successfully by following LC subject application guidelines as well as CSH program guidelines; for example, a story (fiction) about events involving President George Washington would have at least the following two subject entries, in which differences are seen in the subdivision for the name entry and in the value of the second indicator:[5]

> 600 10 Washington, George, ‡d 1732-1799 ‡v Fiction
> 650 _0 Presidents ‡z United States ‡v Fiction
> 600 11 Washington, George, ‡d 1732-1799 ‡v Fiction
> 650 _1 Presidents ‡v Fiction

Nonfiction biographical works (including autobiographies) of individuals will have similar headings, but normally without subdivision, following CSH program guidelines. In both cases, at least *two* headings are to be entered. The first heading is the individual's name in its valid entry form, and the second is the "class of persons" or field of endeavor with which the biographee is most commonly associated. In some cases, the name of a place, event, or organization with which the person is associated will also be a useful access point.

There are three important differences between standard and CSH use in the assignment of subdivisions. The first is in the application of the subdivision —**Biography,** which is not authorized for use under personal names in standard practice. CSH use for individual biographies of members of ethnic groups, however (including American Indian groups) does call for the free-floating subdivision **—Biography** to be added to the class of person entry for individual biographies in children's catalogs. The second major difference is the use of geographic subdivisions in "class of persons" headings: the subdivision **—United States** is not used in CSH subject entries unless the term is broad or international in scope, so that the place name is required for accurate interpretation, as in the case of **Folklore—United States,** to differentiate U.S. folklore from folklore in general. The opposite is true of standard subdivision practice, in which the geographic subdivision is routinely used for any topic that could reasonably be interpreted as varying from place to place. The same principle applies to standard LCSH headings that include the word *American,* such as **American wit and humor,** or **Short stories, American;** the CSH equivalents are **Wit and humor** and **Short stories.** The third important difference in application is in the use of specific *and* broader entries in the same bibliographic record. In standard LCSH practice, a broad term is not used in addition to a specific term, if the broad term encompasses it. The rule in both standard and CSH practice is to be as specific as the content of the work, or *coextensive* with the scope of the work. In CSH practice, however, the use of specific and broad terms is encouraged when the inclusion might provide better access to the work.

The following example illustrates all three differences between standard and CSH subject entries; these are headings that would be applied in the case of a juvenile biography of John Chapman (the legendary American apple seed and sprout planter):

> 600 10 Appleseed, Johnny, ‡d 1774-1845 ‡v Juvenile literature.
> 650 _0 Apple growers ‡z United States ‡v Biography ‡v Juvenile literature.
> 600 11 Appleseed, Johnny, ‡d 1774-1845.
> 650 _1 Apple growers.
> 650 _1 Horticulturists.

In this example, the two standard subject entries, identified by the 0 in the second indicator position, have subdivisions that are not used in CLS practice: **—Juvenile literature** and **—United States.** The third CSH entry, **Horticulturists,** has no matching standard entry, because the term is broader than, and encompasses, the specific term **Apple growers.** Also, both the specific term and the broad term designate "professions," so the subdivision **—Biography** is not used. By using a second indicator of 1, the cataloger alerts searchers looking at the record that the term in that field has been assigned according to CSH practice, even if it is a standard term or subdivision.

A different modification of subdivision practice for use in children's and young adult catalogs is encountered in headings for adapted versions of works. The following example is for a film version of Samuel Beckett's *Malone Dies*. The title portion of the name-title entry has been modified for CSH use, replacing the original French title with the English-language title by which English-speaking readers know the work. Note that no form subdivision is available for use in the CSH program as a counterpart for the subdivision —**Juvenile films.** Subject headings for this work would include the following:

> 600 10 Beckett, Samuel, ‡*d* 1906-1989. ‡*t* Malone meurt ‡*v* Juvenile films.
>
> 600 11 Beckett, Samuel, ‡*d* 1906-1989. ‡*t* Malone dies.

In this example, the first indicator 1 represents the form of the surname (single), which controls filing. The second indicator in a 6XX field, as noted previously, represents the authority for or the source of the subject heading, in this case the CSH list.

Works about other works and adaptations of other works with known authors are always (and only) entered under the authorized entry for the author of the original work. This is especially helpful in collocating all forms, versions, adaptations, editions, and so forth, of the same work, because the titles on the items often vary. If the entries were under item title, this would force such variations away from each other alphabetically and create great difficulty for searchers who wish to find all iterations of a work. The only titles that may be accessed directly under their titles in subject entries are anonymous works and works that have been assigned a uniform title as their main entry. Uniform titles used as subjects are entered in MARC field 630. A children's play based on such a work might have such subject entries as:

> 630 00 Cantar de mío Cid. ‡*l* English ‡*v* Juvenile drama.
>
> 630 01 Cantar de mío Cid. ‡*l* English ‡*v* Drama.

In this example, the first indicator 0 represents that there are no nonfiling characters in the entry. AACR2 prescribes omission of leading articles in uniform titles, so a zero indicator is used for any uniform title used as a subject or name entry. In addition to uniform titles for individual works, titles of series and collective titles are entered in 630 fields when they are the subject of other works. Note that the CSH list provides for the subdivision —**Drama** to be used instead of the standard subdivision —**Juvenile drama.**

Each type of name heading is entered in a different field number. For example, corporate-body names are tagged 610, conference names are in field 611, and geographic or place names are given in field 651. The most commonly used subject field tag, however, is 650. It is used for topical subjects, including any identifiable topic for fictional works, and names of fictional characters. A children's book about coral snakes will have the following entries:

> 650 _0 Micrurus ‡v Juvenile literature.
> 650 _1 Coral snakes.

For many nonfiction works, no subdivision is required for juvenile subject entries. Yet there are a number of exceptions. Some are listed in the CSH list, while others are available as free-floating subdivisions for either standard or CSH headings. Others are listed in the CSH instructions. For example, all works of juvenile fiction should have a topical entry if possible. The well-known work *Charlotte's Web* might have the following subject added entries:

> 650 _0 Spiders ‡v Juvenile fiction.
> 650 _0 Death and dying ‡v Juvenile fiction.
> 650 _1 Spiders ‡v Fiction.
> 650 _1 Death and dying ‡v Fiction.

Many additions and modifications have been made to enhance use of children's materials. Some are modified and noted in the CSH list, while others are to be modified by instruction, as seen in the preceding examples. The list includes a number of terms that have been added for the benefit of persons working with children and young adults—terms that younger readers might not think to use as access points. For example, the term **Textures,** which is not used in the standard list, would be of interest to a parent or teacher, but not necessarily to young children. Similarly, the subdivision —**Collections** is no longer authorized as a standard LCSH free-floating subdivision; nevertheless, it is still to be used with certain headings in children's catalogs, such as **Storytelling—Collections,** because of its usefulness to librarians and teachers in making selections for young readers.

Teachers and librarians occasionally develop reading lists for bibliotherapy and independent reading on a variety of topics and levels. The special children's headings in the CSH list supplement standard headings and make it easier to identify material using terms more familiar to younger readers. **Gas,** for example, replaces the standard LCSH term **Natural gas;** the term **Marriage** is modified for CSH use, so that it replaces the main-list term **Teenage marriage.**

Children and young adults are considered the ultimate users of the juvenile catalog. For this reason, the greatest part of the CSH list consists of substitutions for standard LCSH terms. Each year several of the substituted terms also replace terms previously used in the main listing of subject headings. As a result, those terms have been removed from the children's heading list and are now considered standard. Their use as standard headings benefits all catalog users without diminishing children's catalogs in any way. When they are used in catalogs for children and young adults, they continue to have the second indicator set to 1.

Examples of headings removed from the CSH list because they have become standard are **Music camps** (which replaced Camps, Music), **Cave drawings** (which had been spelled with a hyphen in the standard list), and **Roe deer** (which had been substituted for Capreolus). The personal name **Coronado, Francisco Vásquez de, 1510-1554** has replaced Vásquez de Coronado, Francisco, 1510-1554 in the Library of Congress's name authority file, and the replaced name no longer appears in the CSH list. This process is ongoing, and such changes are made with much deliberation.

A number of CSH terms substitute a combined term for one or more single terms. Some examples are **Actors and actresses** (which replaces six LCSH terms), **Lost and found possessions** (which replaces six terms), and **Waiters and waitresses** (which replaces two terms). Some CSH headings replace more than one standard heading without actually combining them. For example, **Babies** replaces both Infants and Infants (Newborn); and **Lesser panda** replaces Ailurus fulgens, Red panda, and Wah. **Kings, queens, rulers, etc.** is used in place of fourteen terms in the main list: Caliphs; Chiefs, Indian; Emperors; Indian chiefs; Monarchs; Pharaohs; Queens; Roman emperors; Royalty; Rulers; Russian empresses; Shahs; Sovereigns; and Sultans!

Popular terms replacing other, less commonly used terms include **Greed** (used for [UF] Avarice and Covetousness), **Luck** (UF Fortune), and **Menstruation** (UF Menstrual cycle). Similarly, shorter forms of headings sometimes replace longer forms: **Baseball—Fiction** is used instead of Baseball stories, for example, and **Jumping bean** replaces Mexican jumping bean. Occasionally the use of some CSH terms seems contradictory, such as **Horror stories** instead of Horror—Fiction and Horror tales, but on examination those terms may be found to be more popular.

Scientific terms are frequently replaced with more popular terms, even though children and youth are not likely to use the popular term to a great extent either; for example, **Livebearers (Fish)** replaces Poeciliidae, and **Isopods** replaces Isopoda. Some terms, however, truly are more common, such as **Snakes,** used for Serpents, and **Test tube babies,** used for Fertilization in vitro, Human. For older children and youth who are more familiar with the natural world and who may be studying scientific topics, it is recommended that both the popular term *and* the scientific term be used in the bibliographic record as access points. When both terms are used in the same catalog, however, some accommodation to the reference structure will be required—for example, using *See also* or *RT* (related term) references to resolve conflicts.

Both ALA and LC's CSH program recommend use of both specific and broad headings as useful access points. Although this practice would be good to apply generally, LC's standard policy for subject heading assignment has in the past led to decreased use of this obvious and helpful aid to catalog users. The CSH program does, however, recognize that young people and teachers frequently refer to topics in more inclusive groupings than other people might. For example, a person might use the term *space* to refer to any of a number of more specific topics, such as space travel, space exploration, astronomy, the universe, and so on. Whenever such broad terms are available in either the main list or the CSH list, they should be used as access points *in addition to* the more specific terms. Some general terms are specified in the CSH list to even replace main headings, such as **Dogs** in place of Puppies, or **Chickens** instead of Chicks.

The CSH list provides special treatment for works in non-English languages and for bilingual works in languages that have been established in the CSH list. Headings follow two patterns: the first is for informational and recreational works in a language, including bilingual works; the second is for works designed for instruction and practice in reading the language, commonly referred to as *readers*. The heading for the first broad grouping follows the pattern **French language materials, Chippewa language materials,** and so on. This type of heading may in turn be followed by the subdivision **—Bilingual** when the work is in both English and the language named in the heading. The second pattern is the same term without the word *materials;* this type of heading may be used alone or followed by any applicable free-floating subdivision, including the special CSH language subdivisions: **Hebrew language, German language—Collections, Spanish language—Readers.**

In addition to heading modification, a number of subdivisions have special applications. Besides **—Collections,** mentioned earlier, the following subdivisions are used only in children's catalogs:**—Cartoons and comics, —Guides** (use differs from the standard LCSH practice), **—Habits and behaviors,** and **—Wit and humor.** On the other hand, the subdivision **—**Illustrations is not used; instead, the subdivision **—Pictorial works** replaces it in CSH practice. The particular CSH use guidelines for the subdivision **—Biography** are quite different from those of standard LCSH practice and include a specific *limitation* in that the subdivision may only be used in topical entries under names of ethnic groups (including the older category Indians) and under subject fields in which no specific term designates the profession or contributions of the biographee; for example, the Biography subdivision may not be used under **Teachers** or under **Baseball players,** because those terms designate professions.

Headings and free-floating subdivisions in the standard list that begin with the words *Children, Children's,* or *Juvenile* are to be used without those words in CSH headings; the same is true for headings ending with such phrases as *for children* or *in children.* An example of the first type is **Plays,** which is used for Children's plays, One-act plays, and School plays. Examples of the second type are **Separation anxiety,** used instead of Separation anxiety in children, and **Strangers,** which replaces Children and strangers.

Although this chapter reflects the practices of the Children's Literature Section at the Library of Congress and most MARC record vendors, it must be pointed out that other lists are available to aid in the subject cataloging of materials included in catalogs that are used by children and young adults. In particular, the *Sears List of Subject Headings*, though designed primarily for public library use, does include terms believed to be more commonly understood and used by the general English-speaking population. This list is also available in Spanish, which provides catalogers for all types of audiences the opportunity to add headings for materials in English or in Spanish, or both. This level of cataloging enhancement can only improve access for our many readers, at all levels and of many backgrounds. In addition, the book *Subject Headings for School and Public Libraries* (Libraries Unlimited) is soon to appear in a bilingual edition. That list includes terms as well as names that appear frequently in both school and public libraries. The same approach should be taken for any language that reflects the audience or collections or both of a library with a significant non-English-dominant population. Many lists exist for assistance in those languages, and in some cases there are lists specifically for catalogs used by children or young adults or both. Future works, whether in print or electronic form, should be considered that will aid catalogers in providing continuously expanding access to the collections we organize.

CONCLUSION

Both ALA's guidelines and the Library of Congress's Children's Subject Headings program are outgrowths of the clear need to modify standard access to and arrangement of materials in catalogs intended for children and young adults. The purpose of these guidelines is to increase the likelihood that younger readers will find what they want and need, in terms they use and understand. Both sets of guidelines outline modifications of terminology and access-point selection that advance that purpose. The result is that catalogers will write longer, more inclusive bibliographic records, supplying both specific and general vocabulary as subject access points and assigning headings that reflect adult, child, and youth language use. In headings for the youthful reader, superfluous terms related to youth are omitted, and special subdivisions are added to others to increase their comprehensibility. These guidelines do not foster more or faster cataloging, but are undoubtedly better for the catalog user. We are still indebted to Charles Ammi Cutter for his clear statements of our objectives in cataloging, including his admonition that "the convenience of the public is always to be set before the ease of the cataloger."[6] He further took care to point out that both guidelines and thought are required to achieve our purposes, stating, "Cataloging is an art, not a science. No rules can take the place of experience and good judgment, but some of the results of experience may be best indicated by rules."[7]

NOTES

1. Library of Congress, Policy and Standards Division, Library Services, *Library of Congress Subject Headings Supplementary Vocabularies: Free-Floating Subdivisions, Genre/Form Headings, Children's Subject Headings*, 31st ed. (Washington, DC: Library of Congress, Cataloging Distribution Service, 2009).
2. MARC standards for curriculum enhancements [fields 521, 526, 658], published online at www.loc.gov/marc/bibliographic/ecbdhome.html.
3. Joanna F. Fountain, "Guidelines for Standardized Cataloging for Children," in *Cataloging Correctly for Kids: An Introduction to the Tools,* 4th ed., ed. Sheila S. Intner, Joanna F. Fountain, and Jane E. Gilchrist (Chicago: American Library Association, 2006).
4. Blank positions are represented in examples by an underscore.
5. Subfield delimiters are represented in examples by a ‡ (double dagger, or diesis). Note, however, that many printers do not accommodate this character, so this symbol is also sometimes represented by a | (pipe) or a $ (dollar mark).
6. Charles A. Cutter, "Rules for a Dictionary Catalog: Selections," in *Foundations of Cataloging: A Sourcebook,* ed. Michael Carpenter and Elaine Svenonius (Littleton, CO: Libraries Unlimited, 1985), 66.
7. Ibid.

RESOURCES

Abridged Dewey Decimal Classification and Relative Index. 14th ed. Dublin, OH: OCLC Online Computer Library Center, 2004.

Anglo-American Cataloguing Rules. 2nd ed., 2002 rev. with updates. Chicago: American Library Association, 2002.

Association for Library Collections & Technical Services/CCS Cataloging of Children's Materials Committee. "Guidelines for Standardized Cataloging of Children's Materials." In *Cataloging Correctly for Kids: An Introduction to the Tools,* 4th ed., edited by Sheila S. Intner, Joanna F. Fountain, and Jane E. Gilchrist. Chicago: American Library Association, 2006. Originally published in *Top of the News* 40 (Fall 1983): 49–55.

"Cataloging for Children: A Selective Bibliography." *ALCTS Newsletter* 1, no. 4 (1990): 40–41.

"Children's Subject Headings." In *Library of Congress Subject Headings. Supplementary Vocabularies,* 31st ed. Washington, DC: Library of Congress, Cataloging Distribution Service, 2009.

Cutter, Charles A. "Rules for a Dictionary Catalog: Selections." In *Foundations of Cataloging: A Sourcebook,* edited by Michael Carpenter and Elaine Svenonius. Littleton, CO: Libraries Unlimited, 1985.

Dewey Decimal Classification and Relative Index. 22nd ed. Dublin, OH: OCLC Online Computer Library Center, 2003.

"Juvenile Materials, D500." In *Subject Cataloging Manual: General Cataloging Procedures.* Washington, DC: Library of Congress, Cataloging Distribution Service, 1992.

Library of Congress Authorities (topics, names, titles). http://authorities.loc.gov.

Library of Congress. Network Development and MARC Standards Office. *MARC 21 Format for Bibliographic Data.* Washington, DC: Library of Congress, Cataloging Distribution Service, 2009. www.loc.gov/marc/bibliographic/ecbdhome.html.

Library of Congress. Subject Cataloging Division. *LC Classification Schedules, A–Z* (LCC). Washington, DC: Library of Congress, Cataloging Distribution Service (dates vary).

———. *Classification and Shelflisting Manual.* Washington, DC: Library of Congress, Cataloging Distribution Service, 2008.

———. *Library of Congress Rule Interpretations.* Washington, DC: Library of Congress, Cataloging Distribution Service, 2005.

———. *Library of Congress Subject Headings* (LCSH). 31st ed. Washington, DC: Library of Congress, Cataloging Distribution Service, 2009.

———. *Subject Headings Manual.* Washington, DC: Library of Congress, Cataloging Distribution Service, 2008, with updates, 2009–.

CHAPTER 8

Sears List of Subject Headings

Joseph Miller

Two sources of subject headings are available for cataloging children's materials. The first is *Library of Congress Subject Headings* (LCSH) in conjunction with the modified list of the Library of Congress's Children's Subject Headings (formerly called the Annotated Card or AC headings) used by the Library of Congress for children's materials only. The second source is the *Sears List of Subject Headings* (Sears). Both lists are subject authority environments entirely complete within themselves, and a library will use either one or the other, but rarely both.

The need for alternative authority lists was felt early in the twentieth century. In 1923, when the first Sears list appeared, the Library of Congress's *Subject Headings Used in the Dictionary Catalogs of the Library of Congress* and the American Library Association's *List of Subject Headings for Use in Dictionary Catalogs* already existed. Then as now, the Library of Congress (LC) tailored its subject headings to its own needs, which are those of a very large research library and quite different from the cataloging needs of small libraries. It was with this difference in mind that Minnie Earl Sears (1873–1933) consulted the catalogs of a number of small libraries that she considered well cataloged and put together a list entitled *List of Subject Headings for Small Libraries*. Beginning with the sixth edition (1950), the list was given her name and has since been known as the Sears list. The Sears list has never been intended exclusively for cataloging children's materials. It is meant to be used in any kind of small library.

The original goal of the Sears list was to remain as close as possible to the practices of the Library of Congress in order to make it possible for a library to change over from Sears headings to LC headings when it grew larger. Since 1923, however, the two worlds of Sears and LCSH have grown more distinct and separate, although they still share important common ground. Both are alphabetical subject lists, not true thesauri. Both are based on the principle of pre-coordinated subject strings with the use of subdivisions rather than discrete terms to be coordinated by the end user. Both are based on literary warrant and make no attempt to establish headings before there are library materials requiring such headings. And both are devised to implement Cutter's rule for the cataloging of materials to the greatest possible level of specificity.

COMPARING SEARS AND LCSH

Although Sears continues to conform to the practices of the Library of Congress to a considerable degree, there are nonetheless a number of differences between the two lists. A quick way to know if a library uses Sears or LC headings is to check the catalog: Sears has **Religious holidays** while LC has **Fasts and feasts,** and Sears has **Litigation** where LC has **Actions and defenses.** (Sears has **Pigs** and LC has **Swine,** although the LC Children's Subject Headings also has **Pigs.**) In general, Sears has fewer technical terms, preferring the common names of things to the scientific names. There are other differences as well. Beginning with the fifteenth edition (1994), Sears converted all its remaining inverted headings to the uninverted form, while LC still maintains a combination of inverted and uninverted headings. For example, **Education, Elementary** in LC is now **Elementary education** in Sears. In some cases the vocabulary itself differs. For example, in the seventeenth edition (2000) Sears canceled all its headings for **Indians of North America, Indians of Mexico, Indians of South America,** and the like, in favor of the single heading **Native Americans,** which may be subdivided geographically by continent, country, region, state, and so on. (The heading **Native Americans** is another quick identifier of a Sears library.) Sears also differs from LC in its use of subdivisions. Sears allows for direct geographic subdivisions rather than indirect. For example, Sears would have **Bridges— Chicago (Ill.),** where LC would have **Bridges—Illinois—Chicago.** These are all differences that must be kept in mind when LC MARC records or LC Cataloging-in-Publication (CIP) data are being adapted for a catalog using Sears headings.

The greatest difference between the two lists is that the Library of Congress establishes in its list every heading that has been used in its catalog, with the exception of subject strings involving standard geographic or free-floating subdivisions. The Sears list aims instead to be a pattern or model for the creation of headings as needed. As a result it is less detailed and complete than LCSH but also much smaller, more flexible, and less expensive. In Sears, for example, at the heading for **Animals** there is a general reference note authorizing the creation of headings for types of animals and species of animals as needed. Likewise, at **Dogs** there is a provision for creating headings for types of dogs and breeds of dogs as needed. The cataloger is not encouraged to put a book about collies under **Dogs,** but in very small libraries that is always an option. Even when there is no general reference note in Sears providing for kinds of things and names of specific things under the heading for the thing, it is implied by the nature of the system that those headings can always be created.

When there is a need for subject headings not included in the Sears list, librarians can establish new subjects in the form they feel best describes the contents of the book or is most likely to be found by their users. They can always use or adapt headings from the CIP or LC MARC records, from periodical indexes, or from other cataloging and indexing sources. These new headings are established as Sears headings and are incorporated into the library's subject authority file by attaching them to the appropriate broader term from the Sears list and by establishing cross-references to any narrower or related terms already used in the catalog.

The Sears list is also greatly expandable with the use of subdivisions. Throughout the list general references give instructions on the application of topical and form subdivisions. An example of a very complete general reference, which draws the distinction between two similar but not interchangeable subdivisions, can be found under the heading **Ethics:**

SA [See also] types of ethics, e.g. **Business ethics;** ethics of particular religions, e.g. **Christian ethics;** names of individual persons, classes of persons, types of professions, and types of professional personnel with the subdivision *Ethics,* e.g. **Librarians—Ethics; Shakespeare, William, 1564-1616—Ethics;** etc., and subjects with the subdivision *Ethical aspects*, e.g. **Birth control—Ethical aspects** {to be added as needed}.

For every subdivision provided for in the Sears list there is a general reference with specific instructions on its use. For subdivisions that are also subject headings, the general reference introducing the subdivision is appended to the entry for the subject heading, as with **Ethics** above. Subdivisions that are not also subject headings, such as *Ethical aspects*, also have a freestanding entry with a general reference. A complete list of the subdivisions provided for in the Sears list appears in the front matter of the printed volume. Other subdivisions can be established by the cataloger, if needed.

Unlike LCSH, the Sears list is used almost exclusively in combination with the *Dewey Decimal Classification* (DDC). In view of that fact, every heading in the Sears list is assigned one or more numbers from the most recent abridged edition of the *Dewey Decimal Classification*, published by OCLC. These DDC numbers in Sears are meant only as pointers to the place or places in the Classification where materials on a particular subject are most likely to be dealt with, not as a guide for classifying any individual item. The numbers should not be assigned to books or other materials without first consulting the schedules and tables of the DDC itself. The Sears headings also serve as access vocabulary in OCLC's *Abridged WebDewey* database.

FEATURES OF THE SEARS LIST

The Sears list is produced both as a print volume and in a web-based version. In print the entire Sears list is contained in one handy volume, while LCSH is now published in five very large volumes, with cross-references spanning the set. A new edition of the Sears list appears every three years, while a new edition of LCSH is published every year. In print the Sears list is correspondingly cheaper. The web-based version of Sears is not free, as LCSH on the Web is, but it emphasizes ease of use as a high priority.

In 2008, the H. W. Wilson Company published a new Spanish translation and adaptation of the Sears list entitled *Sears: Lista de Encabezamientos de Materia*. This volume, which contains an exhaustive index linking it heading-by-heading to the English Sears, is of special interest to libraries that want to provide Spanish-language access for their Spanish-speaking users. A fully integrated web-based version of the two lists together, English and Spanish, is currently in development.

In the twenty-first century, cooperative cataloging and the use of MARC records extend even to small libraries. There is sometimes a mistaken impression that only LC subject headings are compatible with the MARC formats. There has always been, in fact, full provision in MARC for the use of Sears headings. In the MARC 21 format, Sears headings in the 650 field are coded with the value 7 in the second indicator position and the word *sears* in subfield 2. In the OCLC MARC format, Sears headings are identified by the value 8 in the second indicator position without a subfield 2. Most vendors are able to supply MARC records with Sears headings.

The "Principles of the Sears List of Subject Headings," which can be found in the front of every edition, serves as a substantial introduction both to the Sears list and to the practice of subject cataloging in general. The principles and all the other front matter of the print volume, including the list of subdivisions, are available in the web version of Sears as a PDF document. The principles detail the process of establishing new subject headings and cross-references. The principles also provide guidance in assigning topical and geographic headings to individual works of fiction, drama, and poetry, contained in nine rules or suggestions, which vary in significant ways from the practice of many catalogers in this area.

CONCLUSION

The same standards of subject analysis are applicable to Sears as to other subject heading lists, but the shortness and simplicity of the Sears list make it an attractive alternative to LCSH for many small libraries and libraries devoted primarily to children's materials.

RESOURCES

Chan, Lois Mai. *Cataloging and Classification: An Introduction.* 3rd ed. Lanham, MD: Scarecrow Press, 2007.

Chan, Lois Mai, Phyllis A. Richmond, and Elaine Svenonius, eds. *Theory of Subject Analysis: A Sourcebook.* 2nd ed. Littleton, CO: Libraries Unlimited, 1990.

Cutter, Charles. *Rules for a Dictionary Catalog.* 4th ed. Washington, DC: U.S. Government Printing Office, 1904.

Dewey, Melvil. *Abridged Dewey Decimal Classification and Relative Index.* 14th ed. Edited by Joan S. Mitchell et al. Dublin, OH: OCLC, 2004.

Foskett, A. C. *The Subject Approach to Information.* 5th ed. London: The Library Association, 1996.

Intner, Sheila S., and Jean Weihs. *Standard Cataloging for School and Public Libraries*. 4th ed. Santa Barbara, CA: Libraries Unlimited, 2007.

Sears List of Subject Headings. 19th ed. Edited by Joseph Miller; Barbara A. Bristow, Associate Editor. New York: H. W. Wilson, 2007.

Sears List of Subject Headings: Canadian Companion. 6th ed. Edited by Lynne Lighthall. New York: H. W. Wilson, 2001.

Sears: Lista de Encabezamientos de Materia: Nueva traducción y adaptación de la Lista Sears. Iván E. Calimano, Editor; Ageo García, Editor Asociado. New York: H. W. Wilson, 2008.

Taylor, Arlene G. *Introduction to Cataloging and Classification*. 10th ed. Santa Barbara, CA: Libraries Unlimited, 2006.

──────. *The Organization of Information*. 3rd ed. Santa Barbara, CA: Libraries Unlimited, 2009.

CHAPTER 9

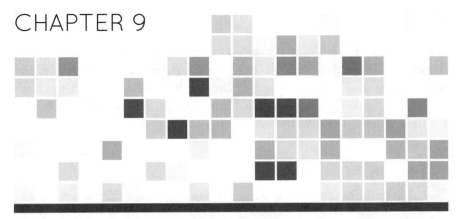

Dewey Decimal Classification

Julianne Beall

The Dewey Decimal Classification (DDC)[1] system can play an important role in facilitating access to children's materials, both on library shelves and in online systems. It can help provide multilingual access. This chapter focuses on what catalogers need to know to apply the DDC successfully, whether for copy classifying or original classifying, followed by suggested sources for learning more.

EDITIONS OF THE DDC

For libraries using the DDC, the American Library Association's *Guidelines for Standardized Cataloging for Children*[2] call for use of the *Abridged Dewey Decimal Classification and Relative Index*[3] (Edition 14 or the most current edition); this chapter assumes that catalogers are using the latest abridged edition. The abridged edition is designed to meet the needs of general collections with up to twenty thousand titles.

Catalogers using the abridged edition should not assume that the full edition[4] (Edition 22 or the most current edition) is of no interest. Full DDC numbers are often found in cataloging copy. The abridged number for a work may be the same as the full number for a work—or it may be the same but shorter. At most, a standard full number needs only to be shortened. Catalogers with access to a full edition may find specific topics not named in the abridged edition; they can then check the abridged edition to see where to shorten the number. Do you need to know where to class a work about cooking insects—for example, *Bug-a-licious* by Meish Goldish?[5] Edition 22 has a Relative Index entry:

Insects—food—cooking   641.696

The Abridged Edition 14 number is 641.6 (Cooking specific materials). The Abridged Relative Index has nothing about cooking insects.

ABRIDGED WEBDEWEY, WEBDEWEY, AND MAPPED TERMINOLOGY

Abridged WebDewey[6] and WebDewey[7] are updated web versions of the latest abridged and full editions, respectively, offered by OCLC as a subscription service. Both the abridged and full versions offer efficient web searching and browsing as well as a feature that allows catalogers to add notes about a library's local practices. Both versions have electronic-only Relative Index terms to improve access, but WebDewey has many more such terms. Both have been updated quarterly, but work has begun on a new version (2.0), which will be updated more frequently. Monthly listings of new and changed entries are available free at www.oclc.org/dewey/updates/new/default.htm. The monthly listings give selected updates, but for complete access to all updates, catalogers need to consult Abridged WebDewey or WebDewey.

Abridged WebDewey has Library of Congress Subject Headings (LCSH), headings from LC's Children's Subject Headings,[8] and Sears subject headings[9] mapped to the Dewey numbers. For example, the handicrafts number 745.594 (Decorative objects) has mapped headings such as **Jack-o-lanterns, Party decorations,** and **Valentines.** The mappings from *Subject Headings for Children* reflect Abridged Edition 13, not having been updated for Edition 14; but the other two mapped terminologies have been updated for Edition 14.

WebDewey has editorially mapped LCSH, LCSH mapped from *People, Places, and Things,*[10] and statistically mapped LCSH. Only the editorially mapped LCSH have been fully updated for Edition 22.

CHOICE OF NUMBER

The basic classes of the DDC are organized by disciplines or fields of study. At the broadest level, the DDC is divided into ten main classes, which together cover the entire world of knowledge. The same topic can be studied in more than one discipline—for example, animals in zoology (590) and animal husbandry (636). The first decision catalogers must make in choosing a Dewey number is what discipline or field of study is appropriate for the work in hand. Does the work belong to a particular discipline, or does it cover multiple disciplines, as many children's works do? If it covers many disciplines, catalogers should look for the interdisciplinary number.

The Relative Index can help catalogers find numbers to consider. For example, catalogers classifying *The Wild Side of Pet Dogs* by Jo Waters[11] might look under "Dogs" in Abridged Edition 14:

Dogs	636.7
Dogs—animal husbandry	636.7
Dogs—zoology	599.77

The first line—with nothing between "Dogs" and the number 636.7— indicates that 636.7 is the interdisciplinary number for dogs. The second line says that 636.7 is also the animal husbandry number, and the third line says that 599.77 is the zoology number. Catalogers should always look in the schedule at least for the number tentatively chosen, and often they will find it useful to check more than one place in the schedule. In the schedule at 599.77 (Dog family) is a note saying to class interdisciplinary works on dogs in 636.7. All the members of the dog family named in 599.77 and its subdivisions are wild animals—coyotes, foxes, and wolves—not domestic dogs. In the schedule at 636.7 (Dogs), the subdivisions list breeds of domestic dogs, most of which are often pets. *The Wild Side of Pet Dogs* treats both domestic dogs and their wild relatives; the interdisciplinary number 636.7 is appropriate. In this case a note in the schedule indicates which number is interdisciplinary, but often the Relative Index is the only place that the interdisciplinary number is indicated. Often the quickest way to find the interdisciplinary number for a topic in Abridged WebDewey or WebDewey is to browse the Relative Index—instead of doing a keyword search.

If catalogers look in the Relative Index of Abridged Edition 14 for "Pets," they will find:

Pets   636.088
Pets
    see Manual at 800 vs. 398.24, 590, 636

The first line indicates that interdisciplinary works on pets are classed in 636.088. The second line refers to a note in the Manual that gives advice about choosing among four areas where animals are commonly classed: literature (belles-lettres), folk literature, zoology, and animal husbandry. That Manual note is not needed for *The Wild Side of Pet Dogs*, but it might be useful for another work. In the schedule at 636.088 (Animals for specific purposes) is the note "Including animals raised for food, hides, sport, work; laboratory animals; pets." An example of a work about pets classed in 636.088 is *Pets: Cats, Dogs, Horses, and Camels, Too!*[12]

Why not put a book about pet dogs in 636.088 instead of 636.7? Both numbers are subdivisions of 636 (Animal husbandry). What rule says that a taxonomic grouping like *dogs* should get preference over a function or purpose grouping like *pets*? In this case, the short answer—no history or philosophy here!—is the rule of zero, which is explained in the introduction to Abridged Edition 14 (section 5.7 E):

> Subdivisions beginning with zero should be avoided if there is a choice between 0 and 1 – 9 at the same point in the hierarchy of the notation. Similarly, subdivisions beginning with 00 should be avoided when there is a choice between 00 and 0.[13]

In other words, 636.7 is preferred over 636.0.

Catalogers need to keep in mind the hierarchical nature of the DDC when choosing a number. The notational hierarchy of the DDC is obvious because it is visible, with longer numbers more specific than and subordinate to shorter numbers in the same class, as in the following example:

394   General customs
394.2   Special occasions
394.26   Holidays
394.262   Holidays of March, April, May
394.2627   May Day

The structural hierarchy of the DDC, explained in section 4.18 of the introduction, is less obvious:

> *Structural hierarchy* means that all topics (aside from the ten main classes) are part of all the broader topics above them. The corollary is also true: whatever is true of the whole is true of the parts. This important concept is called *hierarchical force*. Certain notes regarding the nature of a class hold true for all the subordinate classes, including logically subordinate topics classed at coordinate numbers. . . .
>
> Because of the principle of hierarchical force, hierarchical notes are usually given only once — at the highest level of application. . . . In order to understand the structural hierarchy, the classifier must read up and down the schedules (and remember to turn the page).[14]

Catalogers seeking a number for *Cinco de Mayo* by Ann Heinrichs and Kathleen Petelinsek[15] won't find "Cinco de Mayo" in the print Relative Index (though they will find it in Abridged WebDewey as mapped terminology and in WebDewey). If they look in the Relative Index under "Holidays" and choose the interdisciplinary number 394.26, then look in the schedule at 394.26 (Holidays), they will find this class-here note: "Class here carnivals other than pre-Lenten and related festivals . . . ; festivals; independence days; patriotic, seasonal, secular holidays." Cinco de Mayo is a patriotic holiday, a seasonal holiday, and a secular holiday—but that does not mean catalogers should class the work right at 394.26, because class-here notes have hierarchical force. Catalogers need to look down in the hierarchy to see if there is a more specific number that is appropriate, in this case 394.262 (Holidays of March, April, May).

Because Cinco de Mayo is a holiday of Mexico, why not use the number given as an example in the add note at 394.269 (Historical, geographic, persons treatment): "Add to base number 394.269 notation T2—1–T2—9 from Table 2, e.g., holidays of Mexico 394.26972"? At 394.269, following that add note, is this class-elsewhere note: "Class historical, geographic, persons treatment of specific holidays and of specific kinds of holidays in 394.261–394.267." That class-elsewhere note has hierarchical force over all possible specific numbers built with the add instruction; thus, the specific holiday Cinco de Mayo belongs in 394.262, not in 394.269+. An example of a work correctly classed in 394.26972 is *The Festivals of Mexico* by Colleen Madonna Flood Williams,[16] because that work covers "Mexico's many festivals and holidays." The class-here note at 394.26 mentions "festivals," and that note has hierarchical force; hence, festivals are classed in 394.26 and appropriate subdivisions of 394.26.

NUMBER BUILDING AND BUILT NUMBERS

The DDC relies heavily on number building ("the process of constructing a number by adding notation from the tables or other parts of the schedules to a base number").[17] Catalogers need a basic understanding of number building just to check numbers in catalog records—and to make logical decisions about where to shorten a number, if it is longer than allowed in a library's catalog.

Many Dewey numbers are built with notation from Table 1 Standard Subdivisions (T1) or Table 2 Geographic Areas, Historical Periods, Persons (T2), or both. For example, the DDC number 577.0911 for ecology of frigid zones, used for *An Arctic Ecosystem* by Greg Roza,[18] is built by adding from Table 1 and Table 2, as shown:

577　　Ecology ("Class here biomes, ecosystems . . .")
091　　Treatment by areas, regions, places in general (from Table 1)
1　　　Frigid zones ("Class here polar regions"; from 11 Frigid
　　　　zones in Table 2)

Notation from Table 1 can be added without special instructions, but all other notation can be added only with special instructions. The special instructions for adding from Table 2 in this case are found at T1–091 Treatment by areas, regions, places in general: "Add to base number T1–091 the numbers following T2–1 in notation T2–11—T2–19 from Table 2, e.g., Torrid Zone T1–0913." The built number 577.0911 is not found in Abridged Edition 14, but the pieces and instructions needed to build the number are found there. The built number 577.09113 (built with T2–113 North frigid zone) is found in Edition 22, with the Relative Index term Arctic ecology.

History numbers illustrate direct addition of Table 2 numbers. General instructions for building history numbers are found at 930–990 (History of ancient world; of specific continents, countries, localities; of extraterrestrial worlds). Special instructions for specific countries and localities are found where needed. History numbers for countries appear already built in the Relative Index of Abridged Edition 14, just above the corresponding Table 2 notation—for example:

United States	973
United States	T2–73

As the Relative Index entries for countries suggest, the history number for a specific area is also the interdisciplinary number for that area. The class-elsewhere note at 900 (History, geography, and auxiliary disciplines) confirms this: "Class interdisciplinary works on ancient world, on specific continents, countries, localities in 930–990."

In Abridged Edition 14, numbers for history of a specific U.S. state or Canadian province are not already built; only the Table 2 number appears in the Relative Index. To build a number for a specific state, one must find the Table 2 number for that state (e.g., Arizona T2–791), then follow the instructions at 974–979 (Specific states of United States): "Add to base number 97 the numbers following T2–7 in notation T2–74—T2–79 from Table 2, e.g., Arizona 979.1 . . . ." An example of a work classed in 979.1 is *Arizona* by Barbara A. Somervill,[19] an interdisciplinary work covering such topics as the land, people, history, government, and economy of Arizona.

The abridged edition has very few built numbers. The full edition has more—including built numbers for all the U.S. states and Canadian provinces—and the full WebDewey has many more numbers already built. But no version of the DDC has an exhaustive list of all the numbers that can be built with the system.

SEGMENTATION IN DDC NUMBERS

Segmentation is "the indication of logical breaks in a number by a typographical device, e.g., slash marks or prime marks."[20] Here are key parts of the statement about segmentation policies and procedures:

- One aid to reduction of the full DDC number is the segmentation provided in DDC numbers assigned by such centralized cataloging services as . . . the Library of Congress and the Library and Archives Canada.

- The segmentation is indicated by a prime mark ('), a slash mark (/), or other comparable indicators.
- The segmentation mark indicates the end of the abridged number (including, if applicable, the end of the abridged standard subdivision in the abridged number).[21]

In WebDewey, segmentation is shown with a slash mark, and the segmented number is clearly labeled—for example, Segmented Number: 599.53/6. The full number for Orcinus (Killer whale) is 599.536; the abridged number for a work on that topic is 599.53. A work on that topic with the DDC number assigned by the Library of Congress will similarly have a slash mark showing the end of the abridged number (e.g., in the record for *Killer Whales* by Sandra Markle):[22] 599.53/6. The prime mark is used for segmentation in DDC numbers when Cataloging-in-Publication data are printed in the book. DDC numbers not assigned by the Library of Congress, Library and Archives Canada (LAC), or another central cataloging agency commonly do not have a segmentation mark.

The rules for segmentation changed during the life of Edition 22. The Library of Congress implemented the change in September 2005,[23] and Library and Archives Canada implemented it in March 2006.[24] Prior to the change, the rules called for a segmentation mark at the start of every standard subdivision (notation from Table 1) as well as at the end of the abridged number; after the change, the rules have called for only one segmentation mark, at the end of the abridged number. For example, the following number for *Mount St. Helens* by Jen Green,[25] assigned before the change, has two slashes, the first before the zero that marks the start of the standard subdivision T1–09 Geographic treatment, the second at the end of the abridged number: 551.21/09797/84. The same number assigned to a later book, *Volcano! The 1980 Mount St. Helens Eruption* by Gail Blasser Riley,[26] has only one slash, before the final 84: 551.2109797/84. The abridged number locates Mt. Saint Helens in Washington state (T1–09 plus T2–797 Washington); the full number locates Mt. Saint Helens more specifically in Skamania County, Washington (T2–79784).

DDC AND MARC 21

For DDC, the field in the MARC Bibliographic Format with which catalogers most need to be familiar is 082 Dewey Decimal Classification

Number.[27] Here are two examples of the 082 field, both for *Wolves* by Seymour Simon:[28]

Tag	1st Indicator	2nd Indicator	Subfield a	Subfield 2
082	0	0	$a 599.74/442	$2 20
082	0	4	$a 599.773	$2 22

The first indicator value 0 means that the DDC number is from the full edition; if the DDC number were from the abridged edition, the first indicator value would be 1. The second indicator value 0 means that the DDC number was assigned by the Library of Congress. The second indicator value 4 means the number was assigned by an agency other than LC. When LC does copy cataloging and copies the DDC number without reviewing it, the second indicator is 4. Subfield a contains the DDC number itself. Subfield 2 gives the edition number—in the first 082 field, Edition 20; in the second, Edition 22. The Library of Congress record for *Wolves* by Seymour Simon has only the first 082 field given in the preceding table (082 00 $a 599.74/442 $2 20). The DDC number in $a was correct at the time it was assigned—though it is now obsolete—and LC is not able to go back and update DDC numbers when they change. The $2 value 20 is a warning that a DDC number particularly needs to be checked. The OCLC record for the same work has both the 082 fields shown in the table. The second 082 field was added later (082 04 $a 599.773 $2 22). The number in the second 082 field is the correct number for *Wolves* in Edition 22, and the number is the same in Abridged Edition 14.

New provisions relevant to DDC were added recently to the MARC Bibliographic Format to indicate standard versus optional numbers, to indicate the assigning agency other than LC, to allow assignment of additional DDC numbers for access, and to show how a built number was built.[29] The new provisions can be used now, but it is unclear how soon or how frequently they will appear in cataloging copy.

DEWEY IN MANY LANGUAGES

The DDC has been translated into over thirty languages. Translations of the latest full or abridged editions of the DDC are completed, planned, or under way in Arabic, French, German, Greek, Hebrew, Indonesian, Italian, Korean, Norwegian, Spanish, Swedish, and Vietnamese.

Translations draw attention to areas that need expansion and updating in the standard DDC and lead to improvements. They also make possible multilingual applications of the DDC. Dewey summaries in seven languages have been used to provide multilingual access in the World Digital Library (WDL), which is available free at www.wdl.org. The DDC numbers are hidden in WDL, but librarians will recognize the "topics" as DDC captions. The experimental DeweyBrowser catalog developed by OCLC Research has tag clouds presenting Dewey captions associated with Dewey numbers in WorldCat records. The tag clouds provide visual representations of the number of titles in each class of the three main DDC Summaries. The tag clouds are available in six languages. The full interface—including the feature that allows refinement of searches by audience level (e.g., kids and preschool)—is available in four languages. DeweyBrowser is available free at http://deweybrowser.oclc.org/ddc-browser2/.

Recently the Dewey summaries have been made available in nine languages (Arabic, Chinese, English, French, German, Portuguese, Russian, Spanish, and Swedish) at http://dewey.info. More languages are planned. The summaries can be used for many purposes and used immediately for noncommercial purposes.[30] They are presented in a linked data form that makes it easy for machines or humans to manipulate them. Librarians could, for example, copy and paste them into Word and convert them to tables. The captions might be used on a library website or for signage in the stacks or for library guides—to help patrons whose first language is not English or to support nonnative-language learning.

CONCLUSION

To apply DDC successfully, catalogers especially need to understand the core concepts and rules that affect choice of number and number building and to know how to find information about updates to the DDC. They also need to understand segmentation and the MARC 21 field 082. Catalogers should be aware that DDC can help in providing multilingual access to library materials.

RESOURCES

Core Concepts and Rules

Chan, Lois Mai, and Joan S. Mitchell. *Dewey Decimal Classification: Principles and Application*. 3rd ed. Dublin, OH: OCLC Online Computer Library Center, 2003.

Dewey Training Courses. www.oclc.org/dewey/resources/teachingsite/200801/default.htm.

Introduction to the Dewey Decimal Classification—Abridged Edition 14. http://connexion.oclc.org/html/corc/help/en/Ab14Intro.html.

Other Useful Sources

025.431: The Dewey Blog. www.ddc.typepad.com.

Abridged WebDewey User Guide. www.oclc.org/support/documentation/dewey/abridged_webdewey_userguide/.

Available RSS Feeds. www.oclc.org/dewey/syndicated/rss.htm.

Cataloguing and Metadata: LAC Dewey Decimal Classification Policy. www.collectionscanada.gc.ca/cataloguing-standards/040006-2208-e.html.

Classify. http://deweyresearch.oclc.org/classify2/.

Dewey Decimal Classification Glossary. www.oclc.org/support/documentation/glossary/dewey/glossary.htm.

Dewey Decimal Classification: Summaries. http://dewey.info.

European DDC Users Group, Technical Issues Working Group. Projects. www.slainte.org.uk/edugit/projects.htm.

European DDC Users Group, Technical Issues Working Group. Services. www.slainte.org.uk/edugit/services.htm.

New and Changed Entries. www.oclc.org/dewey/updates/new/.

NOTES

1. DDC, Dewey, Dewey Decimal Classification, and WorldCat are registered trademarks of OCLC Online Computer Library Center, Inc.
2. *Guidelines for Standardized Cataloging for Children*, www.ala.org/ala/mgrps/divs/alcts/resources/org/cat/ccfkch1.cfm.
3. *Abridged Dewey Decimal Classification and Relative Index*, devised by Melvil Dewey, 14th ed., edited by Joan S. Mitchell, Julianne Beall, Giles Martin, Winton E. Matthews Jr., and Gregory R. New (Dublin, OH: OCLC Online Computer Library Center, 2004).

4. *Dewey Decimal Classification and Relative Index*, devised by Melvil Dewey, 22nd ed., edited by Joan S. Mitchell, Julianne Beall, Giles Martin, Winton E. Matthews Jr., and Gregory R. New (Dublin, OH: OCLC Online Computer Library Center, 2003).

5. Meish Goldish, *Bug-a-licious* (New York: Bearport, 2009). Library of Congress record at http://lccn.loc.gov/2008032802; WorldCat record at www.worldcat.org/oclc/236117423.

6. www.oclc.org/dewey/versions/abridgedwebdewey/

7. www.oclc.org/dewey/versions/webdewey/

8. *Subject Headings for Children: A List of Subject Headings Used by the Library of Congress with Dewey Numbers Added*, 2nd ed., edited by Lois Winkel (Albany, NY: OCLC Forest Press, 1998).

9. *Sears List of Subject Headings*, 19th ed., edited by Joseph Miller and Barbara A. Bristow (New York: H. W. Wilson, 2007).

10. *People, Places and Things: A List of Popular Library of Congress Subject Headings with Dewey Numbers Added* (Dublin, OH: OCLC Forest Press, 2001).

11. Jo Waters, *The Wild Side of Pet Dogs* (Chicago: Raintree, 2005). Library of Congress record at http://lccn.loc.gov/2003024750; WorldCat record at www.worldcat.org/oclc/54022390.

12. Charles F. Baker III, ed., *Pets: Cats, Dogs, Horses, and Camels, Too!* (Peterborough, NH: Carus, 2005). Library of Congress record at http://lccn.loc.gov/2005029833; WorldCat record at www.worldcat.org/oclc/62090814.

13. Introduction to the Dewey Decimal Classification—Abridged Edition 14, http://connexion.oclc.org/html/corc/help/en/Ab14Intro.html.

14. Ibid.

15. Ann Heinrichs and Kathleen Petelinsek, *Cinco de Mayo* (Chanhassen, MN: Child's World, 2006). Library of Congress record at http://lccn.loc.gov/2005025680; WorldCat record at www.worldcat.org/oclc/61479537.

16. Colleen Madonna Flood Williams, *The Festivals of Mexico* (Philadelphia: Mason Crest, 2003). Library of Congress record at http://lccn.loc.gov/2001052214; WorldCat record at www.worldcat.org/oclc/48177272.

17. "Number building," Glossary, Abridged Edition 14, www.oclc.org/dewey/versions/abridgededition14/glossary.pdf.

18. Greg Roza, *An Arctic Ecosystem* (New York: PowerKids Press, 2009). Library of Congress record at http://lccn.loc.gov/2008042718; WorldCat record at www.worldcat.org/oclc/246889264.

19. Barbara A. Somervill, *Arizona* (New York: Children's Press, 2009). Library of Congress record at http://lccn.loc.gov/2007037923; WorldCat record at www.worldcat.org/oclc/173218653.

20. "Segmentation," Glossary, Edition 22, www.oclc.org/Support/documentation/glossary/dewey/#Segmentation.

21. "DDC Appendix: Segmentation," Abridged WebDewey User Guide, www.oclc.org/support/documentation/dewey/abridged_webdewey_userguide/.

22. Sandra Markle, *Killer Whales* (Minneapolis: Carolrhoda Books, 2004). Library of Congress record at http://lccn.loc.gov/2003025944; WorldCat record at www.worldcat.org/oclc/54046918.

23. "Segmentation Marks in DDC Numbers," *025.431: The Dewey Blog*, http://ddc.typepad.com/025431/2005/09/segmentation_ma.html.

24. Library and Archives Canada, "Change in DDC Segmentation Policy on Full DDC Numbers," www.collectionscanada.gc.ca/obj/040006/f2/040006-13-e.pdf.

25. Jen Green, *Mount St. Helens* (Milwaukee, WI: Gareth Stevens, 2005). Library of Congress record at http://lccn.loc.gov/2004056711; WorldCat record at www.worldcat.org/oclc/56386957.

26. Gail Blasser Riley, *Volcano! The 1980 Mount St. Helens Eruption* (New York: Bearport, 2006). Library of Congress record at http://lccn.loc.gov/2005028041; WorldCat record at www.worldcat.org/oclc/61704800.

27. Library of Congress, Network Development and MARC Standards Office, MARC 21 Format for Bibliographic Data, "082—Dewey Decimal Classification Number," www.loc.gov/marc/bibliographic/bd082.html.

28. Seymour Simon, *Wolves* (New York: HarperCollins, 1993). Library of Congress record at http://lccn.loc.gov/92025924; WorldCat record at www.worldcat.org/oclc/26363489.

29. The new provisions were added to MARC 21 in Update No. 9 (October 2008). See subfields m (Standard or optional designation) and q (Assigning agency) in 082—Dewey Decimal Classification Number, www.loc.gov/marc/bibliographic/bd082.html. See also 083—Additional Dewey Decimal Classification Number, www.loc.gov/marc/bibliographic/bd083.html; 085—Synthesized Classification Number Components, www.loc.gov/marc/bibliographic/bd085.html.

30. Dewey.info carries this notice: "This work is licensed under a Creative Commons Attribution-Noncommercial-No Derivative Works 3.0 Unported License by OCLC Online Computer Library Center, Inc. Permissions beyond the scope of this license may be available at www.oclc.org/dewey/about/licensing/. All copyright rights in the Dewey Decimal Classification system are owned by OCLC. Dewey, Dewey Decimal Classification, DDC, OCLC and WebDewey are registered trademarks of OCLC."

CHAPTER 10

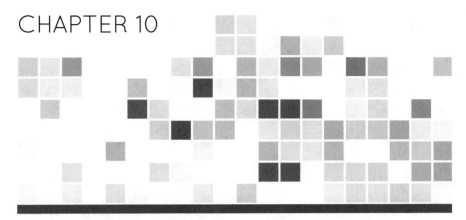

Cataloging Nonbook Materials

Sheila S. Intner and Jean Weihs

Materials intended for children's education, information, and recreation are issued in a great variety of physical formats, including books, maps, recordings of many kinds, pictures, games, printed music, electronic databases, and many more. Libraries and media centers catering to children have a long tradition in collecting them. Since 1978, when the second edition of the *Anglo-American Cataloguing Rules*[1] (AACR2) was first issued, catalogers have been able to integrate the cataloging of all physical formats into one workflow and display the results in the same catalog.

Beyond description and access, tools used to provide subject access, including subject heading lists such as *Library of Congress Subject Headings* and *Sears List of Subject Headings*, and classifications such as the *Dewey Decimal Classification* and *Library of Congress Classification*, though originally designed for collections of books, are also applicable to other types of materials. The MARC format used to computerize cataloging data has long been integrated so that it can be applied to any type of material.

The question arises whether to file cataloging for all materials into one public catalog or maintain separate catalogs for individual types of materials. We recommend putting all catalog information into one public catalog. This lets searchers see everything the library has available at once. If a library has one integrated catalog, it automatically allows a search for individual types of media, but the reverse is not true. If separate catalogs for individual media are established, they do not automatically allow for integrated searches.

From the library's perspective, integration means that staff members with the greatest expertise in cataloging do it all, thus ensuring the best possible results. All the materials the library buys are given equal opportunities to be selected and used. From the children's perspective, such a policy enables them to look something up in the catalog and see all the available editions of a desired work or all the materials a library or media center has on a desired subject or by a particular author, regardless of format. A young searcher may not have any particular type of material in mind and be open to using any or all of them. If the catalog is computerized, as most are in the twenty-first century, searches can be limited to a single medium when children want only one type of material. With this capability, a search for videos about pets or images of London can be retrieved without also retrieving all the books, games, maps, electronic resources, and other materials that are about those subjects.

The paragraphs that follow explain how catalog records are prepared—records that can be integrated into a single public catalog display.

DESCRIPTION AND ACCESS

At this writing, doing standard descriptive cataloging means using the current version of AACR2, although a new revision that will supersede it, titled *Resource Description and Access*[2] (RDA), has just been released and is being tested. RDA, organized by area of description instead of physical format, differs in appearance from AACR2, but the entries that result from application of its rules are expected to be much the same as they were.

AACR2's first chapter sets out a general descriptive cataloging standard that applies to all forms of materials. Eleven chapters follow, each covering the special issues that relate to a specific format group, including books and other printed texts (which are not discussed in the present chapter), maps and other cartographic materials (chapter 3), manuscripts (chapter 4), printed music (chapter 5), recorded music (chapter 6), motion pictures and videorecordings (chapter 7), graphics (chapter 8), electronic resources (chapter 9), three-dimensional materials (chapter 10), microforms (chapter 11), and continuing resources, such as magazines and newspapers (chapter 12).

AACR2 emphasizes that its descriptive standard applies to all materials, stating: "The rules cover the description of, and the provision of access points for, all library materials commonly collected at the present time. The integrated structure of the text makes the general rules usable as a basis for cataloguing uncommonly collected materials of all kinds and library materials yet unknown."[3]

Most of the instructions in the eleven specific chapters refer catalogers to the general rules in the first chapter, giving different rules only when necessary, such as for material specific details or the physical description of materials. For example, the rules for transcribing the main title, called *title proper*, for each of the eleven special chapters begin by instructing catalogers to do what it says in rule 1.1B. Similarly, rules for transcribing editions, publication, distribution information, series, and standard numbers follow this form. Special instructions are given regarding general material designation, material specific details, and physical description as well as in a selection of parts of other areas.

Material specific details (area 3) apply to maps and other cartographic materials, printed music that contains musical presentation statements, and serially issued continuing resources. Data about a map's scale, projection, coordinates, and equinox are entered in this area as are the musical presentation statements and the numbering and dating information given for serials. A serially issued map might have two statements of material specific details: one relating to the scale and so forth, and one relating to the serial numbering and dating.

Physical format is indicated in three places in a bibliographic description: immediately after the main title (area 1); in the descriptive area pertaining to physical description (area 5); and optionally in notes giving additional details about the physical description (area 7). The first indication of format, following the main title, gives a searcher an early warning of an item's physical format. It is called the *general material designation,* or GMD. GMDs are taken from lists in AACR2 and consist of a word or brief phrase indicating a generic medium.[4] They are given in the catalog record in lowercase letters in singular form enclosed in square brackets, because they are supplied by the cataloger, not transcribed directly from the item being cataloged. Following are examples of GMDs for four nonbook titles:

Piggi-billa the porcupine [art reproduction]
Cool moves! [game]
Aaron's hair [kit]
Pumping heart [model]

The second indication of format provides more precise information for the searcher, naming the physical format specifically as part of the extent of the material. The third indication gives even finer details, as shown in the catalog records for the same titles (see figure 10.1).

When the bibliographic description is completed, descriptive headings are made for the persons and bodies responsible for creating the nonbook material and for its title(s), exactly the way these are done for books. The headings are made according to the rules in Part 2 of AACR2. Headings are divided into the first, most important one, called the *main entry,* and the rest of the headings, called *added entries.* The principal creator of the material is designated its main entry heading. If there is no person or body primarily responsible for it, the first one named on the material or the title may be selected as the main entry. Rules in AACR2 chapter 21 guide catalogers in making appropriate decisions about main entries. Two provisions of rule 21.1B2, which covers instances in which corporate body headings are appropriate, refer to recordings and maps. Three special sections of chapter 21 cover art works, musical works, and sound recordings.[5]

After the main entry is selected, other authors of written text, composers of music, artists, performers, production companies, and the like, responsible for the creation of the nonbook material and mentioned in the description, are candidates for added entry headings. The main title of the material and other titles found on the material and mentioned in the description, such as variations of the main title, series titles, and titles of parts (known as *analytic titles*) are candidates for added entries as well. An exception to the list of potential title added entries is the main title when it is the main entry. A second, identical added entry is not needed for it if that is the case.

The balance of AACR2's Part 2 is devoted to explaining how to put headings into proper form. Rules for establishing personal, corporate body, and geographic name headings as well as uniform title headings are given in chapters 22 through 25, respectively. Chapter 26 covers the creation of references. These rules apply to headings for all types of materials, regardless of the physical forms in which they appear.

When the work of establishing the proper form of headings is completed, the descriptive part of cataloging is completed. Next, catalogers turn to describing the content of materials, known as *subject access* or *intellectual access.*

FIGURE 10.1 **CATALOG RECORDS FOR ITEMS WITH DETAILED PHYSICAL FORMAT INDICATIONS**

Kemp, Roslyn Ann.

Piggi-billa the porcupine [art reproduction] / Roslyn Ann Kemp. — [Brisbane?] : Boolarong Publications in association with Queensland Aboriginal Creations, [19--]
  1 art reproduction : col. ; 33 x 25 cm.

Reproduction of original bark painting.

Cool moves! [game]. —Livermore, CA : Discovery Toys, c2000.
  12 penguins, 40 game cards, 1 game board : plastic and cardboard, col. ; in box 12 x 12 x 6 cm. + 2 instruction cards.

"Strategy game that helps develop thinking and fine motor skills"—Container. Game board forms the lid of a container storing the game pieces.
  For children 8 years up.

Munsch, Robert.
  Aaron's hair [kit] / Robert Munsch. — Toronto : Scholastic, c2000.   1 book, 1 sound cassette ; in hanging bag 26 x 24 cm.

Narrated by Robert Munsch.
Text illustrated by Alan & Lea Daniel.
Summary: When Aaron hurts his hair's feelings by saying he hates it, his hair runs away and jumps onto other people and into trouble.
  ISBN 0-439-98716-4 (book). — ISBN 0-439-98759-8 (cassette).

Pumping heart [model]. -- Skokie, Ill. : Lindberg, [20--].
  1 model (various pieces) : plastic ; 29 cm. high in container 31 x 24 x 7 cm. — (Natural science series)

Assembly instructions (4 p.) has title: The Visible pumping heart.
  "Life-like continuous action pumps blood thru the visible heart chambers"— Container.
  Intended audience: for use by doctors, educators, students and schools for study demonstration purposes.

SUBJECT ANALYSIS: INTRODUCTION

To maintain an integrated catalog, the same tools used to select subject headings and classification numbers for books are used for the nonbook materials. The standard tools for subject headings are *Sears List of Subject Headings* (Sears; see chapter 8 in this book) and *Library of Congress Subject Headings* (LCSH; see chapter 7 in this book). Both of these subject lists are applicable to nonbook materials. The standard tools for classifying materials are Dewey Decimal Classification (see chapter 9 in this book) and Library of Congress Classification. Both are applicable to nonbook materials, although the Library of Congress Classification is not covered in this book.[6] Libraries that use other subject lists or classifications can apply them to nonbook materials as well as to books.

In considering the content of materials, more than one aspect is important. A distinction is made between what the content is about (subject matter) and what it is (form or genre). In the past, when catalogers dealt mainly with books, they emphasized what the books were about, but sometimes the genre was recognized as well, as in a dictionary of economics. The subject is economics; the genre is a dictionary. When they worked with nonbook materials, however, catalogers concentrated mainly on form, rather than subject matter. A motion picture about dogs would be assigned a subject heading and class number for motion pictures, not for dogs.

The paragraphs that follow describe how subject headings and call numbers are assigned to nonbook materials considering both subject matter and form/genre. Which aspect takes precedence is less important in computerized catalogs in which both can be represented by using appropriate keywords or by limiting searches by physical form, or both.

SUBJECT HEADING ASSIGNMENT

The general approach to assigning subject headings to nonbook materials as well as to books involves three simple-sounding steps:

1. Read, view, hear, or run the material technically to gather data about content. Focus on subject-rich parts of the material, such as titles, about files, summaries, introductions, and so on.
2. Record in your own words what the material is about, what it is, what the creator's approach is, and any other important features.

Make sure each topic you list has enough material to satisfy a searcher looking for material on that topic.

3. Match the terms you listed with authorized headings for those subjects in the subject heading list, known as the *subject authority*. If necessary, qualify the main heading with subdivisions to create a heading that exactly matches the term.

For most subject areas, topic takes precedence over form and genre. Secondary aspects that qualify the main subject, such as location, time period, and subtopics, can be added to the main subject. For example, a documentary videorecording titled *Keep On Walking: Joshua Nelson, The Jewish Gospel Singer* is about at least three things: Joshua Nelson, gospel singing, and Jews or Judaism. Secondary aspects are that Mr. Nelson is an African American and the material is biographical as well as being a documentary video-recording. The distributor's description explains that Mr. Nelson is a Jewish African American who composes and sings gospel music. He is interested in using his music to create a bridge among people of different races. The Library of Congress assigned the follow subject headings to this material:

1. **Nelson, Joshua.**
2. **African American Jews—Biography.**
3. **Gospel musicians—United States—Biography.**
4. **Biographical films.**
5. **Documentary films.**
6. **Feature films.**

Policy makers at the Library of Congress offer guidance on how to assign LCSH headings to various types of materials in a publication titled *Subject Headings Manual*.[7] One of its instructions is to give a subject heading for every topic mentioned in an item's summary note. This direction highlights how elements of bibliographic description provide some of the subject-rich information that informs subject cataloging. It also demonstrates that topical headings take precedence over form and genre headings, although these are not neglected in the example.

Sears subject headings are similar in principle to LCSH, but are broader and use simpler language. Small collections that cater to non-scholarly searchers may not need the specificity and complexity of LCSH. The Sears volume includes a user manual in its introductory pages.

In applying Sears subject headings to the videorecording mentioned earlier, the first, fourth, and fifth subject headings would be the same. The second and third subject headings would become four subject headings— for example, **African-Americans—Biography; Jews—Biography; Gospel music; Musicians—Biography** (or **Black musicians—Biography**). There is no subject heading for feature films.

CLASSIFICATION AND CALL NUMBERS

Classification numbers are the most important part of call numbers— combinations of characters that indicate the locations where materials are shelved—identifying their primary subjects. Call numbers are created by adding distinguishing elements to the classification numbers to identify individual items. These elements include Cutter numbers (alphanumeric codes devised by Charles Cutter) or letters that stand for main entries, dates, and title letters.

Two policy issues are of concern in classifying nonbook materials: what system to use for classification and whether to keep nonbook materials on separate shelves or integrate them with the library's books. Over the years, classification systems have been developed for a number of nonbook material formats, such as the Alpha-Numeric System for Classification of Recordings (ANSCR).[8] Usually the special classifications are limited to one physical format or a specific subject area or a combination of these. However, Dewey Decimal and Library of Congress classifications, which are the most popular general classification systems used by libraries in North America, are also applicable to nonbook materials.

The advantages of using the same classification for book and nonbook materials are that expert classifiers can handle all materials, more options are available for shelving (discussed in the next paragraph), and the call numbers that result express subject matter in familiar terms for members of the public browsing for materials. For those reasons, it is recommended that Dewey Decimal or Library of Congress classification be used for nonbook materials.

Libraries have four choices about shelving book and nonbook materials: (1) integrate them all into one classification sequence; (2) separate materials by physical format, but follow the same classification sequence for each one (this can be done by adding a collection prefix before or above the classification numbers or letters); (3) separate books from nonbook materials, but combine all the nonbook formats and follow the classification sequence in both areas; and (4) integrate some nonbook formats with the books and treat other formats separately or in different combinations, following the classification sequence in each area. The key feature in shelving is to take advantage of the classification sequence for shelf placement, no matter how the parts of each individual collection are deployed. The result will be more satisfying for browsers and reflect the subject matter of the materials more effectively. For example, a young person interested in volcanoes may start by reading a book and then want pictures of an actual volcanic eruption. It is likely that his or her attention will be drawn to a videorecording about volcanic activity when the videorecording is housed with all materials about volcanoes.

Classification numbers reflect the principal subject of a nonbook item. Its physical format can be included in a full call number by use of a collection prefix or a format suffix, if that is desired. It is more likely that a student browser will seek nonfiction nonbook materials by their topics than by other access points, although teachers and parents may seek materials by physical format. Fiction, however, is another story, because children and youth often turn to stories to learn about subjects in which they are interested, and adults employ stories to introduce new subjects. Catalogers sometimes exclude fiction materials—book and nonbook—from classification in order to save time, arguing that members of the public prefer shelf arrangements for fiction by author and title. Perhaps the best practice locally is to classify nonbook fiction the same way fiction books are classified.

MARC CODING

MARC 21[9] is the standard computer markup language for bibliographic data. MARC has been designed with appropriate fields to code all the data needed to catalog nonbook materials in all physical formats. Average catalog records representing nonbook materials are, typically, somewhat longer than those representing books. The additional length of nonbook catalog records is attributable mainly to the larger number of people and corporate bodies responsible for the content of the materials that warrant mention. Much of this additional information appears in descriptive areas 1 (statement of responsibility; MARC tag 245) and 7 (notes). It also means more added entries are made (fields 700 and 710), along with the authority work the headings require. Among the more important notes for nonbook materials are the system requirements note (MARC tag 538), summaries (MARC tag 520), and audience notes, such as reading grade level (MARC tag 521). Summaries are particularly important for nonbook materials, some of which cannot be easily browsed and must be selected for use based solely on the information given in their catalog records. Contents notes (MARC tag 505) name individual works gathered on one recording, website, or other item. The greater complexity of some nonbook formats is described in coded data in several of the control fields (MARC tags 006, 007, and 008). Special control fields are defined for selected nonbook formats, such as the 028 field, used for publisher/distributor numbers for printed music, musical recordings, and videorecordings.

OTHER CONSIDERATIONS

In order to catalog nonbook materials accurately, catalogers should have the hardware needed to view and hear the materials. There is no substitute for obtaining bibliographic data firsthand. This does not mean, however, that a videorecording cataloger is obliged (or, some might say, entitled) to watch movies for hours in the process of cataloging them. Nonbook materials have to be "read" technically, the same as books, as quickly as possible. Good worksheets bearing repetitive data as default values help speed the process. Access to large databases of cataloging for nonbook materials, such as OCLC's WorldCat, which contains records for more than a billion items of which, perhaps, 10 percent are in nonbook formats, increases the possibility of finding source copy. Unfortunately, CIP for nonbook materials, which was never a large program, ended years ago.

When cataloging is obtained from an outside source, such as a school district or cooperative processing center or commercial organization, librarians and media specialists should be clear about insisting, politely, that their policies be followed regarding the fullness of nonbook catalog records, rules used for description, name and subject authorities used, classification used as the basis for call numbers, and so on. They should resist the suggestion that separate, nonstandard treatments for some or all nonbook formats is easier or better for young patrons. On the contrary, applying the same knowledge about one format to all of them is much easier and more efficient than learning multiple systems for different material formats. Librarians and media specialists need to remember that making local changes to source catalog records is costly and time consuming. If the records are clear and accurate and contain enough information for identification and retrieval, it is better to avoid additional editing.

CONCLUSION

Best practices indicate that creating one database for all materials without regard to physical format provides the most service to members of the public. Increasing numbers of catalog users live far from the libraries whose catalogs they search, either because they are in different towns or go to different schools. They depend on what the catalog tells them to decide whether making the effort to obtain the materials is worthwhile. For these remote searchers, it is imperative that catalog records contain enough accurate information to make the decisions. Good cataloging facilitates all people's ability to find what they seek in library collections. Good cataloging for kids should facilitate kids' abilities to find what they seek among all the wonderful materials awaiting them in library collections.

RESOURCES

Andrew, Paige G. *Cataloging Sheet Maps: The Basics.* New York: Haworth Information Press, 2003.

Cole, Jim, and Wayne Jones, eds. *E-serials Cataloging: Access to Continuing and Integrating Resources via the Catalog and the Web.* New York: Haworth Information Press, 2002.

Dreissen, Karen C., and Sheila A. Smyth. *A Library Manager's Guide to Physical Processing of Nonprint Materials.* Westport, CT: Greenwood Press, 1995.

Fritz, Deborah A. *Cataloging with AACR2 and MARC21: For Books, Electronic Resources, Sound Recordings, Videorecordings, and Serials.* Chicago: American Library Association, 2004.

Hsieh-Yee, Ingrid. *Organizing Audiovisual and Electronic Resources for Access: A Cataloging Guide.* Englewood, CO: Libraries Unlimited, 2000.

McKnight, Mark. *Music Classification Systems.* Lanham, MD: Scarecrow Press, 2002.

Olson, Nancy B. *Cataloging of Audiovisual Materials and Other Special Materials: A Manual Based on AACR2 and MARC 21.* With the assistance of Robert L. Bothmann and Jessica J. Schomberg. 5th ed. Westport, CT: Libraries Unlimited, 2008.

Roe, Sandra K., ed. *The Audiovisual Cataloging Current.* New York: Haworth Information Press, 2001.

Schultz, Lois, and Sarah Shaw, eds. *Cataloging Sheet Music: Guidelines for Use with AACR2 and the MARC Format.* Lanham, MD: Scarecrow Press; Music Library Association, 2003.

Urbanski, Verna, et al. *Cataloging Unpublished Nonprint Materials: A Manual of Suggestions, Comments, and Examples.* Lake Crystal, MN: Soldier Creek Press, 1992.

Weber, Mary Beth. *Cataloging Nonprint and Internet Resources: A How-to-Do-It Manual for Librarians.* New York: Neal-Schuman, 2002.

Weihs, Jean. *The Integrated Library: Encouraging Access to Multimedia Materials.* 2nd ed. Phoenix, AZ: Oryx Press, 1991.

Weitz, Jay. *Music Coding and Tagging: MARC 21 Content Designation for Scores and Sound Recordings.* Belle Plain, MN: Soldier Creek Press, 2001.

HELPFUL WEBSITES

Authority Tools for Audiovisual and Music Catalogers: An Annotated List of Useful Resources. Robert Bratton, ed. www.olacinc.org/drupal/?q=node/13.

Online Audiovisual Catalogers. www.olacinc.org.

NOTES

1. *Anglo-American Cataloguing Rules*, 2nd ed., 2002 revision, 2005 update (Chicago: American Library Association; Ottawa: Canadian Library Association; London: Chartered Institute of Library and Information Professionals, 2005. Abbreviated AACR2.

2. Joint Steering Committee for Development of RDA, "Full Draft of RDA," www.rda-jsc.org/rdafulldraft.html.

3. AACR2, 1.

4. AACR2, 1–12.

5. AACR2, rules 21.16–21.23, pages 21.31–21.41.

6. For guidance on how to apply Library of Congress Classification to materials, see Lois Mai Chan, *A Guide to the Library of Congress Classification*, 5th ed. (Englewood, CO: Libraries Unlimited, 1999).

7. This tool, which, until 2009, was titled *Subject Cataloging Manual: Subject Headings*, is available as a file in *Cataloger's Desktop* and *Classification Web* subscription publications available from the Cataloging Distribution Service (CDS) of the Library of Congress.

8. ANSCR: Alpha-Numeric System for Classification of Recordings. Available from Brodart, Inc., 500 Arch Street Williamsport, PA 17701.

9. MARC 21 is available at www.loc.gov/marc/bibliographic/ecbdhome.html.

CHAPTER 11

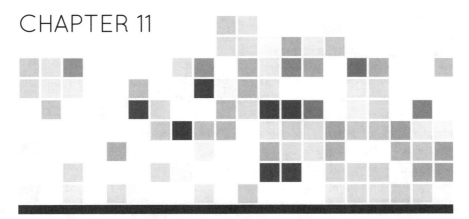

How the CIP Program Helps Children's Librarians

Joanna F. Fountain and Michele Zwierski

CIP, or Cataloging-in-Publication, is a cooperative program begun in 1971 by the Library of Congress (LC) in partnership with U.S. publishers. Publishers send prepublication information for forthcoming books to LC electronically so that cataloging data, prepared in advance of publication, can be printed in the book. Today approximately 3,800 publishers participate in the program.

The CIP program attempts to cover materials that are likely to be collected by most libraries in the United States, primarily English-language books, but also including books in or translated into Spanish. Certain materials are not eligible for the CIP program, such as consumable materials (materials meant to be cut out or written in); transitory materials (such as calendars and phone books); textbooks below the secondary level; instructional books; "tie-ins" (to television, movies, etc.); music scores; mass market publications; self-published materials; and audiovisual materials. For a complete list of exclusions, with explanations, see the CIP web page at http://cip.loc.gov. Even with these exclusions, CIP data are created for a significant percentage of monographs published in the United States, including a large number of juvenile trade books.

PROGRAM DESCRIPTION

CIP data are located on the verso of the title page (or sometimes on the last pages) of a book. These bibliographic data are created by LC cataloging staff and presented in "catalog card" format. The information includes: creator name(s); title(s); series title(s); notes (including summaries); subject headings (both Library of Congress Subject Headings for adults and LC's Children's Subject Headings); and classification (both LCC and Dewey). Publishers send prepublication data either electronically or in hard copy to LC under an agreement that also requires them to follow up by sending LC a copy of the finished book immediately upon publication.

In addition to the CIP data to be printed in books, an electronic version of the data called MARC-CIP (MAchine Readable Cataloging CIP) is created. These records are available for free download from LC's online catalog (http://catalog.loc.gov), or they can be purchased in batches with a weekly subscription. Large libraries, bibliographic utilities such as OCLC, commercial cataloging services such as Auto-Graphics, and book wholesalers often subscribe. In turn, they make the records available to their customers or users.

Because the electronic CIP records are available before the book is published, publishers and wholesalers can use these records to advertise forthcoming materials. Libraries receiving CIP data can in turn pre-order and announce these new and desirable materials to their users.

Because the CIP data are created from prepublication information, it is possible that by the time the book is actually available, some information may be incorrect. In using the CIP data, it is important to compare them with the title page and other sources in the book itself, and to revise products based on the data so that the local cataloging record accurately represents the material in hand. CIP data do not include curricular enhancements, publication data, audience information, contents notes, or other useful retrieval information; therefore—whether in print or electronic format—CIP data must always be treated as high-quality but incomplete cataloging.

CIP AND LOCAL CATALOGING

When material arrives in a library, a catalog record must be created before access and circulation can take place. If a book contains CIP data, quality cataloging already exists, and a librarian needs only to capture that record for local use. Books published without CIP data require that someone on the library's staff produce the cataloging, look for another library's cataloging to copy, or set the item aside to wait for cataloging to appear in whatever sources the library uses. Books with CIP data can get to the shelf sooner.

When CIP data are available, libraries with card catalogs can simply type cards directly from the data, adding the missing data from the item in hand. Libraries with an online catalog have other options for taking advantage of CIP data. MARC-CIP records may be distributed by or available through a publisher, a bibliographic utility, or a commercial provider. Libraries belonging to a bibliographic utility will find MARC-CIP records available to be exported. MARC-CIP records are also available for free downloading from the LC catalog. In short, no matter how a library builds its catalog, the CIP program can save time and money.

An important part of the cataloging process is to verify the accuracy of the CIP data. During the publication process, descriptive elements can change, and the record must be corrected in order for the material to be successfully accessed. For example, the exact title or the order of author names may have been changed prior to actual publication. The CIP data block, once printed in the book, cannot be changed, but the MARC-CIP records frequently are verified and updated when the book arrives at LC. Publishers send finished copies of their books to LC for its collection as their final responsibility in the CIP process. It remains the responsibility of the local library to make the appropriate changes or to check for complete and updated records for books for which there is a CIP record. Either way, local records based on CIP information should be reviewed with the book in hand. Some libraries choose not to complete the CIP data by adding information missing from the records, such as the physical description portion of the cataloging record (MARC field 300), but the data are required in standard "second-level" catalog records (AACR2, 1.0D2).

SERVICE BENEFITS

In addition to the time and resources saved during cataloging, the CIP program provides service benefits. As mentioned, CIP data have potential as a marketing tool for publishers and book wholesalers. Libraries benefit from obtaining high-quality bibliographic information about forthcoming publications before they are issued as well as immediately on receipt. Also, because the CIP data are printed in the book, anyone holding it can refer to them. Students, bookstore browsers, or parents at home can look at the CIP data and find useful information such as annotations or summaries, intended audience notes, subject areas, classification, and more at a glance. It is not necessary to consult a library catalog to learn the information provided in the CIP.

RECENT RESEARCH

In 2006, McCroskey and Wiechert surveyed school librarians, in part to find out how they were using CIP and what they needed from the program in the future.[1] Two hundred eleven librarians from all over the United States responded. Of these, 129 were from Missouri. Seventy-seven percent of those who cataloged books locally used information from the CIP block, many commenting that they especially appreciated the presence of summaries, subject headings, and Dewey classification numbers. When imported records were used, 97 percent of respondents occasionally changed or added information found in the CIP block; 73 percent often did so; 18 percent seldom or never made changes; and 1 percent did not reply.

These numbers suggest that, although both the strengths and weaknesses of CIP data are recognized, CIP is not used thoughtlessly in creating or uploading records into local systems. Therefore, the only negative outcomes that can be attributed to CIP are caused by the small proportion of catalogers who use it without proper caution. Every record entering a local catalog should be reviewed for accuracy, completeness, and consistency with the library's policies no matter its source, including CIP.

CONCLUSION

The CIP program provides prepublication cataloging for most juvenile trade publications issued in the United States. As such, it is an important information source for children's and young-adult services librarians as well as for catalogers and other librarians and media specialists responsible for producing catalog records for their agencies. Thanks to CIP, materials arrive with cataloging inside and can be placed on library shelves quickly.

RESOURCES

LC CIP website (includes Process, Processing New CIP Materials at the Library of Congress, Frequently Asked Questions, and Why CIP Verification Is Important). http://cip.loc.gov.

McCroskey, Marilyn, and Raegan Wiechert. *School Librarians Depend on CIP: Results of a Survey for the CIP Advisory Group. Report for ALCTS Cataloging of Children's Materials Committee, American Library Conference, New Orleans, LA, June 25, 2006.* Handout provided by the authors.

NOTE

1. Marilyn McCroskey and Raegan Wiechert, *School Librarians Depend on CIP: Results of a Survey for the CIP Advisory Group. Report for ALCTS Cataloging of Children's Materials Committee, American Library Conference, New Orleans, LA, June 25, 2006* (handout provided by the authors).

CHAPTER 12

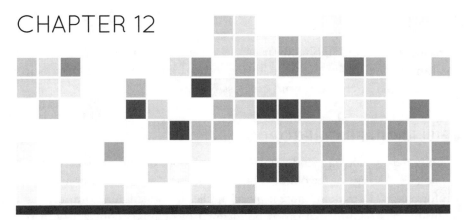

Cataloging for Kids in the Academic Library

Gabriele I. Kupitz

Although children and young adults do use academic libraries and their juvenile collections, it is the university student and his or her mentor, the academic, who are most likely to use the juvenile collections in academic settings for research purposes. The study of children's literature as a serious, scholarly discipline has long cast its magic over researchers. In the 1970s, teachers and academics began to emphasize the value and the interpretation of children's literature, with particular focus on literary analysis.[1] Since that time, the study of children's literature has become a legitimate pursuit, and the corresponding scholarship has both fascinated and involved many academic institutions and their libraries. This chapter examines current practices in the cataloging of children's materials in academic libraries.

CATALOGING OPTIONS

Because scholars use the materials in relation to teaching and research, academic libraries may opt to use Library of Congress Subject Headings (LCSH) and Library of Congress Classification (LCC) numbers in cataloging juvenile materials in order to mirror the cataloging and classification practices in place for other large scholarly collections. Some libraries may choose to use LCSH and Dewey Decimal Classification numbers, which are popular among school and public libraries. All are appropriate depending on the culture of the institution. In addition, other bibliographic enhancements unique to research institutions are possibilities.

BIBLIOGRAPHIC RECORDS

Computer technology and serendipity are tools of the student and the scholar. In the age of the online catalog, bibliographic records offer invaluable information. The axiom "more is more" applies to the online record, although the nuggets of information to be gleaned by scholars contract with the abbreviated computer records needed by most children. Following are examples of differences between full and abbreviated records that might affect typical scholarly projects.

Scrutinizing first edition titles alongside later editions of the same title holds more appeal for the scholar than for the recreational reader. Uniform titles help to identify and organize works. Exact pagination is as crucial to research as are the edition statements.

A 500 note added to the bibliographic records of picture books can highlight the art medium, type of paper, and text type used. This information is of interest to art and illustration students and their professors who peruse picture books for examples of the melding of text and art medium. In some institutions, catalogers record the art medium in genre or physical description notes (coded 538).

Additional 500 notes could be used to record information found only on the dust jacket, translation information often found on the verso of the title page, copyright information, and provenance. Bibliographical references and index information are invaluable additions for students and scholars, as are summary notes, contents notes, audience notes, and the myriad other note possibilities.

In any library, authority work is important, but in large university catalogs it is critical. Names, series, subject headings, and other access points must be as consistent as possible because of the sheer volume of records in the catalog and because of their universal potential to facilitate research. For professional academic catalogers, cataloging materials written for children and young adults requires the same attention and thorough treatment as does cataloging materials for adults, because these juvenile materials are for the on-site as well as the remote researcher.

USEFUL FIELDS

It has been suggested that catalogers use less than 25 percent of the available record fields to provide information for patrons.[2] In addition to 500 (general notes) and 504 (bibliographical references and index notes), the following are some of the fields researchers and patrons welcome.

> 520 Summary note
>   Example: Pictures and rhyming text present some of the many extraordinary things penguins can do. Includes facts about penguins as well as related websites. (From *If You Were a Penguin* by Wendell and Florence Minor. New York : Katherine Tegen Books / HarperCollins Publishers, 2009)
> 521 Audience note
>   Example: "Ages 4–7"—Inside front dust-jacket
> 586 Awards note
>   Example: Batchelder Award (2009); *Booklist* Starred Review (27 July 2008); *Kirkus* Starred Review (10 June 2008); *School Library Journal* Starred Review (1 August 2008).
> 650 _0   Subject heading
>   Example: Penguins ‡v Juvenile fiction.
> 651 _0   Place heading
>   Example: Italy ‡v Juvenile fiction.

Genre headings (coded 655) are key for many searches. At one major university, 1,796 records for books are currently coded with the 655 genre heading **Humorous stories** and include books for children and adults. If the 655 search for **Humorous stories** is modified by adding a subdivision for **—Juvenile fiction** (coded 655, second indicator 0, subfield v, or, Humorous stories ‡v Juvenile fiction), the narrowing of the search now retrieves 742 titles for children and young adults.

Following are suggested possibilities for genre headings that make searching much easier for library staff and patrons, especially teens, because their juvenile-specific subdivisions pull records out from the general academic catalog as they may pull patrons in to the catalog.[3]

> 655 _0 Board books ‡v Juvenile fiction.
> 655 _0 Picture books for children ‡v Juvenile fiction.
> 655 _0 Picture books for children ‡v Juvenile literature.

655 _0 Picture books for children ‡v Juvenile poetry.
655 _0 Young adult fiction.
655 _0 Chick lit.
655 _0 Science fiction ‡v Juvenile fiction.
655 _0 Stories in rhyme ‡v Juvenile fiction.
655 _0 Fantasy fiction ‡v Juvenile fiction.
655 _0 Graphic novels ‡v Juvenile fiction.
655 _0 Novels in verse ‡v Juvenile fiction.

As the world becomes more interconnected and many institutions offer foreign-language study and degrees in specific languages of emphasis, the following genre-specific headings will help patrons find foreign-language materials in academic and large public library collections.

655 _0 Fantasy fiction, German ‡v Juvenile fiction.
655 _0 Fantasy fiction, Japanese ‡v Translations into English ‡v Juvenile fiction.
655 _0 Bilingual books ‡v Juvenile poetry.

CONCLUSION

If all of the above looks daunting, think of this: "even monolingual American children are intrigued with books in other languages. They are especially fascinated by different alphabets. I'm not sure what an American child learns about Japan when she leafs through a Japanese picture book, but it can't hurt to be exposed to the notion that not everybody reads from left to right in the Roman alphabet."[4] Catalogs and their catalogers do make a difference.

RESOURCES

Mann, Thomas. "Why LC Subject Headings Are More Important Than Ever." *American Libraries* 33, no. 10 (October 2003): 52–54.

Maxwell, Robert L. *Maxwell's Guide to Authority Work*. Chicago: American Library Association, 2002.

———. *Maxwell's Handbook for AACR2: Explaining and Illustrating the Anglo-American Cataloguing Rules through the 2005 Update*. Chicago: American Library Association, 2004.

NOTES

1. Jill P. May, *Children's Literature and Critical Theory*, Reading and Writing for Understanding (New York: Oxford University Press, 1995), 23.
2. "Informing the Future of MARC: An Empirical Approach," ALA ALCTS Program at the 2007 ALA Annual Conference in Washington, D.C., Friday, June 22, 2007.
3. Vivian Howard, "Most of the Books I've Read, I've Found on the Floor," *VOYA* 33, no. 4 (October 2009): 298–301.
4. Virginia A. Walter, "The Children We Serve: Five Notions of Childhood Suggest Ways to Think about the Services We Provide," *American Libraries* 40, no. 10 (October 2009): [52]–55.

CHAPTER 13

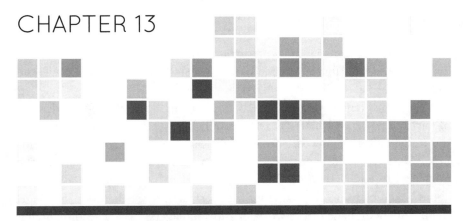

Cataloging for Non-English-Speaking and Preliterate Children

Pamela J. Newberg

For many years, libraries have seen an influx of patrons who are not native speakers of English. An editorial in *School Library Journal* in February 1976 extols the need to reach out to non-English-speaking patrons.[1] Research suggests that the difficulties of cataloging non-English materials have been discussed since the early 1990s.[2] In *Standards for the 21st Century Learner,* published by the American Association of School Librarians (AASL) in 2007, "equitable access to materials" is listed as a key component to education.[3]

Serving non-English-speaking children presents its own set of difficulties with language barriers and availability of resources, but it can be especially frustrating for catalogers who only speak English or do not have skills in the language(s) needed. Whereas the initial language focus for libraries serving children was Spanish, cataloging of materials in a multitude of languages may now be required.

CATALOGING CODE

The cataloging code, whether AACR2 or RDA, can assist with creating MARC records for foreign-language materials. The rules are the same whether a title is in English or another language. The cataloging code also makes searching for materials predictable and consistent. One can always count on the information needed being located in the same place in the catalog record each time it is searched.

There are elements of the MARC record where the consistent addition of tags and codes will enable the non-English speaker to search for and find the information she needs. The 008 field, positions 35–37 (the fixed fields in an OCLC record), contains a three-letter code for the language of the material cataloged. The 041 (Language) code gives additional information about a title by indicating whether the work is in more than one language, the original language of the work, or the language(s) of any accompanying materials. Most library automation systems use one of these codes to filter bibliographic records by language in an advanced search.

Language information can also be recorded in a 546 (Language note) tag. The note is usually worded "Text in [language]." Using the note tag will make the materials available using a keyword search.

UNIFORM TITLES

The use of uniform titles is another cataloging standard that pulls all the various forms of a single work together. According to the MARC 21 standards, a uniform title is "used when a work has appeared under varying titles, necessitating that a particular title be chosen to represent the work."[4] One way to provide access for all translations of a title in the catalog is by using the uniform title to group them together under the title of the original work. In this way users can search for all the translations of a title originally written in English under the English title. A uniform title is recorded in the MARC format in the 240 field and contains the original title (subfield a) and the language of the translation (subfield l).

SUBJECT HEADINGS

Foreign-language subject headings are another way of helping non-English-speaking children find the materials they want. Assigning such subject headings can be nearly impossible though if the cataloger only speaks English. The easiest way to gather foreign-language materials together is by using the Library of Congress's Children's Subject Headings (CSH). The standard CSH subject heading used for foreign-language materials is the name of the specific language followed by "language materials." Examples would be **French language materials** or **Arabic language materials.** These headings work if a collection of foreign-language materials is small and can be browsed easily. In cases of large collections of foreign-language materials or collections that are integrated with English-language materials, it is helpful to have topical subject headings in the language of the materials being cataloged.

In recent years the number of Spanish-language subject thesauri has grown. The oldest of these thesauri is *Bilindex*. First published in 1984, *Bilindex* is "a list of Spanish-English bilingual subject heading equivalents to [the] *Library of Congress Subject Heading* list."[5] The newest version was released in 2009 and is available on CD-ROM or online. The thesaurus works similarly to a Spanish–English dictionary in that one searches for the English heading and finds the Spanish equivalent.

Another Spanish-language thesaurus based on Library of Congress Subject Headings is an online site, http://lcsh-es.org.[6] This thesaurus is free to use but you must register online. The sources of the headings are the Biblioteca Nacional de España, *Bilindex* (1984), Consejo Superior de Investigaciones Científicas (Spain), *Library of Congress Subject Headings*, the Queens Borough Public Library, and the San Francisco Public Library. Be cautious in using this thesaurus because it is not current and has not been checked thoroughly for accuracy.

Two Spanish-language subject heading thesauri that are geared toward school and small public libraries are the Spanish-language edition of the *Sears List of Subject Headings*, titled *Sears: Lista de Encabezamientos de Materia,* and a bilingual version of *Subject Headings for School and Public Libraries.*[7] In the Spanish Sears, every heading from the nineteenth edition of the *Sears List of Subject Headings* is translated according to the most current Spanish and Latin American usage. The list also includes over five hundred subdivisions with instructions on their use. *Subject Headings for School and Public Libraries*, bilingual edition, scheduled to be released in 2010, is based on *Library of Congress Subject Headings.* The bilingual edition is expanded with references, several thousand high-use biographical names, and MARC field tags and subfield codes.

A different, if not unusual, source of foreign-language subject headings for catalogers that speak English is the Dewey Decimal Classification (DDC). DDC is translated into fourteen languages: Arabic, Chinese, French, German, Greek, Hebrew, Icelandic, Italian, Korean, Norwegian, Russian, Spanish, Swedish, and Vietnamese. A cataloger could conceivably look up the DDC number assigned to a work in the corresponding translation and find a broad topical subject heading for that work.

If you subscribe to WebDewey, a future source of foreign-language subject headings could be its experimental space for linked DDC data called Dewey.info. The initial data set to be made available is a linked data version of the DDC summaries in nine languages. With this product you can click on a summary heading and see that heading in Arabic, German, English, Spanish, French, Portuguese, Russian, Swedish, and Vietnamese.

Keep in mind that the use of foreign-language subject headings is not restricted to foreign-language materials. If your library serves a large population of non-English-speaking children, you may wish to add foreign-language subject headings to English materials also. This could facilitate users' transition to English.

VISUAL CATALOGS

Visual catalogs can help non-English-speaking children as well as preliterate children find information through the use of icons in the catalog. Most library patrons are familiar with format icons: those little pictures that indicate whether a title is a book, a compact disc, or an online resource. These icons are generated from the material type coding in the fixed fields of the MARC record. Book cover images also can help the nonreader find familiar characters like Franklin (Bourgeois) or McDuff (Wells).

Subject icons are small icons or pictures of various subjects. Visual catalogs use these icons to allow children to move from broad subject icons, like animals or holidays, to narrower ones, such as dogs or Halloween, and finally to a list of books that match that subject.

Library automation vendors use various methods to create lists of materials linked to a subject icon. Materials to be found under a specific icon can be identified by subject headings (SirsiDynix's Symphony, Surpass Software's Centriva), by classification number (Surpass Software's Centriva), by keyword (Follett's Destiny), or by predetermined lists (TLC's LS2Kids). Most library automation systems allow catalogers to extend their subject choices by creating their own lists of books assigned to an icon, or the system will create a list. In this way, lists of books in a series, by a specific author, or for an assignment can be created and assigned icons for easier access.

CONCLUSION

The thought of cataloging materials in a foreign language may seem daunting. The task of trying to provide access to materials for non-English-speaking or preliterate children may seem impossible. It is not. Cataloging rules, standards, and tools are available to help every step of the way.

NOTES

1. Yolanda E. Rivas, "Reach Out to Your Spanish-Speaking Patrons," *School Library Journal* (February 1976).
2. "Languages of the World: Cataloging Issues and Problems," *Cataloging & Classification Quarterly* 17, no. 1/2 (1993).
3. American Association of School Librarians, *Standards for the 21st Century Learner,* www.ala.org/ala/mgrps/divs/aasl/guidelinesandstandards/ learningstandards/AASL_LearningStandards.pdf.
4. Library of Congress, *MARC 21 Format for Bibliographic Data,* http://desktop .loc.gov.
5. *Bilindex-General 2009,* www.floricantopress.com/BX2009aa.htm.
6. Eda M. Correa and Nashieli Marcano, "Bibliographic Description and Practices for Providing Access to Spanish Language Materials," *Technical Services Quarterly* 26, no. 4 (2009): 299–312.
7. Joanna F. Fountain, *Subject Headings for School and Public Libraries,* 3rd ed. (Westport, CT: Greenwood Press, 2001).

CHAPTER 14

Automating the Children's Catalog

Judith Yurczyk

Whether automating for the first time or changing automation systems, the first step in the automation process is to select an integrated library system (ILS). Each library has its own needs and budget constraints, but with more and more sharing of records, the system you choose is very important. The first step is to outline the needs and specifications for the ILS and then to look at the various system configurations that are available. An integrated library system can operate as an individual site-based system, as a centralized system, or as a hosted system.

PURCHASING AN AUTOMATION SYSTEM

An individual site-based system involves a single library. The ILS can operate independently on one or more computers, or it may be networked among several computers within the library, requiring a server where the data are stored and processed. Resource sharing can be limited with an individual site-based system, because only resources within that single library can be accessed.

In a centralized system, an entire district or multibranch system uses a single centralized server that supports all libraries throughout the district or consortium. Each library has its own collection stored on the central server, in a single database that each library can access. Sharing an automation system decreases maintenance and support costs while increasing resource availability. Centralized systems include Follett's Destiny, Surpass Software's Centriva, TLC's Library Solution for Schools, Book Systems' Atriuum, and Mandarin's Oasis.

A hosted service may be the best solution if limited space, budget, technical staff, and information technology infrastructures are an issue. Software as a Service (SaaS), also known as an Application Service Provider (ASP), is a hosted service, which means a vendor owns and controls the system applications and an off-site server hosts the library's data. The library has access to the applications through the Internet. A hosted service may involve just one library or an entire district or consortium. Hosted service software includes Follett's Destiny, Mandarin's Oasis, CyberTools for Libraries, SirsiDynix's Symphony, and Biblionix's Apollo.

Many software systems are proprietary. Licenses may be purchased from a vendor with restrictions on the use and modification of the applications. In these systems, the user does not have access to the underlying source code and, thus, is not able to make changes to an application. An alternative to the traditional proprietary software or licensing model software systems is a nonproprietary open source ILS. With open source software, the underlying source code is available to the user, and the software is free to use, free to modify, and free to share; it is not necessarily cost-free, however, because there may be costs associated with adapting and supporting it. An open source ILS may be implemented in a single library or in a district or consortium. Open source library management products include Evergreen, Koha, and OPALS (OPen-source Automated Library management System). As an alternative to open source software, companies offering proprietary applications have started to use Application Program Interfaces (APIs) that allow client software and third-party applications to interact with the core system. Through APIs, users are able to write programs to extend functionality of their ILS without the use of the source code. Ex Libris's Open-Platform Strategy and Encore xQuery by Innovative Interfaces are examples of products that use this structure.

The choice of an ILS depends on a number of factors including cost, the library's mission, what you want the system to do, and what it is capable of doing. Before making a choice, you must carefully weigh the advantages and disadvantages of the features, functionality, price, and performance of the software.

RETROSPECTIVE CONVERSION

An automated system will only function well if good data are loaded into it. The foundation of any automation process is the creation of a high-quality database in an electronic format. This database is produced in a retrospective conversion process in which bibliographic data are converted into Machine-Readable Cataloging (MARC) records. MARC 21 is the current standard for these cataloging records. Adherence to the standard is very important, because standards are critical if libraries are to maintain the portability of their files. Portability allows the files to be transferred from one automated system to another without repeating the retrospective conversion phase. Standards are also essential for libraries wishing to participate in resource sharing projects with other libraries, such as the union catalogs of school districts and consortia (e.g., Florida's SUNLINK) and statewide or regional projects (e.g., Wisconsin's WISCAT and Access Pennsylvania).

MARC is a communications format that provides a way to store and move catalog records from one computer to another, but it is not a guarantee of the cataloging content. The structure of the MARC record must meet the MARC 21 standards, but the bibliographic data contained within the record must adhere to the standard rules for describing resources, at this writing the *Anglo-American Cataloguing Rules*, second edition, 2005 revision (AACR2). Depending on the source of the cataloging, the quality of the content may vary. The Library of Congress (LC) creates high-quality MARC records. These same LC records may be available from a bibliographic utility such as OCLC (WorldCat) or may be purchased from a vendor as an online service via the Internet. (See chapter 3 for more information on the MARC format and AACR2.)

OBTAINING A MARC DATABASE

MARC records can be obtained for a library's online catalog in several ways, including manual entry, outsourced vendor conversion, or in-house conversion.

Manual Entry. After the library purchases its automation software, the cataloging staff, other staff, or volunteers can manually create MARC records by entering data from your shelflist cards, catalog cards, or the actual item itself (for books, the title page and verso, or back side, of the title page) into a template in your online catalog system. Many software vendors now provide "easy" entry templates for users without MARC knowledge as well as more advanced templates for users who are already familiar with MARC standards. This is a labor-intensive process. Small collections may benefit from this manual entry approach, but larger collections usually benefit from assistance from an outside vendor.

Outsourced Vendor Conversion. Contracting with a vendor requires the library to either (a) send a catalog card (preferably a shelflist card or a copy of the title page) for each item in the collection, or (b) make a record including brief data such as LCCN or ISBN or both, title, and local information (call number and number of copies) for each item in the old catalog on paper or a disk. The vendor will match the title against its database and provide full MARC records for the "hits" (MARC records that match the LCCN or ISBN). Some vendors will create a MARC record for the "misses" while others will return a list and the library will have to create original records for the misses. The vendor returns the MARC records via FTP (file transfer protocol) or a CD-ROM.

In-house Conversion. There are a number of ways to do retrospective conversion locally, on your own. You can subscribe to an online service and access millions of MARC records over the Internet where you can search for records matching the titles in your library's collection. Matching records are downloaded onto discs or directly into the online catalog after adding local information. Follett's Alliance Plus and Alliance A/V, Brodart's Precision One, and TLC's ITS.MARC are examples of online services that provide millions of MARC records and let catalogers perform their own retrospective conversion. The local library must create the MARC records for titles that have no matches.

Though many online subscription MARC record services are available, there are also many free sources on the Internet. MARC 21 records are available via the Internet using the Z39.50 protocol. With Z39.50 multiple library databases can be searched simultaneously and matching MARC records downloaded into the local library's database. The entire Library of Congress database is accessible and free for downloading by any library by using the Z39.50 protocol. Some library software systems have this capability built in. If the software you choose does not have Z39.50 built in, other products such as ‡biblios.net, eZcat, Surpass Copycat, or BookWhere allow a library to download MARC records from the Library of Congress and from universities and public libraries with Z39.50 servers.

No one method is superior to another. The appropriate method to choose depends on the size of your library's collection and the size of your staff and budget.

PREPARING FOR RETROSPECTIVE CONVERSION

Before automating a catalog or changing ILS vendors, you should complete several important tasks, including making sure the data to be entered are accurate and do not include unwanted records.

Data Cleanup. The first step in cleaning up your data is to weed the collection or remove items that no longer meet the needs of the library users, such as obsolete, damaged, or rarely used items. Next, take inventory of each item in the collection to make sure that the shelflist or existing bibliographic records match the items on the shelves. Last, review spine label standards to be sure all are consistent. Completion of these tasks will simplify the ILS installation process.

Data Enhancement. The data in your catalog are valuable, but they could become more valuable through a data enhancement process. Many vendors enhance LC MARC records provided in their online service with some additional information such as a summary, reading and interest levels, Lexile measures, and Sears subject headings. Additional enhancements such as reading program information, awards, review sources, tables of contents, and cover images can be provided for the records. Data enhanced MARC records improve relevancy and accuracy of search results, and they increase access points so users can find information quickly and easily.

Data Migration. Moving data from one system to a new one can be relatively easy, or it can be a daunting task. Before migrating to a new automated system, doing some data cleanup assists the transfer of data to the new system. As mentioned, some general cleanup can be done in-house, such as weeding the collection, taking inventory, and reviewing spine label standards. Bibliographic records can also be sent to a vendor for additional cleanup, such as repairing any records that have file format corruption, standardizing all records to the MARC 21 format, correcting diacritics, eliminating duplicate records, correctly merging data, and standardizing call numbers and collection codes.

Bar Coding. In addition to creating MARC records, the automation process includes bar coding each item. Barcodes are used to identify and track items. One way to save time is to pre-barcode the collection during inventory or as the collection is weeded to get it ready for automation.

POST-CONVERSION CLEANUP

Some data cleanup is necessary after a retrospective conversion. Cleanup may include creating full MARC records for misses, changing local information regarding the number of copies and volumes for certain items, changing call numbers, or standardizing subject and name headings. This cleanup may be done manually, but that can be very time consuming. Many ILS systems have global editing features to help in this process. Or, a product such as MARC Magician or MARC Report that uses built-in MARC 21 rules and variables may be used to clean up MARC records.

ONGOING MAINTENANCE

Now the library's catalog is automated. What next?

The database of MARC records must be maintained. When new titles are received, MARC records must be added for them. Several sources provide MARC records for new titles. A number of vendors sell MARC records for materials purchased from them and will provide complete processing, including spine labels, catalog cards for a manual shelflist (if one is still maintained), MARC records, barcodes, and book jackets.

When purchasing MARC records from a vendor, make sure the specifications given to the vendor match your system's technical requirements (see chapter 15 for additional information). Before loading the records into the local system, preview them to ensure that information requested in the library's data profile is included and that authority work was done on the name and subject headings. A good way to prevent common coding and cataloging errors in the MARC database is to run the records through a quality control software system such as MARC Magician or MARC Report. These software systems automatically correct many MARC errors and report omissions, which can be corrected manually. After records are loaded into the local system, items are placed on the shelves.

Some vendors will provide MARC records for titles not purchased from them. This service is helpful when a library purchases materials from vendors who do not offer MARC records or who do not have staff who can produce good-quality MARC records, and when titles are donated to the library or purchased from local bookstores.

New MARC records can be obtained from a vendor specializing in MARC records. Some vendors provide online subscription services such as Follett's Alliance Online and Alliance A/V, Brodart's Precision One, and TLC's ITS.MARC. Another source is a bibliographic utility such as OCLC that contains MARC records contributed by member libraries. All these sources operate on a subscription basis, and some are more cost-effective for large libraries and library systems. An alternative, of course, is to catalog the items in-house using the standard tools for bibliographic description, subject headings, and call numbers.

Whatever option is chosen, catalogers need to know their automation system's requirements for importing or creating MARC records. The most important requirement is to know which field contains the holdings information and how that information must be coded. If vendor-supplied MARC records are used, make sure each vendor has the same specification information. All vendors should know the placement of local notes and other notes, such as reading and interest levels, reading program information, award information, and the like. How the automation system indexes various fields such as series and local notes is also important (some systems do not index the 490, 800, or 830 tags). How the system indexes information affects how the MARC records are edited before import. Equally important, MARC format and coding change from time to time. Catalogers need to know how their vendors and the automation system incorporate the changes.

Authority records help in the collocation of works and bring consistency to the database, making the catalog easier to use and aiding users in searching for and finding resources. Authority control within the automation system is important (see chapter 6 for a more detailed explanation of authority control). If the automation system has an authority module, catalogers need to learn the features of their system. Some authority systems are more sophisticated than others. Some systems automatically check the bibliographic records against authority records when the records are being imported or manually created and automatically correct the headings in bibliographic records to match the authority records. Other systems, however, have no direct link between a bibliographic record and its related authority record. No matter how sophisticated or unsophisticated the authority system is, a method should be developed for consistently checking bibliographic records against authority record files and correcting errors.

If the local system does not have authority control, make sure that MARC records purchased from a vendor are subject to strict authority control before they are sent to the library. Also check with the vendor to determine how quickly changes in subject headings, name headings, and call numbers are incorporated into its MARC records.

When changes to name and subject headings occur, catalogers need to determine how to incorporate them into the catalog. If the automation system has global change capabilities, outdated headings can be easily corrected; otherwise, each heading has to be changed individually.

CONTRIBUTING TO A UNION CATALOG

Union catalogs enable libraries to share collections. A union catalog combines MARC records and holdings information from a group of libraries into a single, searchable interface. A union catalog can be small and consist of a group of district libraries sharing the same ILS, or it can be large and include holdings of many different types of libraries (i.e., academic, school, public, special) within a region or state, using multiple ILS systems. Florida's SUNLINK is a statewide union catalog of K–12 public schools. Wisconsin's WISCAT contains holdings of all types and sizes of libraries within that state.

When a library participates in a union catalog, MARC records that meet national standards and holdings information are uploaded into the union catalog, and records are merged to eliminate unwanted duplicate records. Union catalogs allow libraries to download MARC records for use in local online catalogs, thus saving cataloging time. Each union catalog has specific guidelines that libraries need to follow for adding their new acquisitions, keeping holdings information current, and deleting withdrawn holdings.

A library may also choose to add its holdings to a global catalog by becoming part of OCLC's WorldCat, where individual collections are linked together in a huge virtual collection. The library's holdings can be submitted directly to WorldCat, or a consortium can be formed that contributes its holdings collectively to WorldCat. Another option is to use the WorldCat Cataloging Partners service. This service works together with materials vendors by providing OCLC MARC records that match the materials being ordered and automatically sets the library's holdings information into WorldCat.

Participating in a union catalog—whether it is a local district, state, or global union catalog—provides a means for locating and sharing resources. It enables library users to search and borrow resources from their own library and region as well as from libraries outside their region.

CONCLUSION

It is impossible to finish a library's MARC database. Automating a collection and maintaining a high-quality database of MARC records can sometimes seem like a chore, but it is critical to ensuring that teachers and students enjoy the greatest access to library resources. The quality of the library's data directly determines the success of people's searches. In this age of information overload, an even stronger need exists to provide a single place for teachers and students to search for all the information they seek. Your library's catalog can be a gateway to all the information available—if the database is kept in order.

RESOURCES

Breeding, Marshall. "Investing in the Future: Automation Marketplace 2009." *Library Journal* (April 1, 2009). www.libraryjournal.com/article/CA6645868 .html.

⸺. "Library Automation in a Difficult Economy." *Computers in Libraries* 29, no. 3 (March 2009). www.librarytechnology.org/ltg-displaytext.pl?RC=13848.

⸺. "Open Source Integrated Library Systems." *Library Technology Reports* 44, no. 8 (November–December 2008). http://alatechsource.metapress.com/content/r151121q32wv/?p=e7821159a45b45eeb99cbd3b8d6adf08&pi=6.

Schultz-Jones, Barbara. *An Automation Primer for School Library Media Centers and Small Libraries*. Worthington, OH: Linwood Books, 2006.

Understanding MARC Authority Records: Machine-Readable Cataloging. Washington, DC: Library of Congress, 2004. www.loc.gov/marc/uma/index.html.

Understanding MARC Bibliographic: Machine-Readable Cataloging. Washington, DC: Library of Congress, 2003. www.loc.gov/marc/umb/.

CHAPTER 15

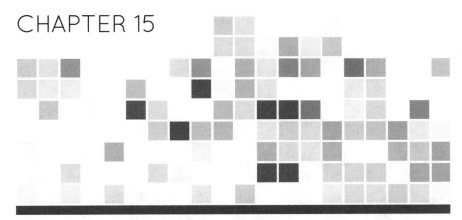

Vendors of Cataloging for Children's Materials

Pamela J. Newberg and Jennifer Allen

Many libraries purchase cataloging from a vendor to save time and money. An initial expenditure of time on the part of the librarian can greatly enhance the entire experience as well as the resulting cataloging (and, often, the processing) product.

Where to get cataloging is the first consideration, and several sources are available. Three major sources are (1) book wholesalers or prebinders, (2) cataloging service or software vendors, and (3) bibliographic utilities.

> *Wholesalers and prebinders.* Hundreds of book and audiovisual wholesalers and book prebinding companies are in business, and most offer some sort of cataloging or processing or both for materials purchased from them. Some also offer cataloging for materials they sell but that may not have been purchased directly from them.
>
> *Cataloging vendors.* Some vendors offer cataloging products and services either online or on CD-ROM. There are also software programs that download MARC records using the Z39.50 protocol.
>
> *Bibliographic utilities.* Not-for-profit bibliographic networks, such as OCLC, also called bibliographic utilities, use computer databases

of member-supplied cataloging records. Libraries using these services sign a membership agreement, often arranged through a local or regional library network.

Whichever route you take, a thorough evaluation of the library's collection will aid considerably in the process. This appraisal is critical if the chosen vendor will be cataloging and processing materials purchased. The basic choices are Dewey or Library of Congress call numbers and Library of Congress or Sears subject headings. After that, the decisions get a bit more complicated.

CALL NUMBERS

Concerns regarding call numbers involve local policies governing the assignment of classification numbers and the addition of book numbers. If Dewey is used, the following questions arise:

- Should the source for the numbers be the abridged edition or the unabridged edition?
- Are the numbers carried to the first slash? Two digits past the decimal? Four digits past the decimal?
- Are author letters or Cutter numbers used? If so, how many characters or digits will be assigned?
- How are the biographies classified? In 921? In B? Will they be shelved in a separate section or mixed with other nonfiction?
- Where are the easy readers and picture books? Are they marked E or P, or something else?
- Are there special collections that require a prefix (for example, reference, professional collection, foreign language, story collections)?
- If automated, in which tag and subfield divisions do the call numbers belong?

SUBJECT HEADINGS

Questions about subject headings include the following:

- What subject authority will be used: *Library of Congress Subject Headings* for adults, the Library of Congress's Children's Subject

Headings (formerly known as Annotated Card or AC headings), or *Sears List of Subject Headings*?

- Is the number of subject headings assigned to an individual item limited?
- Are there other local policies that affect the assignment of subject headings?

READING PROGRAMS

Specialized processing to facilitate reading programs requires asking the following:

- If a reading program is used, how are the books identified?
- If the catalog records are automated, are there special requirements for this field tag (field 521 in the MARC format)?

SERIES

With recent changes to cataloging practice by the Library of Congress regarding how series are treated and recorded in the MARC records LC creates, catalogers may wish to ask the following:

- Where in the MARC record will the series be recorded, and will these series titles be searchable?
- Can the author's name be taken out of the series?
- If the local automation system can't handle 830 field tags, will the vendor put the series title in a 440 tag?

PHYSICAL PROCESSING

Choices about physical processing include the following:

- Does the library want materials to be given covers or not?
- Does the library want cards and pockets inserted into materials, and, if so, where should they be placed?
- Are barcodes going to be applied? If so, where will they be placed on the materials?

OTHER SERVICES

As innovations are made in cataloging and automation, catalogers might want to check with vendors they are considering to determine the following:

- Does the vendor offer Spanish-language subject headings? If so, which thesaurus or subject authority does the vendor use?
- How are the Spanish-language subject headings tagged, and will the coding work with the library's automation system?
- Does the vendor offer subject headings in other foreign languages?
- Does the vendor offer curriculum subject headings? If so, which thesaurus or authority does the vendor use?
- How are the curriculum subject headings tagged, and will the coding work with the library's automation system?
- Are the curriculum headings matched to state or national standards?

Armed with the information gained from answering the preceding questions, you can select vendors who meet most of your needs.

ADDITIONAL CONCERNS

Other vital questions to ask potential vendors include the following:

- Where does the vendor obtain its cataloging records?
- Are the cataloging records reviewed? Do professional catalogers conduct the reviews?
- Does every MARC record have an annotation or summary note?
- How does the vendor handle updates in descriptive cataloging rules, call numbers, and subject headings? For example, how did the company deal with the conversion to ISBN-13? What accommodations were made (if any) for customers whose automation systems couldn't handle the thirteen-digit numbers?
- Does the vendor use authority files? If so, which authority files are used, and how are they maintained?

- Which descriptive cataloging standards does the vendor follow? If the vendor uses AACR2, can the library choose a desired bibliographic level, or does the vendor offer only one level?
- What are the vendor's plans for the implementation of RDA (*Resource Description and Access*)?
- What procedure is used if a question arises about specifications, cataloging, or processing?
- What is the procedure for special cataloging requests?
- Are the library's cataloging specifications kept on file, or must they be submitted with each order?
- How are MARC records sent to the library?

POST-SELECTION ISSUES

If more than one vendor is selected, be sure that each one receives the same specifications for cataloging the library's materials, so records from all of them can be integrated seamlessly into the library's catalog.

The process does not end once a vendor has been selected, contracts have been negotiated, specifications have been recorded and filed, and cataloging products are received. The cataloging records, whether on cards or in a computer file, should be reviewed for completeness, accuracy, and adherence to the library's specific collection and call number requests. Cataloging records need to be evaluated more than once or twice and should be reviewed on an ongoing basis. Changes to a vendor's personnel, policies, and procedures can result in changes to its products that affect the library's catalog positively or negatively.

Vendors should be evaluated periodically for adherence to bibliographic standards and the implementation of changes in standard cataloging practices, call numbers, and subject headings. Attention to problems that crop up, prompt delivery of catalog records and other services, and costs should also be monitored and evaluated periodically. At the same time, the library should be prompt in paying its bills and informing its vendors of such events as initiating new collections, changing library specifications, or implementing new OPACs (Online Public Access Catalogs). Efforts on the part of the library to develop and maintain good relationships with vendors help to ensure that children or adults using the catalog will always receive high-quality service.

DIRECTORY OF VENDORS

U.S. AND CANADIAN WHOLESALERS AND PREBINDERS OFFERING CATALOGING SERVICES

Baker and Taylor
2550 West Tyvola Road, Ste. 300
Charlotte, NC 28217
1-800-775-1800
www.btol.com

Blackwell
6024 Jean Road, Bldg. G
Lake Oswego, OR 97035-8598
1-800-547-6426
www.blackwell.com

BMI Educational Services, Inc.
P.O. Box 800
Dayton, NJ 08810-0800
732-329-6991
Fax 732-329-6994
www.bmionline.com

BookSource
1230 Macklind Ave.
St. Louis, MO 63110
1-800-444-0435
www.booksource.com

Bound To Stay Bound Books, Inc.
1880 West Morton
Jacksonville, IL 62650
1-800-637-6586
www.btsb.com

Brodart Company
500 Arch Street
Williamsport, PA 17701

1-800-233-8467
www.brodart.com

BWI (Book Wholesalers Inc.)
1340 Ridgeview Drive
McHenry, IL 60050
1-800-888-4478
www.bwibooks.com

Children's Plus, Inc.
1387 Dutch American Way
Beecher, IL 60401
1-800-230-1279
1-800-896-7213
www.childrensplusinc.com

Coutts Information Services
1823 Maryland Avenue
Niagara Falls, NY 14302
1-800-263-1686
www.couttsinfo.com

Follett Library Resources
1340 Ridgeview Drive
McHenry, IL 60050
1-888-511-5114
www.titlewave.com

Ingram Library Services
One Ingram Blvd.
P.O. Box 3006
LaVergne, TN 37086
1-800-937-5300
www.ingramlibrary.com

Library Services Centre
131 Shoemaker Street
Kitchener, ON N2E 3B5
Canada
1-800-265-3360
www.lsc.on.ca

Mackin Library Media
14300 W. Burnsville
Parkway
Burnsville, MN 55306
1-800-245-9540
www.mackin.com

Perma-Bound Books
617 E. Vandalia Road
Jacksonville, IL 62650
1-800-637-6581
www.perma-bound.com

Quality Books
1003 West Pines Road
Oregon, IL 61061
1-800-323-4241
www.qbibooks.com

Rainbow Book Company
500 East Main Street
Lake Zurich, IL 60047
1-800-255-0965
Fax 847-726-9930
www.rainbowbookcompany.com

S&B Books Ltd.
3085 Universal Drive
Mississauga, ON L4X 2E2
Canada
1-800-997-7099
www.sbbooks.com

BIBLIOGRAPHIC UTILITIES AND COMPANIES OFFERING CATALOGING PRODUCTION AND SERVICES

Alexandria
1831 Fort Union Blvd.
Salt Lake City, UT 84121
1-801-943-7277
Fax 1-801-943-7752
www.goalexandria.com

Amigos Library Services
14400 Midway Road
Dallas, TX 75244-3509
1-800-843-8482
Fax 972-991-6061
www.amigos.org

Auto-Graphics, Inc.
3201 Temple Avenue,
Ste. 100
Pomona, CA 97168
1-800-776-6939
www.auto-graphics.com

Book Systems, Inc.
4901 University Square, Ste. 3
Huntsville, AL 35816
1-800-219-6571
Fax 1-800-230-4183
www.booksys.com

Brodart Automation
500 Arch Street
Williamsport, PA 17701
1-800-474-9802
Fax 570-326-1479
www.brodart.com

Duncan Systems Specialists
1193 North Service Road West
Units C7–C10
Oakville, ON L6M 2V8
Canada
905-338-5545
Fax 905-338-1847
www.duncansystems.com

Follett Software Company
1391 Corporate Drive
McHenry, IL 60050
1-800-323-3397
www.FollettSoftware.com

Gaylord Bros.
7282 William Barry Blvd.
North Syracuse, NY 13212
1-800-448-6160
Fax 1-800-595-7265
www.gaylord.com

Infor Library and Information Solutions
550 Cochituate Road, 3rd Fl., West Wing
Framingham, MA 01701
1-800-825-2574
www.libraries.infor.com

Library of Congress
101 Independence Avenue SE
Washington, DC 20540-4281
1-800-255-3666
www.loc.gov

London West Resource Centre
708 Gideon Drive
London, ON N6P 1P2 Canada
1-800-387-5958
Fax 1-519-641-6863
www.lwrc.com

The MARC of Quality
3830 S. Highway A1A #4-167
Melbourne Beach, FL 32951
1-321-676-1904
www.marcofquality.com

MARCIVE, Inc.
P.O. Box 47508
San Antonio, TX 78265
1-800-531-7678
www.marcive.com

OCLC
6565 Kilgour Place
Dublin, OH 43017
1-800-848-5878
www.oclc.org

SirsiDynix
101 Washington Street SE
Huntsville, AL 35801
1-800-917-4774
www.sirsidynix.com

TLC The Library Corporation
Research Park
Inwood, WV 25428
1-800-325-7759
www.TLCdelivers.com

VTLS Inc.
1701 Kraft Drive
Blacksburg, VA 24060
1-800-468-8857
Fax 1-540-557-1210
www.vtls.com

BIBLIOGRAPHY

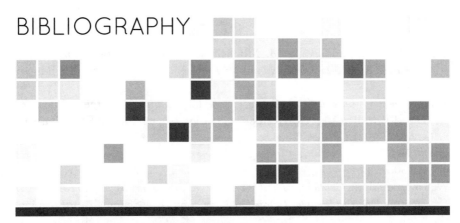

Virginia M. Overberg and Brigid Burke

PRIMARY TOOLS

GENERAL MANUALS

Chan, Lois Mai. *Cataloging and Classification: An Introduction.* 3rd ed. Lanham, MD: Scarecrow Press, 2007.

Hsieh-Yee, Ingrid. *Organizing Audiovisual and Electronic Resources for Access.* 2nd ed. Westport, CT: Libraries Unlimited; Santa Barbara, CA: ABC-CLIO, dist., 2006.

Intner, Sheila S., and Jean Weihs. *Standard Cataloging for School and Public Libraries.* 4th ed. Westport, CT: Libraries Unlimited; Santa Barbara, CA: ABC-CLIO, dist., 2007.

Kaplan, Allison, and Ann Riedling. *Catalog It! A Guide to Cataloging School Library Materials.* 2nd ed. Worthington, OH: Linworth Books, 2006.

Library of Congress. *Cataloger's Desktop.* http://desktop.loc.gov (subscription).

Notes for Serials Cataloging. Edited by Cecilia Genereux and Paul D. Moeller. Westport, CT: Libraries Unlimited; Santa Barbara, CA: ABC-CLIO, dist., 2009.

Olson, Nancy B. *Cataloging of Audiovisual Materials and Other Special Materials: A Manual Based on AACR2 and MARC 21.* With the assistance of Robert L. Bothmann and Jessica J. Schomberg. 5th ed. Westport, CT: Libraries Unlimited; Santa Barbara, CA: ABC-CLIO, 2008.

Pennell, Charlie, and Suzanne Ellison. *Cataloguer's Toolbox.* http://staff.library.mun.ca/staff/toolbox.

Surratt, Brian E., and Anne M. Mitchell. *Cataloging and Organizing Digital Resources: A How-to-Do-It Manual for Librarians.* New York: Neal-Schuman, 2005.

Taylor, Arlene G. *Introduction to Cataloging and Classification.* With the assistance of David P. Miller. 10th ed. Westport, CT: Libraries Unlimited; Santa Barbara, CA: ABC-CLIO, dist., 2006.

The Library Corporation. *Cataloger's Reference Shelf.* www.itsmarc.com/crs/ CRS0000.htm.

Weber, Mary Beth. *Cataloging Nonbook, Electronic, Web and Networked Resources: A How-to-Do-It Manual for Librarians.* New York: Neal-Schuman, forthcoming.

Weihs, Jean, and Sheila S. Intner. *Beginning Cataloging.* Santa Barbara, CA: Libraries Unlimited/ABC-CLIO, 2009.

DESCRIPTIVE CATALOGING

Anglo-American Cataloguing Rules. 2nd ed. Chicago: American Library Association, 2005.

Fritz, Deborah E. *Cataloging with AACR2 and MARC21: For Books, Electronic Resources, Sound Recordings, Videorecordings, and Serials.* 2nd ed., 2006 cumulation. Chicago: American Library Association, 2006.

Gorman, Michael. *The Concise AACR2.* Chicago: American Library Association, 2004.

Haynes, Elizabeth, and Joanna F. Fountain. *Unlocking the Mysteries of Cataloging: A Workbook of Examples.* Westport, CT: Libraries Unlimited; Santa Barbara, CA: ABC-CLIO, dist., 2005.

Intner, Sheila S., Susan S. Lazinger, and Jean Weihs. *Metadata and Its Impact on Libraries.* Westport, CT: Libraries Unlimited; Santa Barbara, CA: ABC-CLIO, dist., 2005.

Maxwell, Robert L. *FRBR: A Guide for the Perplexed.* Chicago: American Library Association, 2007.

———. *Maxwell's Guide to Authority Work.* Chicago: American Library Association, 2002.

———, and Margaret F. Maxwell. *Maxwell's Handbook for AACR2, Explaining and Illustrating Anglo-American Cataloguing Rules through the 2003 Update.* 4th ed. Chicago: American Library Association, 2004.

Miksa, Shawne D. *Introduction to Resource Description and Access: Cataloguing and Classification in the Digital Era.* London: Facet Publishing, forthcoming.

Mortimer, Mary. *Learn Descriptive Cataloging.* 2nd North American ed. Friendswood, TX: Total Recall Publications, 2007.

Understanding FRBR: What It Is and How It Will Affect Our Retrieval Tools. Edited by Arlene Taylor. Westport, CT: Libraries Unlimited; Santa Barbara, CA: ABC-CLIO, dist., 2007.

Welsh, Anne, and Sue Batley. *Practical Cataloguing: AACR, RDA and MARC 21.* London: Facet Publishing, 2009.

MARC FORMAT

Ferguson, Bobby. *MARC/AACR2/Authority Control Tagging: Blitz Cataloging Workbook.* 2nd ed. Westport, CT: Libraries Unlimited; Santa Barbara, CA: ABC-CLIO, dist., 2005.

Fritz, Deborah, and Richard J. Fritz. *MARC 21 for Everyone: A Practical Guide.* Chicago: ALA Editions, 2003.

Furrie, Betty. *Understanding MARC Bibliographic: Machine-Readable Cataloging.* 7th ed. Washington, DC: Library of Congress, Cataloging Distribution Service, 2003.

———. *Understanding MARC Bibliographic: Machine-Readable Cataloging.* In conjunction with the Data Base Development Department of the Follett Software Company. 7th ed. http://loc.gov/marc/umb/.

Library of Congress. Policy and Standards Division. *MARC Standards.* http://loc .gov/marc/.

MARC 21 Format for Bibliographic Data. Washington, DC: Library of Congress, 1999. Update 1 (2000)–Update 9 (2008).

OCLC, Inc. *Bibliographic Formats and Standards.* 4th ed. Dublin, OH: OCLC, 2008–. Also available online at http://oclc.org/bibformats/en/.

Understanding MARC Authority Records: Machine-Readable Cataloging. Washington, DC: Library of Congress, Cataloging Distribution Service, 2004. Also available online at www.loc.gov/marc/uma/index.html.

CLASSIFICATION

Chan, Lois Mai. *A Guide to the Library of Congress Classification.* 5th ed. Westport, CT: Libraries Unlimited; Santa Barbara, CA: ABC-CLIO, dist., 1999.

Dewey, Melvil. *Abridged Dewey Decimal Classification and Relative Index.* Edited by Joan S. Mitchell, Julianne Beall, Winton E. Matthews Jr., and Gregory R. New. 14th ed. Albany, NY: OCLC Forest Press, 2004.

————. *Dewey Decimal Classification and Relative Index.* Edited by Joan S. Mitchell, Julianne Beall, Winton E. Matthews Jr., and Gregory R. New. 22nd ed. Albany, NY: OCLC Forest Press, 2003.

Library of Congress. *ClassificationWeb.* http://classweb.loc.gov (subscription).

Library of Congress. Subject Cataloging Division. *LC Classification Outline.* 7th ed. Washington, DC: Library of Congress, 2003. Also available online at www .loc.gov/catdir/cpso/cco/.

McKnight, Mark. *Music Classification Systems.* Lanham, MD: Scarecrow Press, 2002.

OCLC, Inc. *Dewey Decimal Classification—New and Changed Entries.* www .oclc.org/dewey/updates/new/.

————. *WebDewey.* http://connexion.oclc.org/corc.html (subscription).

Scott, Mona L. *Dewey Decimal Classification, 22nd Edition: A Study Manual and Number Building Guide.* Santa Barbara, CA: Libraries Unlimited, 2005.

SUBJECT HEADINGS

Aikawa, Hiroko. *Guidelines on Subject Access to Individual Works of Fiction, Drama, etc.* 2nd ed. Chicago: American Library Association, 2000.

BILINDEX-GENERAL 2009: A List of Spanish-English Bilingual Subject Heading Equivalents to Library of Congress Subject Heading List. MountainView, CA: Floricanto Press, 2009.

Calimano, Iván E. *Sears Lista de Encabezamientos de Materia.* New York: H. W. Wilson, 2008.

Chan, Lois Mai. *Library of Congress Subject Headings: Principles and Application.* 4th ed. Westport, CT: Libraries Unlimited; Santa Barbara, CA: ABC-CLIO, dist., 2005.

Ganendran, Jacki, and Lynn Farkas. *Learn Library of Congress Subject Access.* 2nd North American ed. Friendswood, TX: Total Recall Publications, 2007.

Library and Archives Canada. *Canadian Subject Headings* (CSH). www .collectionscanada.ca/csh/index-e.html.

Library of Congress. Library of Congress Authorities. http://authorities.loc.gov.

Library of Congress. Moving Image Genre-Form Guide. http://loc.gov/rr/mopic/ miggen.html.

Library of Congress. Subject Cataloging Division. *Library of Congress Subject Headings.* 31st ed. Washington, DC: Library of Congress, 2009.

Library of Congress Subject Headings Supplemental Vocabularies: Free-Floating Subdivisions, Genre/Form Headings, Children's Subject Headings. Washington, DC: Library of Congress, 2009.

Olson, Hope A., and John J. Boll. *Subject Analysis in Online Catalogs.* 2nd ed. Westport, CT: Libraries Unlimited; Santa Barbara, CA: ABC-CLIO, dist., 2001.

SALSA de Topicos: Subjects in SALSA. Chicago: ALCTS, 2007.

Satija, Mohinder P., and Dorothy Elizabeth Haynes. *User's Guide to Sears List of Subject Headings.* Lanham, MD: Scarecrow Press, 2008.

Sears List of Subject Headings. 19th ed. Edited by Joseph Miller and Barbara A. Bristow. New York: H. W. Wilson, 2007.

Sears List of Subject Headings: Canadian Companion. 6th ed. Edited by Lynne Lighthall. New York: H. W. Wilson, 2001.

FILING

ALA Filing Rules. Chicago: American Library Association, 1980.

Carothers, Diane Foxhill. *Self-Instruction Manual for Filing Catalog Cards.* Washington, DC: Library of Congress, 1981.

Library of Congress Filing Rules. Prepared by John C. Rather and Susan C. Biebel. Washington, DC: Library of Congress, 1980.

CATALOGING FOR CHILDREN

Boyce, Judith I., and Bert R. Boyce. "A Reexamination of Shelf Organization for Children's Books." *Public Libraries* (September/October 2002): 280–83.

Children's Catalog. 19th ed. New York: H. W. Wilson, 2006 (annual supplements).

Frierson-Adams, Vickie. "Cataloging Juvenile Monographs in an Academic Library." *Technical Services Quarterly* 20, no. 1 (2002): 39–47.

Karpuk, Deborah J. *KidzCat: A How-to-Do-It Manual for Cataloging Children's Materials and Instructional Resources.* New York: Neal-Schuman, 2007.

Middle and Junior High School Library Catalog. 10th ed. Edited by Anne Price and Juliette Yaakov. New York: H. W. Wilson, 2009 (annual supplements).

Woodbury, Sara. "Subject Access to Children's Picture Books." *Technicalities* 23, no. 2 (March/April 2003): 8–12.

FURTHER READING AND STUDY

Ballard, Terry. *Typographical Errors in Library Databases.* Rev. February 2009. www .terryballard.org/typos/typoscomplete.html

"Children's Subject Headings." In *Library of Congress Subject Headings. Supplementary Vocabularies: Free-Floating Subdivisions, Genre/Form Headings, Children's Subject Headings.*, 31st ed., CSH-1–CSH-17. Washington, DC: Library of Congress, 2009.

Joint Steering Committee for Development of RDA. *RDA Online.* www .rdaonline.org/index.html.

Librarians' Internet Index. http://lii.org.

Librarian's Yellow Pages. Larchmont, NY: Garance, 2009. Also available online at www.librariansyellowpages.com.

"Library Journal Gold Book." http://goldbook.libraryjournal.com.

Library of Congress. *Online Catalog.* http://catalog.loc.gov.

Northern Lights Internet Solutions, Ltd. *Publishers' Catalogues.* www.lights .ca/publisher/.

OLAC (Online Audiovisual Catalogers). www.olacinc.org/drupal/.

Outsourcing Cataloging, Authority Work, and Physical Processing: A Checklist of Considerations. Edited by Marie A. Kascus and Dawn Hale. Chicago: American Library Association, 1995.

GLOSSARY OF ABBREVIATIONS

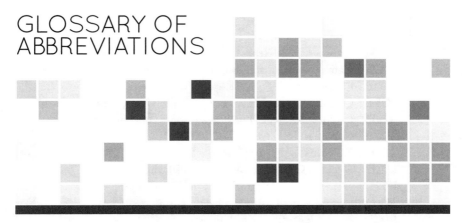

Compiled by Sheila S. Intner and Joanna F. Fountain

AACR2 *Anglo-American Cataloguing Rules,* 2nd edition
AASL American Association of School Librarians (a division of the American Library Association)
AC Annotated Card (program of the Library of Congress); now called Children's Subject Headings program
ALA American Library Association
ALCTS Association for Library Collections & Technical Services (a division of the American Library Association)
ANSCR Alpha-Numeric System for Classification of Recordings
API Application Program Interface
ASP Application Service Provider
AUSMARC Australian MARC
AUTOCAT Cataloging discussion list
BIC Book Industry Communication (Bibliographic Standards Technical Subgroup)
BT Broader Term (reference in a subject heading list or thesaurus)
CANMARC Canadian MARC
CatSIG Cataloging Special Interest Group
CCM Canadian Committee on MARC
CCS Cataloging and Classification Section (of the Association for Library Collections & Technical Services, ALA)

CD-ROM   Compact Disc Read-Only Memory

CDS   Cataloging Distribution Service (of the Library of Congress)

CIP   Cataloging-in-Publication

CLS   Children's Literature Section (of the Library of Congress)

CSH   Children's Subject Headings (program of the Library of Congress)

DC   Dewey Classification; *see also* DDC

DCD   Decimal Classification Division (of the Library of Congress)

DDC   *Dewey Decimal Classification; see also* DC

DVD   Digital VideoDisc

FICU   Find, Identify, Clarify, Understand

FISO   Find, Identify, Select, Obtain

FRAD   *Functional Requirements for Authority Data*

FRBR   *Functional Requirements for Bibliographic Records*

FRSAD   *Functional Requirements for Subject Authority Data*

FTP   File Transfer Protocol

GMD   General material designation; *see also* SMD

ICDL   International Children's Digital Library

IFLA   International Federation of Library Associations and Institutions

ILL   InterLibrary Loan

ILS   Integrated Library System

ISBD   International Standard Bibliographic Description

ISBN   International Standard Book Number

ISSN   International Standard Serial Number

JSC   Joint Steering Committee (for Revision of AACR)

LAC   Library and Archives Canada (formerly National Library of Canada)

LC   Library of Congress

LCMARC   Original version of MARC, instituted by the Library of Congress

LC/NACO   Library of Congress/Name Authority Cooperative (of the Program for Cooperative Cataloging)

LCC   Library of Congress Classification

LCCN   Library of Congress Control Number

LCRI   *Library of Congress Rule Interpretations*

LCSH   *Library of Congress Subject Headings*

MARBI   Machine-Readable Bibliographic Information Committee (American Library Association)

MARC   MAchine-Readable Cataloging (a bibliographic record communication standard)

MARC 21   First international version of the MARC standards

NACO	Name Authority Cooperative of the Library of Congress's Program for Cooperative Cataloging
NAF	Name Authority File
NT	Narrower Term (reference in a subject heading list or thesaurus)
OCLC	Online Computer Library Center (formerly Ohio College Library Center)
OCLC MARC	A version of MARC designed by and for OCLC
OPAC	Online Public Access Catalog
PCC	Program for Cooperative Cataloging (Library of Congress)
PZ	Library of Congress Classification schedule for Juvenile Belles Lettres
RDA	Resource Description and Access; descriptive cataloging rules expected to supersede AACR2 in 2010
RLIN	Research Libraries Information Network
RT	Related term (reference in a subject heading list or thesaurus)
RTSD	Resources and Technical Services Division (of the American Library Association; former name of the Association for Library Collections & Technical Services)
SA	See Also cross-reference (reference in a subject heading list or thesaurus)
SaaS	Software as a Service
SAC	Subject Analysis Committee (of the Cataloging and Classification Section of the Association for Library Collections & Technical Services)
SACO	Subject Authority Cooperative (of the Library of Congress's Program for Cooperative Cataloging)
SMD	Specific material designation; *see also* GMD
SUNLINK	Florida's K–12 public school union catalog
UF	Used For (reference in a subject heading list or thesaurus)
UK	United Kingdom
UNIMARC	Universal Machine-Readable Cataloging (an international version of MARC devised before MARC 21)
URL	Uniform Resource Locator
USMARC	United States MARC
Utlas	University of Toronto Libraries Automated System
WDL	World Digital Library
WEMI	Work, Expression, Manifestation, Item
WISCAT	Wisconsin statewide union catalog
XML	Extensible Markup Language
Z39.50	A client-server protocol for searching and retrieving information from remote computer databases maintained by the Library of Congress

CONTRIBUTORS

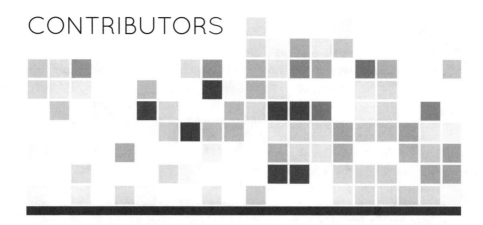

Jennifer Allen is the acquisitions and cataloging manager at Perma-Bound Books in Jacksonville, Illinois, having started as a copy cataloger at the company eleven years ago. A former English teacher and school librarian, Jennifer finds her experience in the schools indispensable when working with customers. She is a member of the American Library Association (ALA) and chair of the MicroLIF Community and has served as a member of the Cataloging of Children's Materials Committee of the Cataloging and Classification Section of the Association for Library Collections & Technical Services (ALCTS, a division of ALA). Jennifer is also a board member of the Educational Book and Media Association (EBMA).

Julianne Beall is assistant editor of the Dewey Decimal Classification, Dewey Section, Library of Congress, a position she has held since 1986. From 1977 to 1986, she was a Decimal Classification Specialist for the Decimal Classification Division (DCD), Library of Congress. She received both her PhD in English literature and her MLS from the University of California, Los Angeles. She is the Dewey Section liaison to the Subject Analysis Committee (SAC) of the Cataloging and Classification Section, Association for Library Collections & Technical Services. She has worked closely with many Dewey translators—training, answering questions, and reviewing drafts. She is currently responsible for editing the DDC psychology, economics, law, medicine, management, and literature schedules, plus Table 3 and Table 5. She also writes for *025.431: The Dewey Blog*.

Brigid Burke has been a professional cataloger for fifteen years, working for a book jobber as well as in school, public, and academic libraries. Currently she is working on two grant-funded digital projects at Fairleigh Dickinson University and is in the process of building and customizing the university library's digital repository. She taught cataloging and classification for seven years at Rutgers University's School of Communication, Information, and Library Studies (now the School of Communication and Information). She has taught the School's automation and networking course and teaches introductory religion courses in the Philosophy and Religion Department at Montclair State University. She lives in western New Jersey with her four cats.

Lynnette Fields is a catalog and metadata librarian and assistant professor of Library and Information Services at Southern Illinois University Edwardsville (SIUE), where she is responsible for cataloging serials and electronic resources. Prior to her position at SIUE, she was a cataloging trainer for The MARC of Quality, the database consultant for the Lewis and Clark Library System (Edwardsville, Ill.), and a cataloging librarian at the St. Louis Public Library. Lynnette is a Serials Cataloging Cooperative Training Program (SCCTP) trainer and has been an adjunct instructor for the University of Missouri, School of Information Science and Learning Technologies. She holds an MA in library science from the University of Missouri.

Deborah A. Fritz is co-owner of The MARC of Quality, Inc., a Florida-based company that provides training, software, and database services to help librarians create better MARC records. She currently teaches an extensive array of cataloging workshops around the United States and abroad. Before starting her own business, she was a cataloging trainer at a multitype library consortium and, before that, was in charge of retrospective conversion at a large bibliographic utility. She has also been a cataloger at various libraries. She is the author of *Cataloging with AACR and MARC21* (ALA Editions 2007), coauthor of *MARC 21 for Everyone* (ALA Editions 2003), and codeveloper of several MARC processing programs, including "MARC Report," "MARC Global," and "OSMOSIS." She earned her master's degree in library science at the University of Toronto.

Lynne A. Jacobsen is head of technical services at Warren-Newport Public Library, Gurnee, Illinois, where she has worked since 1994. She also catalogs at the College of Lake County (Illinois) and teaches cataloging and classification for the Library Technical Assistant program. Previously, she was a cataloger at Cook Memorial Public Library in Libertyville, Illinois. Lynne received her undergraduate degree in physical education from the University of Illinois, Urbana-Champaign, and her MLIS from Northern Illinois University. She served as intern to the Cataloging of Children's Materials Committee in 1995-96 and contributed chapters to the third and fourth editions of *Cataloging*

Correctly for Kids. She is the author of "Warren-Newport: Testing Innovative Design Concepts" (*ILA Reporter*, February 1998).

Gabriele I. Kupitz is a librarian in the Harold B. Lee Library at Brigham Young University in Provo, Utah, where she catalogs juvenile literature and special collections materials. In 2007, Gabi served on the Batchelder Committee of the American Library Association's Association for Library Service to Children (ALSC) and has served as chair of the Cataloging of Children's Materials Committee of the Cataloging and Classification Section of the Association for Library Collections & Technical Services (CCMC/CCS/ALCTS, a division of ALA). She also has served as past CCMC liaison to the Committee on Cataloging: Description and Access (CC:DA), the CCS/ALCTS committee concerned with the *Anglo-American Cataloguing Rules* and *Resource Description and Access*.

Kay E. Lowell is archival services librarian and professor, University Libraries, at the James A. Michener Library of the University of Northern Colorado (UNC) in Greeley, where she has also managed the catalog department. She has served in both public and technical services roles in academic, health sciences, and public libraries. She has served as an intern, member, and chair of the ALCTS Cataloging and Classification Section, Cataloging of Children's Materials Committee as well as being the committee's liaison to the ALA Committee on Cataloging: Description and Access (CC:DA). She received an MLS from SUNY Buffalo and an MET in Educational Technology from UNC and has done doctoral-level work in visual literacy and instructional design. She lives in Greeley with her husband, two daughters, two cats, and a variety of fish.

Joseph Miller received his MLS degree from the School of Information Science and Policy at the State University of New York at Albany, the only library school founded by Melvil Dewey still in existence. (The School is now the Department of Information Studies in the College of Computing and Information.) At the H. W. Wilson Company, he worked for a number of years in Subject Authorities and is now vice president for cataloging and general reference. He has been the editor of the *Sears List of Subject Headings* since the fifteenth edition (1994). He has participated on the Subject Analysis Committee (SAC) and the Cataloging of Children's Materials Committee of the Cataloging and Classification Section of the Association for Library Collections & Technical Services (ALCTS, a division of the American Library Association). He is also a library user and the proud holder of a library card from the New York Public Library.

Pamela J. Newberg is an assistant professor and manager of resource processing and description (otherwise known as cataloging) at the University of Northern Colorado. In her previous life, Pam was the manager of the cataloging department for Follett Library Resources in McHenry, Illinois. She holds an MLS from Dominican University, an MM from DePaul University, and an MAT from

National-Louis University. She has worked as a cataloger, children's librarian, automation librarian, and teacher in a number of settings including school, public, academic, and special libraries. She has served as a vendor liaison, member, and chair of the Cataloging of Children's Materials Committee of the Cataloging and Classification Section of the Association for Library Collections & Technical Services (ALCTS, a division of the American Library Association).

Virginia Overberg is the manager of book cataloging for Baker and Taylor, Inc., in Bridgewater, N.J., having previously worked as a department trainer and cataloging policy manager. She has served on the Cataloging of Children's Materials Committee of the Cataloging and Classification Section of the Association for Library Collections & Technical Services (CCMC/CCS/ALCTS, a division of the American Library Association) as both a past member and liaison. She is a representative to the Cataloging-in-Publication Advisory Group and the MicroLIF Community. In her spare time she is a runner and triathlete as well as a nationally certified running coach. When she isn't training or coaching, she enjoys quilting and square dancing. She lives in central New Jersey with her husband.

Judith Yurczyk is a research analyst at the Follett Software Company in McHenry, Illinois, where she serves as the company's cataloging/MARC resource. She writes the "Tag of the Month" (accessible on Follett Software's home page), responds to the "Ask MsMARC" inquiries, and plays an integral part in maintaining Follett's Alliance MARC record databases. She is the author of the *MARC Bibliographic Format Guide* and *MARC Authority Format Guide* and has developed MARC workshops, which she presents nationally and internationally. She received her MLS from the University of Wisconsin, Milwaukee. She is a member of the American Library Association, the Association for Library Collections & Technical Services (ALCTS) and its Cataloging and Classification Section (ALCTS/CCS), and Online Audiovisual Catalogers (OLAC). She has served as a member of the ALCTS/CCS Cataloging of Children's Materials Committee and the Vendor Relations Committee.

Michelle Zwierski is the head of cataloging for the Nassau Library System on Long Island, New York. After receiving her MLS from the University of North Texas, she practiced as a cataloger, specializing in nonprint materials and working at academic libraries in Virginia, Connecticut, and Texas before joining the Austin Public Library as a branch manager. In addition to her current cataloging responsibilities, she presents workshops to member library staff on technical services topics. She also is an adjunct instructor at the Palmer School of Library and Information Science. In her free time, she plays bass in several community orchestras on Long Island, having earned a Bachelor of Music degree from the University of Wisconsin, Madison and a Master of Arts degree at the Yale School of Music before beginning her library career.

SUBJECT INDEX

See also Figure Index, page 223.

FIGURE INDEX

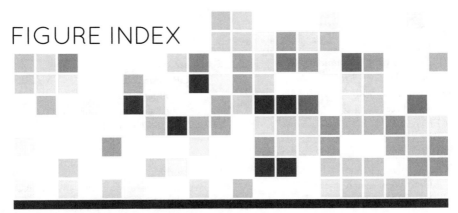

See also Subject Index, p. 213.

You may also be interested in

RDA Toolkit: Use the resources in the online RDA Toolkit to navigate from AACR2 to RDA. RDA—included in the toolkit—is the new unified standard for resource description and access, designed for the digital world and an expanding universe of metadata users. The RDA Toolkit also includes user-created and sharable workflows and mappings, views of RDA content by table of contents and by element set, and links to other relevant cataloging resources.

Introducing RDA: A Guide to the Basics: Author Chris Oliver, cataloguing and authorities coordinator at the McGill University Library and chair of the Canadian Committee on Cataloging, offers practical advice on how to make the transition from the Anglo-American Cataloguing Rules (AACR) to Resource Description and Access (RDA).

Cataloging Cultural Objects: A Guide to Describing Cultural Works and Their Images: This is a must-have reference for museum professionals, visual resources curators, archivists, librarians, and anyone who documents cultural objects (including architecture, paintings, sculpture, prints, manuscripts, photographs, visual media, performance art, archaeological sites, and artifacts) and their images.

Magic Search: Getting the Best Results from Your Catalog and Beyond: Rebecca S. Kornegay and Heidi E. Buchanan, experienced reference librarians, and Hildegard B. Morgan, an expert cataloger, present the 467 best-performing LCSH subdivisions that speak to the kinds of research questions librarians handle every day. This handy reference format and index offers a useful tool to keep for quick reference rather than a cumbersome tome to be read from cover to cover.

Order today at www.alastore.ala.org or 866-746-7252!

ALA Store purchases fund advocacy, awareness, and accreditation programs for library professionals worldwide.